The World Needs Dialogue!
Three: Shaping the Profession

This edition first published in 2021

Dialogue Publications
The Firs, High Street
Chipping Campden
Glos GL55 6AL UK

All rights reserved

Book Copyright © Dialogue Publications, 2021
All individual authors featured in this publication retain copyright for their work

Without limiting individual author's rights reserved, no part of this publication
may be reproduced, distributed or transmitted in any form or by any means, including
photocopying, recording, or other electronic or mechanical methods, without
the prior written permission of the publisher, except in the case of brief quotations
embedded in critical reviews and certain other non-commercial uses permitted
by copyright law. For permission requests, write to the publisher at the address above.

Typeset by Ellipsis, Glasgow, Scotland

Ordering Information:
Quantity sales – Special discounts are available on quantity purchases by
libraries, associations and others. For details, contact the Special Sales Department
at the address above.

The World Needs Dialogue! / Three – 1st ed.

Classifications:
UK: BIC – Society (JFC): Cultural Studies and JFF: Social Issues)
US: BISAC – SOC000000 Social Science

Hardback: 978-1-9161912-7-3
Ebook: 978-1-9161912-8-0

Printed in Great Britain and the USA

Contents

Chairman's Foreword   v
Editor's Introduction   vi

Section One
Shaping Education Through Dialogue

Dialogue and Decision-Making in Leadership Coaching   3
Mechtild Beucke-Galm

Dialogue in Teacher Training at the University Level   21
Heike de Boer & Daniela Merklinger

Overcoming Challenges to Dialogue in Professional Higher Education   39
Timo Nevalainen

Section Two
Shaping Corrections Through Dialogue

Threshold Dialogue to Change a System   59
Jane Ball

Dialogue within Decision-Making   79
Peter Garrett

Live Facilitation of the Offender Resettlement Journey   97
Jane Ball

Dialogue through the Offender Resettlement Journey   105
Jane Ball

Section Three
Shaping Social Work Through Dialogue

Community Dialogues on Homelessness   125
Rebecca Cannara

Dialogue and Managing Societal Conflicts   145
Bernard le Roux

Transforming Care for the Elderly through Dialogue   159
Lars-Åke Almqvist

Section Four
Shaping Thinking Through Dialogue

What is Professionalism in Dialogue?   179
William Isaacs

Developing Online Professional Dialogue   197
Thomas Köttner

The Container Development Model   215
Peter Garrett

Participants   231

Chairman's Foreword

Welcome to this record of a significant week! The Academy of Professional Dialogue's third annual international conference, 26th to 30th October 2020, was reassuringly similar and yet strikingly different from the previous two. Things had evolved significantly with the Covid-19 pandemic, and we took full advantage of the changing situation amongst and around us.

As before, all the materials, considerations and presentations were designed, authored and led by Academy Members who were there throughout the conference. Once again, the full set of Working Papers in this volume were distributed to conference participants well beforehand, and people chose which practitioners to join during the breakout sessions. One major difference was instead of meeting in a physical conference centre, we met in our online Academy Conference Centre. This was specially built for the occasion. The design favoured engagement, allowing us to divide from a large group of several hundred in one room, down to multiple small groupings or pairs in a single minute. And then we could reconvene the whole group again equally quickly. Another change was the welcome of our first accredited organisational member, the largest state agency in Virginia. The combination of these two changes enabled us to extend the number of participants from 80 to over 500, whilst reducing the fees substantially.

The new arrangements were hardly rehearsed before the conference began. A non-profit organisation like the Academy is dependent on the generosity of its Members and they certainly stepped forward in good spirit, hosting, facilitating, singing (I have to mention Eelco de Geus's name) and working behind the scenes. We introduced Brief Encounters, which are short experiential learning sessions led by Members, and featured 21 of them during the five days. As you can see, this was a highly participatory conference with many Members taking direct responsibility for its success. All conference sessions were recorded and are available on the Members' website for ongoing learning.

All three of our annual conferences have been called **The World Needs Dialogue!** with the conference themes appearing in the subtitles of their subsequent publications. The sequence encapsulates our progress in a succinct way – from Volume One, **Gathering the Field**, to **Setting the Bearings** and now **Shaping the Profession**. And that is what is starting to happen. The Virginia Department of Corrections is a living example of a Dialogic Organisation. How this has been achieved is codified and incorporated into the Academy's accredited educational programme. The desire to learn is in the air. Proponents of practical forms of Dialogue (that address specific needs) and those familiar with the more emergent forms of Generative Dialogue (that realise opportunities) are engaged with one another to find a common understanding.

As mentioned, the theme of this conference was *shaping the profession*. The shape of Professional Dialogue is, of course, whatever is needed to shape society, and during the conference we reviewed our collective progress in this regard. We considered substantial work by a dozen different practitioners drawn from Germany, Finland, the UK, Sweden, the USA and Argentina. In the first section of this volume you will find three papers describing how practitioners are *Shaping Education Through Dialogue* in primary, secondary and adult learning. A further three papers were chosen for each of the other three sections. The second section, *Shaping Corrections Through Dialogue,* is demonstrated with dialogic organisational decision-making, and examples of overcoming fragmentation in the criminal justice system. The third section, *Shaping Social Services Through Dialogue,* offers accounts of practitioner work involving homelessness, the interface between local government and individual beneficiaries, and care for the elderly, each showing remarkable results. The final section, *Shaping Thinking Through Dialogue,* includes a foundational paper on professionalism in Dialogue, another on the nature of online dialogue and a third on an archetypal pattern of developmental growth. These are firm strides in shaping society through Dialogue.

The act of shaping is worthy of a little more consideration. There are different ways of shaping things. An architect might shape his or her initial ideas of a building by drawing with a pencil on paper, allowing a design to emerge. Potters shape their pottery with the feel of the wet clay in their hands. A chef might shape the dish according to the raw produce available on the day. We also are interested in the material outcomes – namely the building, the pot and the meal – but let's stay with the act of shaping itself. Something about shaping through Dialogue was revealed in every aspect of this conference. As you read the 12 papers in this volume and follow the conference sessions extracts and the writers' postscripts, you have a chance to sense the shaping process at work. It is a collective act involving multiple nudges – something tangible yet hard to describe.

The accounts generally began with a confused context or a fragmented situation. The practitioners had a sense of how things could work more generatively and productively, despite the evident constraints and complexity. They were deliberately collaborative and respectful, and they sought understanding by giving people the chance to speak and the opportunity to be heard. They encouraged active participation in a process that could begin to define itself rather than be driven to a predetermined outcome. As practitioners they drew on their experience, their passion and their desire for a richer human experience. They were pragmatic, rigorous and hard-working – and also reflective, accepting setbacks and considering possible ways forward carefully. They were changing themselves in the process of working with others. They knew they were endeavouring to shape an ongoing, inclusive and common human story in which everyone could participate. And they wanted to inspire and inform you and the shaping of your work.

Peter Garrett
Chairman, International Board of Trustees,
Academy of Professional Dialogue

Editor's Introduction

If ever a year proved the need for Dialogue, 2020 would be it. And if ever there was a group to demonstrate the interest and skill to match that need, this year's collection of authors did so ably and with articulate enthusiasm.

As Peter has mentioned, our conference theme was *Shaping the Profession*. To us this seemed a natural progression from the first conference's efforts to survey the many fields of dialogic practice (Gathering the Field), then access the collective intelligence available in Dialogic work at different scales (Setting our Bearings) to, this year, beginning to look more closely at three areas of professional Dialogue—education, corrections, and social services—and explore the challenges of advancing the profession itself. Whereas conference papers often tend toward the abstract or theoretical, the work in this volume reflects decades of hands-on, skilled work.

As in previous volumes, the papers here have been written by those from different countries of origin—seven this year—and, as before, we have attempted to respect the authors' nuances of language and sentence structure to give a flavor of the many voices of Dialogue. Practically speaking, this also means using British / European / American spelling and punctuation, as well as the occasional "translator's note" (Lars-Åke Almqvist helpfully lets us know, for example that his company's KASAM evaluation metric is based on a Swedish phrase meaning "a sense of coherence.")

Finally, we have continued our tradition of including a greatly shortened transcript of the smaller-group considerations with the author(s) of each chapter, and a postscript-reflection written some months after the conference, in which authors share how their thinking has continued to develop and deepen over time.

This volume, like the two that have preceeded it, give evidence of a solid progression of intent, determination and collaboration across diverse traditions, levels of skill and personal backgrounds. Like any good dialogue, it is bound to challenge and sustain us as we engage with it and find our ways through it.

Cliff Penwell
Editor
Dialogue Publications

Section One

Shaping Education Through Dialogue

How can education be shaped through Dialogue and how might things change in consequence? In this section we have three very different accounts of ways in which this is already being done, from primary school level through to adult education.

Mechtild Beucke-Galm tells the fascinating story of her dialogic coaching of the leadership team of an innovative German school. The context is a school for 10- to 16-year-olds that had developed a responsive bottom-up power structure with some of the decision-making initiated by pupils, including in conflict resolution and a pupils' council. The main story is the tension between the staff and the adept founder of the school when she shifted her position significantly. Those in the leadership team had to manage changing identities and the shifting power dynamics in themselves and each other. The series of Dialogues that Mechtild facilitated provided the necessary environment of challenge, safety and sensitivity for them to find a viable resolution.

In contrast, Daniela Merklinger and Heike de Boer's university courses, also in Germany, help primary school teachers to develop dialogic skills for use in the classroom. This requires a break in the normal, rarely dialogic patterns of classroom discourse. Typically, the teacher directs and the students are expected to report someone else's thinking rather than thinking for themselves, and are evaluated accordingly. Daniela and Heike describe one of their teacher students managing conflict between pupils in a very different way. She stepped back from being the directive authority and instead facilitated and witnessed conversations between the pupils involved. The pupils not only discovered for themselves what lay behind their conflict but were moved to change their behaviour in relation to each other.

Timo Nevalainen tackles the nature of education itself. Rather than proposing that there should be education about Dialogue, or even education for people to practice Dialogue, Timo takes a more radical stance. He advocates education should itself be a form of Dialogue. Without shared understanding and coherent action, he believes we will continue to suffer social fragmentation and divisiveness. If education is a form of Dialogue, then knowledge is not a 'thing' to be found in books or lectures and then applied, but a process co-created by the participants themselves and enriched by whatever sources prove helpful. The entrepreneur school where he works in a university in Finland has been developing such an approach in an impressively practical and successful way during the past decade.

– P.G.

Dialogue and Decision-Making in Leadership Coaching

Mechtild Beucke-Galm

Over the last 30 years, coaching has developed from a niche practice into an accepted form of consulting, and is now a part of the repertoire of personnel development offers in almost all companies. In the educational sector, reflecting on one's own professional practice has an even longer tradition. It began to take hold in the 1970s, when teams of teachers attached importance not only to their academic competence but also to making the interaction between teachers and students the subject of their own learning. In the early 2000s, when running a school began to be considered by educational professionals as a leadership function instead of an administrative task, school principals also started to reflect with a coach their on leadership.

A Systemic and Dialogic Approach to Coaching

People often associate the term *coaching* with a form of supervision, where a specialist helps a client to develop special skills. This approach, having developed from the practice of providing support to top athletes, is based on the coach's expert knowledge, with coaching organised around it. This approach can be found also in business or in schools, when former managers or principals move into the coaching field and use their knowledge of management or running a school for coaching. This 'expert coaching' is not what I am referring to here. I use the term *coaching* for a process, where I reflect with clients on their questions without telling them what to do. I accompany and guide clients in an exploration of 'difficult' situations and the underlying assumptions which have driven their actions and behaviours. My special knowledge is about development of individuals, groups and organisations, and about creating insights through observing the process with the client.

My background is in systemic organisational consulting, systemic family therapy and dialogue.
    With this perspective I have the whole system in mind; I distinguish between the system and its environment and focus also on the relationships between the two. For example, when

working with an educational client I look first at the specific school (the system) and at such factors as the parents, the facilities, the school authorities and the city administration (the environment). Then I look at three levels: the *person*, the *group* and the *organisation*. Regardless of whether I work with an individual or a team, I ask myself, which part of the client's topics do I need to reflect on, and at which level? On the level of the person, I look at the individual preferences; on the level of the group I reflect on social dynamics; and, on the level of the organisation, I put the attention to structure and its culture. I explore with the client their inner models and look at the connections between reactions across the environment, between behaviour and mental models. Sometimes one level is in the foreground and sometimes another – it is important not to remain in one level, but to include all levels and to make the connections between them visible.

Besides the systemic approach, my coaching is based on dialogue. Working dialogically means meeting the client as an equal, with an open, explorative and non-evaluative attitude. I accept their questions without reservation, as I am interested in their 'reality'. In my model, the client's views of reality – and mine – is not 'the truth', but is a construction whose usefulness only emerges in action. I do not assume that I know what is right and what needs to be done. I work with the belief that – through the process of describing, questioning, responding and commenting – new insights perspectives will open up for the client. I deeply trust in the process, and am confident that the relevant insights will emerge.

In this paper I would like to present an excerpt of my work as a case study and present a coaching process with the leadership team of a school. I will use two perspectives:

1. A chronological one: How did the engagement start? What happened during the time of the consultation, and how did it continue after the conclusion of the sessions?
2. A conceptual one: What were the effects of my systemic-dialogical approach, with its focus on decision-making and communication?

The School and its Context

As it so often does, the coaching engagement started with a phone call. A deputy headmaster wanted guidance for the next phase in the development of his school. "Our headmistress is retiring", he said, "And we would like to consciously shape this transitional phase and the beginning of a new era with the help of an external consultant". Our conversation revealed two interesting aspects. First was the concept of "a new era" itself, as the school had a special pedagogical approach in which all children of a district are included and taught together. Second was the importance of the headmistress: she had co-founded the school and managed it for 15 years. With her departure, an era would come to an end. I was familiar with the school and remembered it as interesting and lively. I quickly determined to have a first conversation with some of the school's leadership and gain a first impression. When I arrived at the school on the agreed-upon date, the entire leadership team was waiting for me. I got to know the members, learned a lot about the school itself and more about the background of the request. In the end we agreed to work together for two years.

To start a coaching process it is necessary to know the context of the client or organisation. In this example, the context is a comprehensive school for children between 10-16, with all-day operation. It sees itself as a school for all children of the neighbourhood and has created a special pedagogical programme. The school life is characterised by reformed pedagogical concepts, adapted to the present day. In addition to traditional subject teaching, individualised learning and group learning through projects plays an important role alongside learning social skills. The school is organised in classes of 25 and by year-groups. That is, the classes for young people of one age have a common area in the school; for example, all classes for the ten-year-olds are on the same corridor. Thus the pupils have two social frames of reference: their own class and their year-group. In addition to the classrooms, the hallway has been set up as a learning environment with material for self-learning, which can be used by all pupils of the year-group for self-organised learning.

The pupils are involved in the responsibility for social life at school from the very beginning; a student might work by helping in the arbitration council (conflict resolution office), or by keeping certain areas of the school clean, or by helping to prepare festivities, or by being a member in the pupils' council, which is consulted by the teachers when important decisions are to be made in a class or at school.

Teachers are grouped in fixed teams, assigned to the different year-groups, organising their work rather autonomously. Each teacher is part of such a team and therefore knows all pupils of that age. The teachers meet for weekly exchanges, and each team regularly has its work reviewed. The members of the school leadership team have a double function. All of them work as teachers in a team and in a class. They are also responsible for the overall management of the school. Leadership responsibilities include looking after the school programme, the quality of teaching, teacher deployment, compliance with legal requirements, the culture of the school, parental work, public relations and many other areas. The leadership team meets weekly to discuss and decide on current and long-term issues. Overall, one could say that the school gives high priority as well to the development of professional learning, education and social skills.

In this school, the principles of *team consideration* and *bottom-up* play a special role. This can be seen, for example, in the organisation of decision-making processes. All questions and impulses for the further development of the school begin with discussions in the class teams, preparing the basis for decisions. Afterwards, any arguments and exploration of the premises behind decisions are brought to the conference of the whole staff, where they are discussed and debated again. The decision itself is made through a voting process that collectively includes all colleagues. Whatever the majority of the college is in favour of applies. The headmistress can intervene, but only through the right to veto. In the school leadership team of six members, the principles of 'teams' and 'hierarchy' intersect because all members are not only school management but also part of a class team.

The leadership team is the developing, coordinating and controlling organ of the school. Members cooperate well, each receiving the same attention for their thoughts and concerns – the headmistress or her deputy does not dominate the discussions. However, on closer observation there is one distinction between the leadership functions. The headmistress, the deputy headmistress and the pedagogical director have fewer teaching duties than the others, allowing more time for developing concepts and greater powers of shaping and decision-making. Although the headmistress and deputy headmistress do not have any responsibility for the personnel – that role sits with the school supervisory authority – they do have the authority to issue instructions in work planning, and they have control with regard to the quality of teaching and the pedagogical approach.

The Coaching Structure

In the first interview with the leadership team I had suggested a bimonthly rhythm, working together for half a day each time we met. Our coaching session would consist of two phases: a dialogue phase and a decision-making phase.

The dialogue phase was a joint thinking process in which the different perspectives were expressed, making visible in the room the different, new, unfamiliar and perhaps irritating ideas. This created a space in which thoughts were not filtered or evaluated and in which the coexistence of contradictions was accepted, providing room for options and possibilities. Here, implicit connections between different perspectives were inquired into and individual assumptions about the context and its mode of operation became seen. In leadership teams, it is not so common to think together and communicate in this way. Leaders and managers tend to respond quickly and assume that fast decisions are expected of them. In complex situations, however, decisions do not gain their quality through speed, but through an understanding of the situation – of the relevant contexts and of the essential questions in detail. Leaders need dialogue in order to gain this understanding.

The dialogue phase began with a 'check-in' to prepare the ground for this conversation. With the check-in a space is built in which people could talk about what they consider as relevant, even if it is unpleasant or unsettling. Children need such a 'container' in order to develop and learn. By my observation, adults need a protected space as well to try themselves out and develop.

The building of a container happens first through one's own attitude as coach, holding a genuine interest in the people and what they do. The coach's attitude is the model to which the client orientates. While I was familiar with the context of the school, I was interested to learn what the headmistress's retirement would mean for each of them and how they would introduce the topic of her departure into the coaching sessions. I wanted to explore the topics with respect and attentiveness. People notice how they are approached, and this determines their own attitude toward the coaching.

We often started the dialogue phase with a simple inquiry: "What is currently occupying you as a member of the leadership team, and why is that relevant to you?" One by one each described what was on his or her mind. They listened to each other and were in contact with each other. They were interested in the perceptions and interpretations of others and were prepared – some of them slowly, others more quickly – to reveal their own beliefs. After the check-in, there were always moments of uncertainty. Which statements from the check-in would be taken up and which would not? How were these topics taken up, how were they responded to and how could this become a 'deep conversation'?

In every dialogue the various pieces of the current situation came together and revealed an overall picture. The whole picture was then jointly viewed and commented on. There were various points of reference for the comments; a central one was the retirement of the headmistress. I named as well (from an external position) what I could perceive as a 'Gestalt' of the situation, and what was still unspoken. I also talked about the emotional colouring the group had created with its description, and I shared my associations with it. In this phase, the members of the group were able to experience the mental models and the motives of each of them. For all participants the assumptions and thoughts upon which decisions were to be made, became apparent. Our process created transparency.

The first dialogue sessions were rather bumpy. The discussion process felt as if the group was learning to walk. Over time, however, the dialogues became more fluid. Engaging in dialogue requires skills, abilities and process competence, which the participants developed through practice. These include *self-confidence* and *openness*, *courage* and *trust in the process*.

- *Self-confidence* is assuming that one has something to contribute. This includes becoming aware of one's own inner voice and daring to express it to the outside world, thus standing up for one's own thinking.
- *Openness* is an inner attitude of making oneself permeable to the thoughts and feelings of oneself and those of others. If one keeps oneself open, then one can allow others to impress upon him their 'pictures' or mental models. It is essential not to try to avoid these impressions, for example by having already filled oneself with knowledge and certainty. Openness is the aperture for the 'possible' and the 'unpredictable'.
- *Courage* means taking the risk of putting oneself at the mercy of others, not only to be impressed upon, but also to want to make an impression oneself. *Courage* means to name what is happening, even if it does not fit into the existing culture and interpretation. This is easier with people, contents or contexts that are familiar to us; it is difficult in unknown settings or with persons we don't know well. Courage also includes approaching the foreign without instinctively rejecting it, getting close to it in order to understand what it is – even if it remains foreign.
- *Trust in the process* means assuming that the steps makes sense. This includes not

knowing the result at the beginning of a dialogue, yet still trusting that the outcome will be okay. It requires us to refer to the process itself even while walking through individual steps to create a result.

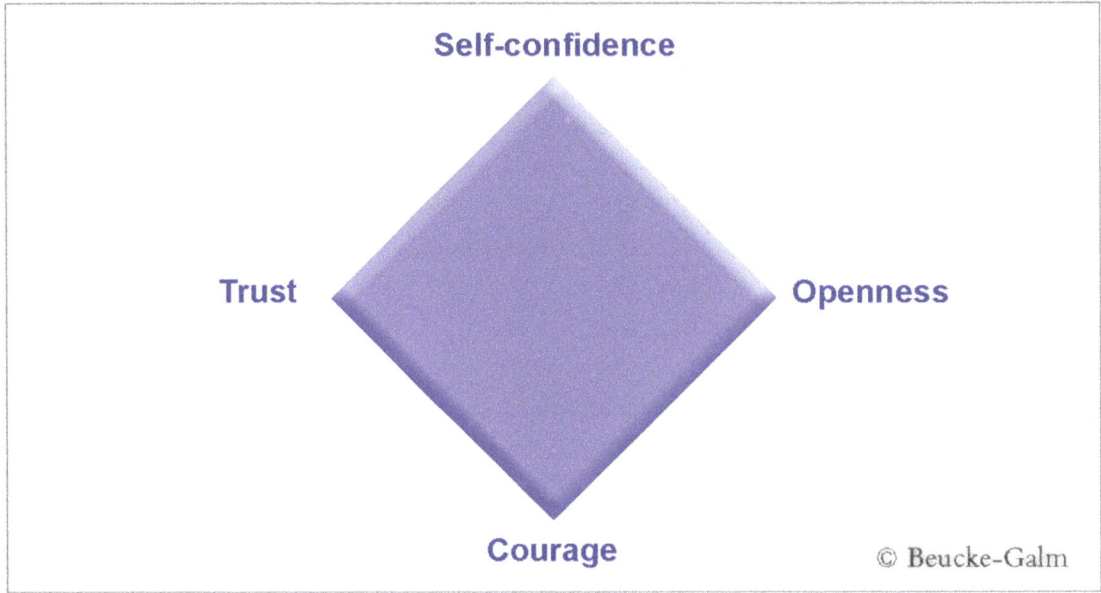

The success of a leadership team is measured by its results. Good results, however, depend on the quality of the learning or decision-making processes. The ability to create processes appropriate to the circumstances is essential. As a member of a leadership team, one must reckon with the unique requirements of every situation. Instead of relying on a logical process or a fixed structure (predetermining that a particular method will lead to the right result), it is important to carefully design the process. In doing so, one has to be aware of what is happening in the 'here and now' in order to be able to identify, what emerges in the process and which steps come next. *Process competence* is an essential skill for every member of a leadership team. The school leadership group gradually learned to observe itself in its assumptions and actions, to exchange and question these observations without lapsing into defensive reactions, and it learned to use individual and collective self-observation to determine starting points for effective leadership action.

Our second coaching phase, separated from the first by a break, had a different focus. It was about making decisions, about closing the more open and expansive part of the conversation. While the dialogue was about 'opening and broadening', this phase had to be about ordering and evaluating, reducing and excluding. Organisations are social systems that unendingly produce a multitude of decisions, each of which follows on from the other, and each of which engenders further decisions. Current decisions depend on previous decisions, which thus act as premises for later ones. The premises behind the decisions determine the scope within which decisions can be made, and are therefore of central importance in leading an organisation.

Communication during decision-making is different from thinking together in dialogue. It is characterised by a different energy and a different pace. While the dialogue phase has a rather meandering, slow and deepening character, the decision-making phase is fast and focused.

From the impressions and insights gained during the dialogue phase, starting points were identified which are relevant to the respective issue and which were now systematically worked through. I supported the leadership team in this phase differently, asking exact questions and providing focused comments. At the end of this phase decisions were taken and agreements made.

Each coaching session ended with two steps. First, the members summarised the agreements they had worked out. They described how they had progressed together in the topics and how they would proceed with them. Then they changed from the organisational level to the group level and the personal level. Everybody described how they had experienced the day's process and evaluated its results, naming an insight he or she had gained as well as what remained open or unresolved.

The Interaction of the Inner and the Outer Dynamic

The topics of the coaching sessions seemed obvious. At the content level, several questions stood out, including: What does the headmistress's retirement mean for the school? What will remain, what will stop? How can the essential elements of the concept be preserved and changed at the same time? I was curious to see how they would begin the consideration and how they would process these questions. Also, I wondered what dynamics these topics would create within the people individually and in the group. In the first sessions, the group started with topics they currently had to deal with as a leadership body; e.g., with the intervention in emerging conflicts or with activities of the staff to introduce new elements into the pedagogical concept. The exchange often began objectively and rationally. As described above, the various observations and assessments were compiled, and then they and I commented on the overall picture and asked some guiding questions.

Over the course of the sessions I noticed a communication pattern developing, where mainly the deputy headmaster and the pedagogical director pushed the group's issues. The headmistress sat next to them, calmly and almost untouched by the conversation. When I introduced my observation – after a phase of silence – suddenly movement emerged. The pedagogical director and the deputy headmaster spoke emphatically about their worries and fear that the power relations between the school and the state authorities would change with the departure of the headmistress. The headmistress, with her networking abilities and her political know-how, had been able to prevent or skilfully control regulatory interventions in the pedagogical development of the school. Now they feared the retirement would create a power vacuum, particularly at a time when the winds of education policy had changed and the new Minister of Education was pursuing other education policy goals.

The fear in the room was twofold: one was that the previous scope for shaping the school would become significantly narrower; and second, the school supervisory authority could appoint a new headmaster who would give priority to a selective pedagogy over the integrative model currently practised. The pedagogical director was clearly annoyed about her dependence on the actions of the headmistress. She felt powerless, and she deeply feared for the survival of the pedagogical concept of the school. For her it was the survival of a life's work in which she – just like the headmistress – had been involved since the foundation of the school. I had noticed the pressure in these two people, which so far had only been expressed on the content level, e.g., in discussions about resolutions to secure the school concept for the next two years. Surprising was the relative calm of the headmistress. I thought perhaps the outburst of the two colleagues must have affected her. The continuation of the school concept also must have been close to her heart. How might her behaviour be understood? Had she, more than a year before her retirement, already withdrawn internally? The answer to this question became apparent in the next coaching session. After the check-in, the deputy headmaster began to talk about the loss that the retirement of the headmistress would mean for him. He turned to her and talked about how much he appreciated working with her, listed what he had experienced and gone through with her over the years, what her strengths were in running the school and what he would miss. Others joined him, and touching moments arose in which the members of the school management were very close to each other – in memory of what they had built together and in anticipation of the coming loss. The headmistress responded by making herself and her performance small: "We managed that together. You will be able to carry on well without me . . ." It seemed as if the feedback of her colleagues had not reached her, or perhaps she could not react to it. When I asked her how her reaction to the appreciative comments could be understood, she reacted again with an ambivalent and superficial explanation. Only when I inquired further it gradually become apparent that for this woman – who was a teacher and headmistress with her body and her soul, who knew how to swim like a fish in the educational policy waters, and who had co-created the school – that the withdrawal from her life's calling as a headmistress threatened her and she could lose her identity. She could not and did not want to imagine the change that would take place in the foreseeable future and did not want to get involved in these thoughts.

The experience of her fear and her resistance had a considerable effect on the leadership team. Her colleagues reacted as if they were frozen. They were confused because their appreciation apparently had not been accepted and remained unaddressed. They were frustrated and angry because the headmistress deflected their fears about the continuity of the school model by arguing that there was still enough time to exert her influence. Her defensive arguments put her two colleagues under even more stress and increased their anxiety. I described the observable recurring dynamic of fear and appeasement, excitement and defensiveness and it became clear to all of them that the energy in the leadership group had been tied up by the impact the inner dynamic of the headmistress had on the group and hindered joint actions.

It was uncertain at this point whether it would be possible to interrupt these dynamics and whether the headmistress would find access to her fear that accompanied the end of her active professional life and could connect to the emotions of her colleagues.

The Revelation of Motive

There were about two months between the individual sessions, and I was curious how the leadership team would process these experiences and where inner stance the headmistress had moved to. Our next session began with a surprise, however. The leadership team wanted my help in preparing a conference in which the college should vote on whether they wanted to actively participate in the founding of a new school with the same concept.

I was speechless at this unexpected turn of events. What had happened to the insights from the last session? How did this leap from an emotional group situation to a very ambitious educational initiative come about? In the course of the conversation it turned out that the headmistress had initiated this idea and proposal. She had interfered in the re-founding of another integrative comprehensive school and had offered herself as interim headmistress for it. In doing so, she brought her college into play as mentors and as a personnel resource. The new comprehensive school could, she suggested, first be established as a branch of this school. The teachers could work in both places and introduce the teachers of the new school to the integrated concept. She herself would manage this branch for the first two years and then hand it over! The headmistress sparkled with energy at the thought of being able to act once again, before her professional life ended, as a founding member of an interesting school and as its first headmistress – this time with the wisdom of the experienced. The fear of losing her professional identity had released enormous energies in her and she had created this opportunity for herself through many conversations and activities with the school authorities and the city administration.

During the coaching it turned out that the college and the members of the leadership team were surprised and fascinated by this unexpected option. The motivation of the headmistress caused a lot of excitement and at the same time a lot of pressure. Linked to it was a dilemma: If the college said "No" to contributing to the founding of a new integrative school, they would miss the historic moment of increasing the number of these type of schools under a conservative government, which preferred more selective school programmes. Who wants to be accused in this way? At the same time, however, if they were to vote in favour of the proposal, the entire college and especially the members of the leadership team would be under extreme work pressure from now on.

For the leadership team to be able to deal with the question and shape a decision-making process, I invited the team members to describe how they experienced the current situation. As I could observe how everyone in the group constantly oscillated between content and emotionality, I directed the attention from the outside inwards to the personal level: "What would this option of a new branch mean? What could a '*Yes*' decision mean for me personally? and, What impact might a '*No*' decision have on me?" Each member spoke about him- or herself. Everybody could feel what moved the others, could hear their desires and concerns and how they understood their responsibility for the school. They saw what political motives moved them – everyone except for the headmistress. She constantly shifted to the political and to the pragmatic level.

After having expressed their personal thought and motives, we moved on to the organisational level: "What would the proposal mean for the teaching staff and the school as a whole? What opportunities and risks might be associated with it? How would the parents react? And what resources would the school authorities make available?" By thinking about different dimensions, I supported the leadership team in identifying the decision premises which would later be relevant for the decision-making process. At the end of this part of the coaching session it emerged that three members were in favour of the headmistress's initiative and three against it. In the second part, we focused on the upcoming conference and the question how the decision could be taken. Should the decision-making process be organised bottom-up in a team-oriented way, as is usually the case, or should in this case the leadership team take the decision top-down and issue a guideline? In the latter scenario, the college would only have advisory but not decisive authority. This consideration about top-down or bottom-up decision-making held an explosive potential, in that it would have a powerful effect on the principle of the school's team orientation. After a surprisingly short discussion, the leadership team decided that the decision-making authority in this instance should lie with the leadership team. In doing so, it departed from the tradition of making key decisions in a multistage, bottom-up process. On the one hand, the existing deadline was an essential criterion, but in my view the ambivalence of the individuals on this issue played a major role. Each member of the leadership team felt conflicted, and therefore hesitated to engage in a bottom-up decision-making process so as not to create an unmanageable dynamic in the college.

Next time we met, the leadership team appeared torn and battered. In the check-in it became clear that this decision process had put the relationship between the college and its leadership team to the test. The content aspects of setting up a branch had driven a wedge into the college. However, the changed decision-making process itself weighed more heavily than the controversy over content. The intention of the leadership team to take this decision itself, only receiving advice from the college, had led to a deep disappointment and, in the following weeks, to a mutual distancing. The individual members also described why this incident had hit them so hard in the college, and how they assessed the current situation in the school. The headmistress was – again and still – only superficially touched by it. Believing that the situation would soon relax, she was already completely occupied with building up the new school branch.

The further extent to which the inner dynamics of the headmistress influenced the leadership team's ability to act became apparent over the course of the coaching. The headmistress talked almost exclusively about the construction of the new school; ending her professional life was no longer an issue, and she was inwardly about to set off for new shores. It seemed as if she did not perceive that the college and the leadership team were threatening to fall apart. The pedagogical director finally broke away and attacked the headmistress: "You act as if there is no retirement and it's business as usual. And you aren't doing your duties as headmistress at all. You are often absent, requests remain unanswered, work is left undone and upcoming decisions are not made". It annoyed the pedagogical director that the headmistress acted as if she would stay, and at the same time did not do her job. She was afraid that the school as a whole might become run-down. When I invited the other members of the leadership team to describe how they experienced the situation, they hesitantly joined in, and it became clear that they all shared the pedagogical director's assessment. They all confirmed that the school was badly managed, and they saw the inability of the headmistress to accept her impending departure from her professional life as causing a repressive dynamic into which her leadership team colleagues (and the entire college) were drawn. In their view this dynamic produced paralysis, anger and disappointment. The issue was now on the table and 'the elephant was visible'.

The violent outburst of the pedagogical director and the feedback from the other school leadership colleagues shook the headmistress. She could not react, shrunk in her chair and one could feel her despair. She asked for guidance and at her request and that of her colleagues, I agreed to work with her individually over the following weeks. Normally I don't work with two parties who relate to each other or are dependent on each other at the same time. In this case I agreed to accompany her for some weeks to give her support and a holding environment In my individual coaching sessions with her, the enormous importance her job and calling as a headmistress had for her and how her identity was shaped by it became apparent. This role had filled her and kept her alive. In the individual sessions she was able to talk about it without having to defend herself or be ashamed.

The effect of the headmistress's reflections (with me) about her fears and her despair, caused by the prospect of her retirement – and her acceptance of those emotions – showed itself in the next team coaching session. After she described more about how she was doing, and gave space to the others to participate, the pedagogical director and the deputy headmistress took a lead and came forward with a suggestion. They proposed evaluating the school over the next two months. All elements and components would be addressed: how they had experienced working at the school over the last five years; what had proven to be successful; where the group had harboured doubts; and what the group was *not* doing – although they talked about it often. In this coaching session, the members of the leadership team agreed upon a systematic evaluation process to take place across several workshops and, as a next step after the evaluation, to adapt or change outdated concept elements. The group also discussed the role and contribution of the headmistress in this evaluation process: she would act as a coach for the college, observe from the sidelines and provide her knowledge and experience in comments and recommendations.

This move shifted the energy in the group and obviously in the college. In the following coaching session the dialogue phase was marked by enthusiastic descriptions about the inspiring evaluation process and how these conversations had led to a shared direction and to common goals. Everybody in the college was interested and involved in the further development of the school and the teachers' collective. They evaluated, selected and created space for something new to happen.

Letting Go is a Prerequisite for Further Development

The experience of this evaluation process enabled the headmistress to accept the end of her career and to start thinking about leaving active professional life. One expression of this acceptance was her commitment to finding a successor. She pulled strings – and she was good at it – on the political backstage to get someone to the school who would fit in with the college and the school concept. The headmistress left the school at the scheduled time. In the last month of her term in office, the college took her on a full day's walk through a region of the country she loved and had chosen for her farewell.

The new school was founded, but not as an annex. In the last two years, it has developed into an independent, integrative school to which the college is committed. This school has a new headmaster who appreciates the concept. He has a different mentality and a tendency to decide more quickly than the former headmistress used to do. I coached the leadership team with the new headmaster in this transition phase for another year and supported them in getting to know their way of working and in working together. It turned out that, in this new combination, the leadership team was able to tackle issues that had previously been taboo.

I finished my coaching after three years. The school had stayed the same and had changed at the same time.

For all of this to happen the headmistress had to let go of her identity-shaping role as the head of a school, accept the loss and her fears about who she would be without that role. Only by letting go could an open space be created in which something new could emerge. Dialogue is essential in these transitional phases, as it has the potential to create and provide such a space.

Looking Back as a Coach

In thinking about this coaching process, the most powerful experience was the connection and interaction between the fear and resistance of the headmistress and the actions of the leadership team. The inner dynamic acted itself out in an outer dynamic. One pivotal moment in the coaching process was my naming of the communication patterns between the headmistress and the pedagogical director. That observation, including how the communication process was structured and how different arguments were coloured emotionally, led to an important discovery and to an understanding of the relevant dynamics.

Accompanying the leadership team, I kept my attention on six dimensions: the group, the individual and the organisation and the content, the process (sequence of arguments), the emotions (the emotional colouring in relationship to the content and the people). Throughout the process my resonance with what happened and how it happened was an important indicator and guideline for me.

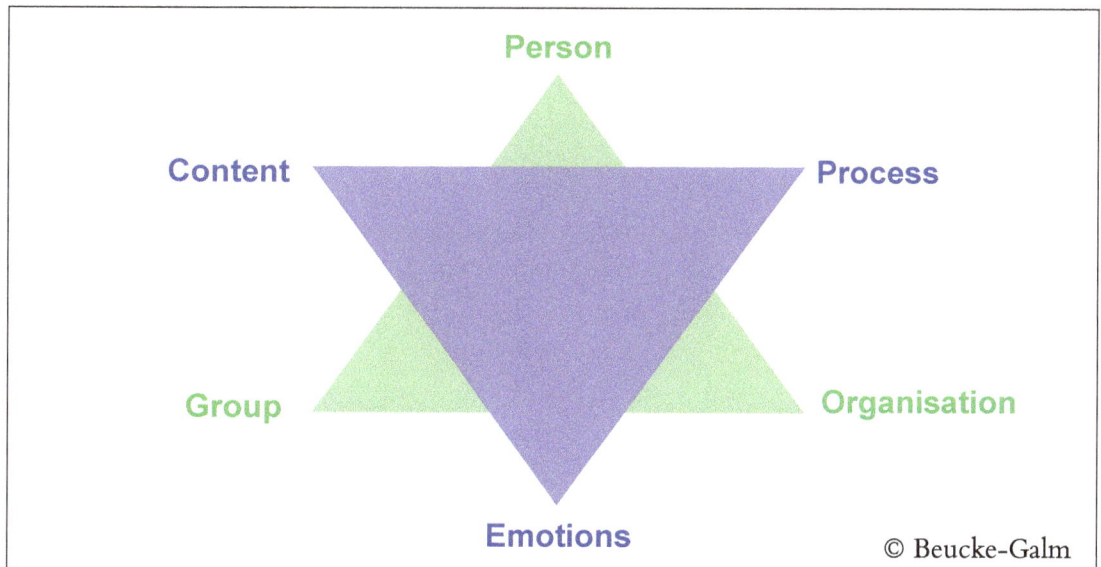

For this coaching assignment I had chosen a two-part structure: first, a phase of opening, widening and deepening the understanding (dialogue); and second, a phase of prioritizing, selecting and closing (decision-making). This structure gave the process a framework in which the topics could unfold and be enfolded again. While working with the group I kept the whole school – its context and the individual people – in mind. The three levels (person, group and organisation) were present throughout, and most of the topics were discussed and reflected on all levels. By again and again distinguishing which aspect of a topic belongs at which level, the leadership team learned to use this model in its day-to-day work. It provided an understanding of where to act.

A special quality in the coaching process appeared in the dialogue phases. In listening with mutual respect and an open mind, there was a threefold readiness in the leadership team: the readiness to engage in the open space, the readiness to engage in a process and the readiness to learn from the observations in the here and now.

The space of Dialogue allows those themes to emerge which could be excluded and rationalised away. They can be expressed and thus be made accessible to the clients and the organisations. Systemically speaking, dialogue opens up the possibility of reintegrating what has been – or would be – excluded from the system. Dialogue is therefore a venture with an unknown outcome. The art of the coach is to know when to keep the process open and when to bring it to a close.

Conference Session Extracts

From a conversation with participants considering the paper with Mechtild Beucke-Galm

Speaker: I struggle with coaching when it comes to the higher-ups or leadership within my institution. As a leader myself, I just find it hard to coach them. It's hard to explain. I have no issues coaching the people that I work with side-by-side or the ones that I supervise, but when it comes to leadership, I have a struggle with the coaching. I was hoping to get some insight on how to handle that.

Speaker: I am an internal coach in the Department of Corrections in Virginia, the United States. My question is about trying to break down the barrier, the walls, that exist in seasoned staff who don't want to hear what dialogue is. And we have higher up people that show a facade. You can tell that the way that they talk is not the way that they act.

Speaker: I'm a counselor at Pocahontas State Correctional Center. I was reading your paper, and in the first part of it there's a lot about the team coaching. When I reflect with clients on their questions, without telling them what to do, I accompany them on an exploration of difficult situations and underlying assumptions. I may not be the highest up the ladder, but for me, leadership starts when you're at the bottom. You have to learn how to hold people accountable. You have to learn how to encourage them to make the right decisions. You have to help them to grow as a person professionally, as well as personally, and be supportive of them for the achievements they make. You have to be able to help them. It's not always someone who's at the top. Sometimes it's that person at the bottom reminding the person at the top that, hey, maybe this will work this way.

Mechtild: I think that it is an important question how one creates and sets up the coaching situation. I'm a person from outside the organisation. So, the border for me is half inside, half outside. On one hand, I get a feeling how the organisation works and on the other hand have enough distance to be able to observe what is not working so well and why, and be able to feed my observation back. I have some distance, and with this position I also have a certain authority to shape the process of coaching. I am not the expert for the topics. The knowledge of the field itself is in the people, the leadership team. Similarly, I do think that it is important for internal coach to position himself or herself in a certain way so that as an internal coach you have an independent authority in what you are doing as a coach. Not what you are doing as a team manager or a dialogue facilitator, but in your coaching role. You should be seen inside the organisation as a certain profession. If you are a coach in the dialogue program where you will help people to become better with their dialogic skills, then you are a coach who has a certain expertise. And with your expertise, you try to help the other person who is not developed yet in their skills. The expertise the other person should develop.

Speaker: To follow what you were saying, whether it's in a group or individual sessions, trust is really important. You have to know that you can speak openly and authentically about what it is that you need to speak about, and know that that trust is going to be able to keep that going. But how to prevent those meetings after the meeting, in little groups and cliques . . . how to get those into the main session and have a more quality conversation?

Mechtild: There is a rule that what is said in a coaching session is not talked about in a different place in the organisation. It is especially important for internal coaches to respect that. If you don't keep that, people will lose trust in the process, maybe not in you, because you are a nice person, but in the process of coaching.

Speaker: Building trust is a very big issue. We talked about the use of what we call the practices in our dialogue training. For y'all who don't know, we'll use Voice, showing Respect, being open-minded and so on. The building of the trust through the listening skills is extremely important so that you can hear everybody and what they're actually saying. Also, we talked about supervisors. Some of them were people who were talking out of the side of their mouth, you know, showing you one thing, but not in their actions.

Speaker: For individuals like myself who work in an institution, we may have the opportunity to dialogue about decision-making when it comes to some things. But sometimes we just check the box to say that we've done it. There are those times when we utilise dialogue in order to make decisions, but a lot of times we don't have that opportunity. Because of Covid we don't have the option to meet as a group as often now.

Speaker: In the community, probation, we conduct dialogue to make a lot of decisions. When we don't there seem to be some hurt feelings, you know. When leadership just has a decision to hand down, sometimes people feel left out. Then on the flip side of that, sometimes people do just want decisions to be made.

Speaker: We talked about the same thing. Sometimes we just have to make an executive decision. It depends on how fast something needs to be taken care of, as well as what type of decision is this being made. I was curious as to how they incorporate correctional officers into dialogues in prisons, because that's a much larger group. We talked about, for instance, the new normal. A new normal taskforce was created on the executive side, and they had dialogue in their decision-making. They invited the units to be a part of it. Then the union had an opportunity to bring in their line staff to have a dialogue about it to push information back up so that the department could come up with a policy that affected my staff more than maybe it affected the executive team. So, my experience with dialogue is that a topic may start at the top, but the department does a pretty good job to filter that information down so others can then dialogue to help make the decision.

Speaker: Because of dialogue, we're able to make more informed decisions. Whereas before we may have done a lot of trial and error, this way around we've gotten something more solid that we can use. So, it's been working to our advantage to have the dialogues and it works to our favour.

Speaker: I just want to commend you for the outstanding and provoking paper that generated such rich conversations this morning. I was fortunate to be in a group with one of your colleagues, and she brought such a rich perspective into the conversation. A lot of what we talked about was just how we are using these principles of coaching here in Virginia, and specific ways for refining it and making it even better instilled in our culture. So, I just commend you! Thank you.

Postscript

The author's reflections, written some months after the conference

When I think back to the workshop, I remember my surprise right at the beginning when I realised that I was facing almost exclusively internal coaches who were interested in learning about coaching on dialogue skills. I immediately asked myself whether my work and my coaching concept would be interesting for them at all, and what I could give to them. I automatically operated with the assumption that in a workshop the speaker should 'deliver'. The participants taught me that it is also about thinking (out loud) together, inviting different perspectives on that topic to emerge and being attentive to what the topic means to different groupings.

In the course of the workshop, two sets of issues came up that stayed with me for a while. One was the role of the internal coach in a hierarchical organisation. The question was how to convince more senior managers in this constellation to trust a colleague as a coach, to trust the other setting and to address their questions and uncertainties in this setting. How can one avoid such coaching sessions becoming small talks and the possibility of the 'protected space' remaining unused? The descriptions of some participants made it clear to me once again how important trust and confidentiality are as a basis and professional standard for successful coaching. For external coaches it seems easy to define this. For internal coaches it is a different story. If the coachee knows about the hierarchically lower position of the coach or if coachee and coach know each other from other contexts, then it is enormously important to introduce the new and different context. The context defines how the relationship can be shaped and how communication can be structured. It is therefore necessary to consciously and carefully establish the other role and the other setting and to persevere with it. For internal (and for external) coaches it is the (basic) principle on which every working alliance is based.

The second set of topics revolved around questions about which context and at what time to introduce dialogue. The participants were surprised at my approach of using dialogue to prepare decisions. I, in turn, was surprised that dialogue was mainly used to achieve a better understanding among each other and to promote cohesion. Through this experience, I would like to pass on to Dialogue Practitioners and change agents that dialogue has a practical meaning in the life of organisations. Well-prepared decision-making processes are crucial for every organisation. An effective decision-making process needs a shared understanding of what is at stake and the strategic challenges. This can be achieved through dialogue.

Dialogue in Teacher Training at the University Level

Heike de Boer & Daniela Merklinger

In addition to my studies, I work as a language teacher in a school in a group with four, fourth-grade children (two boys and two girls) who are learning German as a second language. In one of my lessons a conflict arose between a boy and a girl during the break. I will call them Ahmed and Fatma. Ahmed's parents work all day and he is on his own a lot. Fatma is an only child and grows up protected by her parents. Ahmed is often late to or absent from my language classes. He frequently uses Turkish swear words and is quick to insult. Fatma blames Ahmed for his behaviour. During a break, a conflict had developed between the two which they carried into my classroom.

I sat down with the four children at our group table to talk about the conflict. I asked them not to interrupt one another and to try to speak calmly. Since they were not used to dialogue, this did not work right away. I then asked Fatma and Ahmed to take a moment to think about how the other one felt. At first Fatma said: "I cannot imagine how Ahmed feels, I just want him to no longer offend me".

However, this sentence got the thoughts of the two rolling. Ahmed replied that he wanted to quit insulting Fatma, but that he just didn't know how to get Fatma to stop telling on him. He also said that he has to cook food for himself at noon and therefore just doesn't come out of the house on time. One could read in Fatma's face that she was dismayed and at the same time she was thinking. Then she apologised and even suggested she could call Ahmed from now on so that he is on time for language class. In return, however, she wanted him to stop insulting her and show her more respect. Ahmed was very surprised by Fatma's reaction and made a high and holy promise to improve.

At some point I completely took myself out of this dialogue and just listened. At the beginning, however, it was essential to explain the rules and give impulses.

—Laura Giese, student of primary school education, summer term 2020

The aim of dialogic conversations, in the sense of David Bohm's practice, is to let the emphasis be put on the process (rather than outcomes) so that the implicit and initially unspeakable can surface in a mutual conversation (Bohm 2005, p. 36). This is exactly what the student-teacher and the children succeeded in doing in the small dialogue described above. The student-teacher broke the pattern of judgement and contradiction established between Ahmed and Fatma, and gave the children the opportunity to understand the conflict together.

This does not happen on its own. In the case above, the student-teacher created a framework by giving the children two rules: do not interrupt each other, and try to speak calmly. When that alone was not enough to calm the heated moods, she decelerated the conversation by asking Ahmed and Fatma to consider how the other one felt. In this way, she succeeded in creating a space in which Ahmed could make explicit something that had hitherto remained implicit. He dared to say something very personal, without knowing for sure how Fatma, the other children or the student-teacher would react. Fatma succeeded in changing her perspective. She responded to Ahmed's situation with understanding and offered a surprising solution for Ahmed – and in turn demanded more respect from him.

We have been reflecting together on scenes like this in our dialogue seminars in the current summer semester 2020. For example, even if the student-teacher writes that at some point she *"completely took herself out"*, the seminar group points out that she has done a lot more than this in this situation. She has, as a facilitator, succeeded in creating a 'container', establishing trust and, with a basic attitude that is based on mutual understanding, opened the space for the development of something new. The container in turn enables Ahmed to explain his family context by way of productive pleading. Thus he reaches the heart of Fatma: she feels empathy, she is touched by Ahmed's narration and she wants to find a solution to the situation with him in exchange for more respect from him. Such a situation, as the students agree, is a collective experience that contributes to common understanding and is an example of lived dialogue practice.

This small case study by Fatma and Ahmed illustrates what dialogue can shift at school and how great the chance is to develop common understanding and joint meaning-making in a classroom with dialogical elements. As a prerequisite for students to be able to hold dialogic conversations with others (be they children *or* adults) in the Bohmian sense of dialogue, it is essential that students get to know this form of conversation and gain experience with it. These conversations are geared towards mutual understanding, connecting with others' contributions and opening conversation spaces in which new things can arise. Against this background, this paper focuses on conceptual considerations for dialogue work in teacher training and our first very concrete experiences with it.

Why Dialogue for Teacher Training Is Important

There is a great deal of interest in dialogic forms of conversation in the classroom. *The Routledge International Handbook of Dialogic Education* (Mercer/Wegerif/Major), published in 2019, provides an overview of research on this topic. International research on school talk reveals that communication in the classroom is rarely dialogic. As stated in the handbook, "classrooms are arenas of rapid-fire and complicated patterns of talk consisting of systems of direction and compliance, usually in some form of routine question-and-answer sequences" (Edwards-Groves/Davidson 2019: 126). The common interaction in the classroom is thus still characterised by the teacher setting a topic by asking a question (initiation) and a student usually offering a short answer (response), which is then evaluated by the teacher (evaluation). This *initiation-response-evaluation* scheme was already empirically documented in the seventies (Mehan 1979) and is still the common practice today. Classroom conversations are often characterised by a question-developing conversation style in which short-answer questions from the teacher dominate. This type of classroom conversation is also known as a 'recitation script'; that is, the teacher directs, and the demand on the students is "to report someone else's thinking rather than thinking for themselves and to be evaluated on their compliance in doing so" (Hardman 2019: 153).

At the same time, there are a number of intervention studies that show that teacher-student interaction can be improved through a dialogic pedagogy in the classroom (cf. the research overview by Howe/Abedin 2013). And although research increasingly shows that "dialogic pedagogy can improve student learning outcomes and social-emotional well-being" (Hardman 2019: 152), it also shows that teachers find it difficult to implement (ibid.; cf. also Edwards-Groves/Davidson 2019: 127).

Pupils and thus also students as future teachers lack the experience of a dialogue-based exchange at school. In most cases, they have been socialised at school in such a way that they have sought 'right' answers in results-oriented discussions. They lack the experience to be able to (cf. de Boer 2018):

- express unfinished thoughts,
- allow longer breaks and waiting times,
- suspend their own evaluations,
- trust in the process,
- unfold the 'new' in the joint meaning-making, and
- think together.

Even in university seminars this experience is too rarely enabled. Although students and lecturers take different perspectives on subject-related, didactic and pedagogically relevant content, they usually do so in discussions that aim at making one's point and convincing others of one's own point of view. Often these discussions are conducted by the same people, take place within a framework of self-presentation and are observed by a silent audience. Similar to school, many students at university-level classes are afraid to speak – they fear that they will be embarrassed or make a fool of themselves.

This makes it all the more important for students to become acquainted with dialogical forms of conversation within the framework of university teacher training. This is an important foundation for being able to conduct dialogic conversations geared towards mutual understanding and joint meaning-making with children or adults at school. We also can assume that the experience of dialogue contributes to professionalising one's own conversational behaviour.

Online Seminar: Dialogue as the Basis for Professional Communication Skills

In the summer semester 2020, due to Covid 19 precautions, our dialogue seminar with student-teachers had to take place under completely new conditions. Our earlier seminars were characterised by dialogues in the university setting with the student group and school dialogues with primary school children (de Boer 2019; de Boer 2018; de Boer 2015, Merklinger 2019; Merklinger 2020). However, the University of Koblenz and the Ludwigsburg School of Education (near Stuttgart), our institutions in Germany, offered for the first time a pure online semester without any in-person attendance. The schools in Germany were also faced with great challenges and were closed for a long time, so there was no opportunity to work together with in-room school classes.

Against this background we developed for students at our respective locations a seminar concept in which we balanced the opportunity to gain dialogue experience with primary school children with a higher proportion of tasks for self- and peer-reflection.

The situation with Fatma and Ahmed at the beginning of this article was written by a student-teacher in this context in a reflection task.

As shown below, the seminar concept was based on five building blocks that are all interconnected:

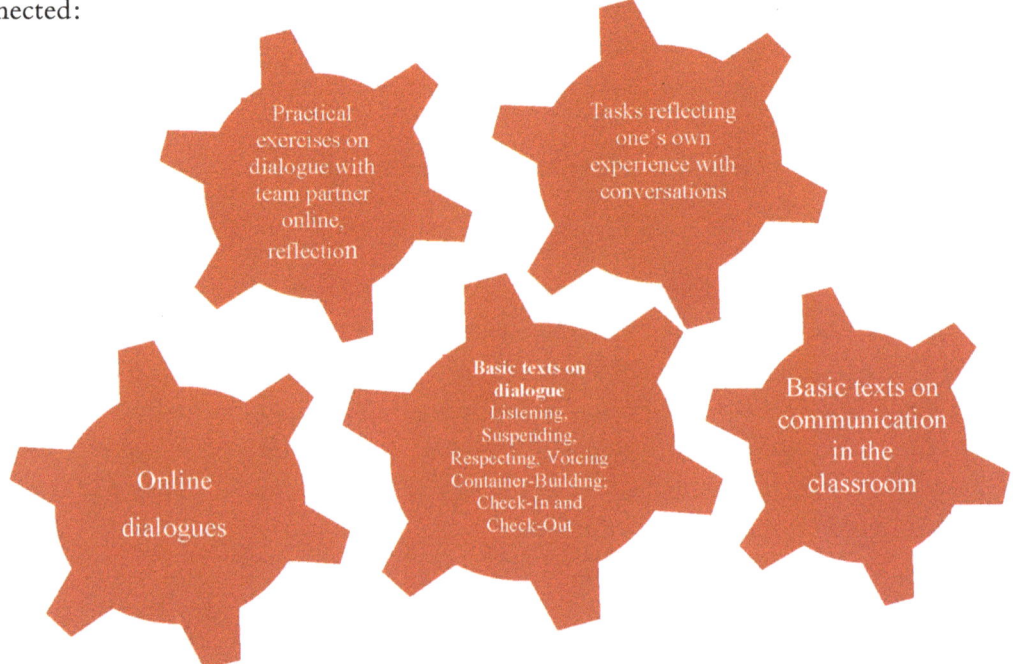

Fig. 1: Components of the online seminar concept, summer semester 2020

Questioning Common Patterns: Students Reflect on their Dialogue Experiences

The experience of online rather than in-person dialogues in the university-seminar environment and with children in their school setting – completely online without personal encounters and conversations – was unfamiliar both for the students and for us lecturers. At first this approach felt quite 'undialogical'. In the following sections we will use original quotations of transcribed excerpts from an online dialogue conducted at the end of the semester to illustrate the student-teachers' experiences and insights. The online dialogue's topic – *What about dialogue has become important to you?* – was particularly revealing.

We describe the students' experiences as 'pattern breaks', moments of realisation or reflection on a long-standing pattern of thought or action. We have divided these patterns into six different forms, each illustrated by student-teacher quotations. During the online seminar students became aware of (and were sometimes confused by) their own existing routines and patterns in their thinking and speaking, as shown by their statements. As a result, they had the opportunity not only to question their conversational behaviour in everyday life, but also their conversational experiences at school and at college or university.

These pattern breaks provide personal insights into the thinking of the students involved, which in this form is unusual for university contexts. We have learned together with and from the students in this dialogue!

Pattern Break One: Process Orientation and Openness to Results

"I have the feeling that this [dialogue] takes a lot of pressure off me in many conversations, so that there is no need for a result".

Before the seminar, this student-teacher had the idea that discussions must lead to results. She reports that she learned through the seminar that things "*can be totally sufficient in the first moment if you just express your thoughts and clarify your ideas behind them*". From her remarks, we could see that she has also changed her idea of conversations to the effect that "*it is perfectly okay if I don't bring any results into the conversation, but only open questions or thoughts that have begun*". It is not surprising that this student-teacher came to the conclusion that the open-endedness of results in a conversation "*takes a lot of pressure off*" of her.

". . . Because I have always waited for the right and perfect answer for myself".

Another student-teacher describes very impressively how the search for the perfect answer led to the fact that it "*always took her a relatively long time*" to speak in seminars. In the first dialogue during the online seminar, she experienced this differently: "*In the first conversation with Christine*, *when we were divided into groups . . . it showed me that it can really be enough to insert a fraction of your thoughts or a question or something like that, and yes – somehow I learned to dare more . . . This was a very important step for me*".

[I found] "that you really do have the time to think about the topic and not to try to produce an answer quickly".

A third student-teacher makes it clear through her statement that the pauses in the dialogue were very unusual for her. She refers to her experience with dialogues using picture books, which she had conducted with primary school children in the previous semester in primary school: "*At the beginning, after three seconds, you thought: 'Okay, now you can have an answer!*'" She realised that the waiting is not only worthwhile for the children, it also makes a difference in the online dialogues in the seminar, where "*we have now taken a minute or two to really think about it*". The phrase '*don't try to produce any answers quickly*' is a contrast to the way she usually experienced conversations in seminars: "*The point is to find quick answers – in case of doubt maybe even 'any answer' seems to serve the purpose*"

Pattern Break Two: Engaging with the Opinions of Others

"that one . . . does not always try so hard to convince others of one's own opinion . . . , but rather to engage with other opinions . . .".

This student-teacher has learned through the seminar "*to realise . . . and make [myself] aware*" that in dialogues she found it difficult to engage with the thoughts of others at the beginning. But "*the longer you were part of it*", she discovered, the more she tried to think along with others and the better she could "*simply take back her own opinion*". Before, she had thought conversations were mostly about "*convincing others of your own opinion . . . or simply presenting it*". To "*be open for other opinions*" and knowing "*that we could continue thinking together in this way helped me a lot*", she said. This also showed her that "*you simply have to listen better*". Another student-teacher states that it's not so easy to suspend one's own opinion in a conversation: "*And it has often happened to me that you want to express your own opinion immediately without holding back at first*". This has become "*extremely important*" to her; she associates this thought with the "*aspect of suspension*", which she has "*not really dealt with before*".

---

* Christine was a tutor in the online-dialogue seminar. She had taken part in the dialogue seminar the semester before, where she also carried out dialogues with children.

As another student-teacher points out, *"When I talk to someone in this way, I make sure that I really hear what they say and that I'm not . . . thinking about something else"*. For her, this also includes letting the person finish what they are saying. She notices that *"I was sometimes so stuck in my convictions . . . It's important that you really get involved with other people and look at things from their point of view . . ."*.

Pattern Break Three: Suspension Instead of Immediate Evaluation

"It has become very important to me in the dialogue . . . to suspend. Because I think we evaluate very often, especially in a school context".

Suspension is an important topic for all students. During the seminar, they got to know Chris Argyris's ladder of interference, which demonstrates how we selectively draw conclusions from data, and applied it to conversational situations from the past that they found challenging. In the online dialogue, one student-teacher points out that she knows the 'ladder experience' well: *". . . I have often observed . . . how quickly I have practically climbed up the ladder of inference within fractions of a second"*. She goes on to say that it is important to her that she tries to *"be aware that I . . . am interpreting and evaluating a situation myself"*. But then she also tries *"to consciously oppose it"*. This thought is taken up by another student-teacher later in the conversation. She says that she has become *"more sensitive to it"* and that she *"notices it more quickly if I'm already at the top of the ladder"*. She has not yet managed to *"immediately stop forming an opinion"*. At the same time, she asks herself *"whether it is really possible to turn it off completely"*. For her, it is more a matter of holding back, not speaking immediately. Then she reports that she does have *"another preconceived opinion, but I am prepared to reconsider it . . . before I express it"*.

"Well, I ask myself . . . whether you have to stop [judging] totally, whether you have to be practically neutral".

Another student-teacher takes up the question of whether the goal realistically can be to stop judging in one's own thoughts. She believes that judging happens *"because it is simply human"*. She understands the process of suspension as follows: *"You just have a fine feeling, and can be so self-reflected that you realise what you are doing and can consciously hold it back"*. She compares suspending with meditation. Some people say, she points out, that *"when you meditate, your head is free, there are no thoughts"*. Others say that thoughts are *"as natural as our heartbeat. And we cannot stop that"*. The question to her, then, is how to deal with the thoughts: *"I can also just *allow the thoughts to come in and then say: 'Yes, okay. But I will also let them go again'. And I ask myself whether this is comparable to suspension. And then then you can use your mind and say: 'Yes, but now I'm going to let it go again'. And you free yourself from these thoughts again, and I think that's already . . . a great expression of self-reflexivity".*

"[Regarding] the core capability of slowing down . . . I have seen how extremely important it is . . . through the different experiences we have had".

Many of the students' statements reflect the practices of slowing down and listening. For example, one student-teacher compares his experience in two online dialogues that took different paths: "*We also compared the [process of a] dialogue on friendship and the [process of a] dialogue on the topic of failure*". He remembers that many "*did not get the chance to speak simply because of the . . . speeding up in the second dialogue . . . including me. I noticed that I didn't get a chance at all*". Even though a pause of 20 seconds feels "*terribly long*" to him, he finds it "*extremely important that you include everyone*". This helps, says the student-teacher, "*that you can look at your own mental and emotional patterns again . . . and those of others.*" Pauses in the conversation are also indispensable for this, because they enable reflection, which can take place at a later time than speaking, says another: "*If you want to give room to thinking . . . then you need . . . the pauses*".

We also emphasise listening as part of the process of deceleration in conversation. "*A very important realisation for me was this* real *listening. So what does real listening mean? That I actually have an open ear and do not spend the whole time thinking, but really* listening *and then being able to promote the flow of thoughts*".

Pattern Break Five: Thinking Together vs. Self-Presentation as Knowledge Expert

"I found this more interesting than factual knowledge, which is what seminars are often about . . . You learn more about the people".

One student-teacher describes experiencing dialogues in a way that is different than seminar discussions, because it is not about "*some kind of self-presentation or that I have to show myself as a knowledge expert . . .*". As a result, he reported that he "*opened up a lot more*" and found what the others were thinking "*much more interesting*", "*even if their thoughts were unfinished*". He enjoyed noticing "*experiences, observations, evaluations – simply meanings they attribute to things.*" Two aspects are interesting here: First, the student-teacher speaks of "*attributing*", i.e., things do not have meaning per se, but the meaning arises in the mind of the observer. He also realises that not having to show himself as a knowledge expert lets him open himself up more in the conversation.

Later in the dialogue, when the students talk about the meaning of "*honest questions*" for a dialogue that is open for results, one student-teacher describes how she experiences questions in the university context: "*We are sitting in the seminar, the lecturer has just given us a lecture and then asks practically what he has just said. Almost no one answers . . . because we know that the lecturer knows, which means it's not an* honest *question. But if the lecturer asks us what we think, then that's something he doesn't know yet and it's an* honest *question*". We should not deny that seminars at the university are also about knowledge transfer. But the question of what students think about lecture content, and how they understand it, does not exclude this level. Rather, many questions cannot be answered without referring to lecture content. The important difference is that everyone – including the lecturer – can potentially learn something new, and an important aspect is *how* the students think about the content presented. In the words of the student-teacher above: "*If you open your eyes and ears to it, you can take a lot with you. You learn more about people*".

Pattern Break Six: Dialogue, Knowledge Transfer and Performance Assessment: Conflicting Ideas

"Oha [OMG] what have I gotten myself into, this system school, . . . which demands these performance assessments from me . . .".

The idea of dialogue and dialogic conversations at school leads students to become aware of and reflect on the fact that joint reflection – the kind that is open to results and to jointly developing meaning in ways that even the initially unspeakable can come to the surface – does not naturally have a place in most educational institutions. For one student-teacher, even as the system demands performance assessments from her, she has the "*wish and interest to work on topics with the children in an experimental, research-based manner, which of course implies completely . . . other forms of questioning*". This also runs counter to experiences she had had in the context of her internship in school: "*Basically it's all about what goal you formulated in your lesson plan; did you reach the goal? Sometimes [it's] a little bit 'how did you reach it?' but actually it's about looking at what didn't work out. Where is there room for such a conversation, where is there room for such a dialogue, where is there room for such an exploratory talk? How can that be formulated as a goal [in a lesson plan]?*"

"We as teachers are too quick to look for the right answer. I actually believe that this is somehow [causing] a tense relationship".

Another student-teacher also questions a procedure she knows from her school internship, where she was told, "*When you ask a question, think about which answer you want to get – think carefully about the aim of the question. It's best to formulate an answer in your head*". Against the backdrop of dialogue, the student-teacher considers this to be "*nonsense*" and "*completely counterproductive*", which she explains like this: "*I'm already pushing all students into the same fairway and I don't allow any opinions left or right of that, because I have exactly one correctly formulated answer in my head . . . I don't allow anything left and right from that*". She believes that "*it is incredibly important . . . that we allow students to . . . give answers that are* not *perfect [and the] same for us. . . . [Students also should be]* allowed to express unfinished thoughts". She thinks that "*pupils have to learn this first*", because she believes that through the conversational modelling that adults show "*especially at school*", "*even children are trained . . . to provide . . . finished answers*". She concludes her statement with the following thought, followed by 25 seconds of silence: "*I believe that this is something where . . . both the students and we as teachers . . . have a lot to learn and a lot of reflection is needed to take the pressure off*".

Final Thoughts

The pattern breaks make it clear that the students' experiences in dealing with dialogue texts, tasks for self-reflection, peer reflections and online dialogues are very complex. In almost all cases, they process their ideas about what they have considered to be 'normal' in conversations they have had in the context of school and university. These experiences are part of their socialisation into conversations, so they take certain practices in conversations for granted. With dialogic practice, they begin to confront these 'old' experiences shaped by their socialisation with their 'new' dialogue experiences, and from this juxtaposition they formulate fresh insights – which leads to a process of transformation. *Transformation,* in this sense, means that these student-teachers:

- question conversational practices that they have hitherto considered 'normal';
- confront these old practices with new dialogic knowledge and experiences; and
- modify their previously held ideas of 'good' conversations against this new background.

The students' very personal statements sometimes point to painful experiences. These reveal that some of the conversational practices they have perceived as normal have hindered their own thinking and speaking – for example, the search for the 'perfect' answer or fast, uninterrupted action in conversation. It also becomes clear that the process of understanding often is hindered because of a bias toward self-presentation, demonstrating factual expertise or hasty evaluation and positioning; these have all restricted the process of mutual understanding.

In the students' written reflections (which are not discussed at length here), through which they studied and processed their experiences in the context of the dialogic practices of voicing, listening, respecting and suspending as documented by David Bohm and William Isaacs, we found many examples in which the experience or observation of being embarrassed or humiliated was addressed, as well as the experience of not being heard and ignored in conversation, or the lack of courage to express one's thoughts aloud.

As a first step toward becoming open to new and dialogue-oriented conversational practices, it is obviously necessary to process the conversational patterns one was socialised into, including the negative experiences and role assignments stored in them; for example, being the quiet, reserved person or the quick, loud, argumentative one.

In order to be able to understand that all roles are important in every conversation, it is important to be aware of one's own practices, and to understand them as changeable. It is necessary to experience and reflect on these as they are prerequisites which can be more or less conducive to dialogue.

Thus, it becomes clear that the tasks for individual self-reflection, in the first place born out of the necessities of the 'Coronavirus conditions', were significant in order to draw out implicit experiences of and ideas for good conversations for the student-teachers. The tasks in the online semester made it possible for students to become conscious of, express and process their formerly implicit experiences and ideas, forming the ground for transformational processes.

Student-Teacher Perspectives on Dialogue in Schools

As a second step, reflecting on one's experience of past conversations in contrast to new experiences in the online dialogues also changes the way students look at school conversations. In this way the dialogue at hand not only reveals pattern breaks, it also lets our students see opportunities to integrate dialogue into their school work, even (as a student says) "*without discussing dialogue as a major concept in its own right*", but rather "*starting in small areas at first*". They recall individual positive examples they have experienced at school; for example, when 'philosophising with children' led children who were previously silent in class to suddenly start speaking more during other lessons.

On the basis of their own reflections and new discoveries, the students formulate an important realisation: "*a culture of dialogue*" from their point of view signals to the children that what they say is important. After all, many children are not at all used to being asked what they think: "*Many children just come into the world with announcements*". From the students' point of view, this also implies open forms of questions "*designed to ask what children think*". In the students' words, it is important to ask "*honest*" questions and not ones where the children "*basically know, I know that myself. Why should they answer me?*"

Students look at their experiences with conversations at school anew against the background of their experiences with dialogue. These insights can be important and also necessary building blocks for change processes, as international research on conversations at school continues to show that the proportion of teachers speaking is too high, short-answer questions are the rule and students rarely get the opportunity to develop their own thoughts (in joint exchange with other students) (cf. the research overview in de Boer 2018; cf. Edwards-Groves/Davidson 2019: 126).

Reflecting on One's Experiences and Making them Fruitful for Dialogue Practice

Even though individual empirical research has shown how the teacher's conversational behaviour can be influenced by targeted intervention training toward dialogue-based conversation (Hardman 2019: 142), too little attention is still paid to the importance of reflection and self-reflection in the context of conversation.

To summarise, at least three different steps are necessary here:

1. reflection on one's own socialisation and biographically shaped conversational practices and roles;
2. engaging in the concrete experience of dialogues; and
3. reflecting on one's own conversational behaviour to see the contrast between self-perception and the perception of others, with the associated opportunity to recognise the 'blind spots' in one's own way of conducting a conversation.

The first step, as presented in this contribution, can be achieved (for example) by studying literature on dialogue and, against that background, reflecting on one's own conversational experiences; the core of the second step lies in experiencing joint dialogues. The third step, however, is more complex to achieve. It is more complex because the desire and the goal of wanting to conduct a dialogue alone does not lead to success. Often the conversation practices acquired over many years are persistently anchored in one's own routines and elude self-perception. Research shows, for example, that the share of the conversation of teachers remains dominant even if it is their explicit aim to open up more space for participation of pupils (compare, for example, Edwards-Groves/Davidson 2019: 127; de Boer 2006). Thus, what is *intended* in terms of dialogue does not automatically lead to *good practice* in dialogue.

Against this background, in past semesters we have worked with student-teachers to empirically examine the dialogues they have conducted in schools (cf. de Boer 2019; de Boer 2018; Merklinger 2020: 67-70). The initial research results of these transcripts show that there is a pronounced difference between self-perception and external perception in conversation: "to the fact that one's own blind spots in the conduct of the conversation not only become visible within a semester, but are also constructively worked on and changed". (de Boer 2019: 2; cf. also de Boer 2018). These blind spots can be experienced by students not only by analysing transcripts of their conversations, but also by receiving individual feedback from trained student-teachers working as tutors; in addition, there is the dialogic exchange in the seminar. This form of research-oriented teaching and learning leads to higher-quality dialogues, as summarised as follows: More breaks and waiting times are realised, and the students only carry out dosed interventions to deepen the conversation. They ask more open questions about the children's experiences and are able to make connections to the children's statements (cf. de Boer 2019: 3).

Establishing dialogue as a theory, method and attitude in the context of teacher education is complex, multilayered and multifaceted. On the one hand, we would like to use this contribution to further reflect with those interested in teacher education on the steps by which future teachers can professionalise their dialogue practice. At the same time, we also ask ourselves which blind spots or implicit assumptions in current dialogical concepts would have to be further spelled out for this common task of establishing dialogue practice in teacher education and schools.

Finally, we would like to emphasise two aspects which we have become aware of in a special way through our cooperation with the students. These aspects are closely related:

- The patterns of conversation and practices experienced over many years at school and university are linked to painful experiences of students not daring to speak and the feeling that they are not being heard.
- The experience of slowing down in conversation is missing. For most students it is new to have conversations in which breaks are possible, in which common reflection and mutual understanding are the main focus.

Only the experience of a 'failed' dialogue without pauses made it clear to the students during the seminar how restrictive conversations, which they had previously considered normal, can be on various levels: few speak, those who think for longer periods have no chance of participating compared to quick speakers, and joint reflection becomes impossible. We did not plan this 'accelerated dialogue' in this way, but it has made us aware of the importance of experiencing the difference – a difference that the students might not even have noticed before engaging in dialogue. Those who are socialised at school and university have generally had no experience of conversations in which there is room for breaks and waiting times in the sense of dialogue.

This observation leads to a special learning realisation: If student-teachers want to have dialogical conversations not only with children at school, but also with colleagues and parents, their own experiences with decelerated dialogues are essential.

We are interested in opening a dialogue with others at the conference.

References

Bohm, D. (German edition 2019). *Der Dialog: Das offene Gespräch am Ende der Diskussion.* Stuttgart: Klett-Cotta.

de Boer, H. (2019). "Students in Dialogue with Children – research-oriented teaching and learning". Available at: https://members.aofpd.org/library/coffee-table/students-in-dialogue-with-children-by-heike-de-boer/ (members' site) (as extracted 11 August, 2019).

de Boer, H. (2018). "Forschend Lehren und Lernen in und durch philosophische Gespräche mit Kindern". In de Boer, Heike/Michalik, Kerstin (Ed.): *Philosophieren mit Kindern – Forschungszugänge und -perspektiven.* Opladen, Berlin, Toronto: Barbara Budrich Verlag, 146-161.

de Boer, H. (2015). "Philosophieren als Unterrichtsprinzip – philosophische Gespräche mit Kindern". In *Heike de Boer & Marina Bonanati (Ed.): Gespräche über Lernen – Lernen im Gespräch.* Wiesbaden: Springer, 233-250.

de Boer, H. (2006). *Klassenrat als interaktive Praxis. Auseinandersetzung – Kooperation – Imagepflege.* Wiesbaden: VS Verlag.

Edwards-Groves, C., & Davidson, C. (2019). "Metatalk for a dialogic turn in early years Classrooms". In N. Mercer, R. Wegerif, & L. Major (Eds.), *The Routledge International Handbook of Research on Dialogic Education* (1st ed., pp. 125-138). (*Routledge International Handbook of Education*). Abingdon, UK: Routledge.

Hardman, F. (2019). "Embedding a dialogic pedagogy in the classroom: What is the research telling us?" In N. Mercer, R. Wegerif, & L. Major (Eds.), *The Routledge International Handbook of Research on Dialogic Education* (1st ed., pp. 139-151). Abingdon, UK: Routledge.

Howe, C. & Manzoorul, A. (2013). "Classroom dialogue: a systematic review across four decades of research", *Cambridge Journal of Education*, 43:3, 325-356, DOI: 10.1080/0305764X.2013.786024.

Mehan, H. (1979). *Learning Lessons. Social Organisation in the Classroom.* London: Harvard University Press.

Mercer, N. & Wegerif, R. & Major, L. (2019). *The Routledge International Handbook of Research on Dialogic Education.* Abingdon, UK: Routledge.

Merklinger, D. (2020). "Literary dialogues on picture books in primary school: The Tiger Prince". Available at: https://members.aofpd.org/library/coffee-table/dialogues-with-second-graders-about-picture-books-daniela-merklinger/ (members' site).

Merklinger, D. (2020). "Oder Wen sieht die Tigerin wie seine Mutter . . ." Perspektiven literarischer Figuren im kollektiven Gespräch über Bilderbücher interaktiv entfalten. In Scherer, Gabriela/Heintz, Kathrin / Bahn, Michael (Ed.): *Das narrative Bilderbuch. Türöffner zu literar-ästhetischer Bildung, Erzähl- und Buchkultur.* Trier: WVT: 57-82.

Conference Session Extracts
From a conversation with participants considering the paper with Daniela Merklinger

Speaker: The thing that really surfaced in our session was the shift of mindset that the teacher can make, even without a lot of dialogic experience, from being the expert to being curious about the thought processes of those they're teaching. That one little shift can make all the difference. Suddenly the emphasis is off the result and it shifts over to putting attention on listening to the students. Such a simple thing and yet it can make such a profound difference in a classroom environment.

Speaker: We talked about having that right answer in our minds when we're teaching people to memorize and regurgitate. Then we're not teaching critical thinking which would involve more of dialogue. In the Department of Corrections in Virginia we are working on a cognitive change in how inmates are thinking and how they're processing their decisions and how they're going to behave going forward.

Speaker: I spent 20 years in the UK education system, so I had an abundance of education, but I'm not sure I emerged from that with a great deal of skill in any of these behaviours. The education system is very much focused on filling this bucket of knowledge. My question for you, Daniela, is to what extent is this sort of thinking having an impact on the sort of education that children today are getting?

Daniela: There is a big international handbook on dialogic education that was published in 2019. There have been several projects of people working with dialogue and education. If you look at the practices all over the world it is still the same as it was in the 1970s: initiation, response, evaluation. Teachers are trained to act dialogically, but even if they try to act that way, they don't. It's really hard to change these routines that you have been socialised into.

Speaker: I think dialogue could be a vessel to allow the students to start thinking about their thinking, because they are thinking about their behaviours. To be able to express the thinking behind their thinking enables a shift in the pattern of their attitudes and beliefs.

Speaker: One thing that we discussed was the unspoken emotional current in the dialogue. Our group felt that people got more out of an in-person group than online. It just seems to flow better with less interrupting each other and more tracking the unspoken, emotional currents.

Speaker: We focused on the experience of silence, and the pauses in dialogue. Most educators are taught to allow a kind of think-time when we are teaching. It reminded me that the pause in a dialogue is good practice. It helps reflection, increases the thinking process and increases participation.

Speaker: I went into our group thinking I was very comfortable with silence. There were two DOC employees, and two of the international folks. I felt myself and the other DOC employee were dominating a little bit, so I had to step back and stop speaking – and then I felt very uncomfortable.

Speaker: How could we work with children in school? And also get them to learn dialogue skills so that they can also use them for themselves? Dialogue skills are life skills. How can we pass on these skills to children or establish them together with children? That was the outstanding thought in our group.

Daniela: How do you implant that idea in schools? We talked about that too. To get it into the school system, you need whole schools and you need a principal who really likes the idea of dialogue and the majority of the teachers working in a system that really want it. If the headmaster doesn't agree, it won't work. The headmaster saying to the colleagues, "We're doing this now" doesn't work either.

Speaker: One way of going about that is to find a language as teachers, right? It's not just about the methods and didactical approaches you have inside the classroom, it's about also how you organise the support for your work. How you work together with colleagues to achieve a mutual goal, to socialise people into becoming aware of the different kinds of conversation there are, what expectations you have of other people and how you look at the world. There is writing about this in the Netherlands, about knowledge learning for qualifications, about socialising people, and then about leaving room for their response and not judging that.

Speaker: I feel that the only way we can progress and make this kind of thinking bigger is to tell the stories and experiences that we have to others, and to try and grow a crowd. I feel that is the central challenge for teachers – to find each other in this reasoning and to strengthen our mutual story.

Speaker: Yeah. And that means taking the time to think about that. So how do you get people involved, given their busy working days where they don't have free time? I mean, I don't know what it is like in the Netherlands, but in Germany, especially in primary school education, they don't get time out of the working day to do that. So what we see is a lot of times the people that really try to get further knowledge, have to do that in their free time.

Speaker: I don't see a lot of wiggle room other than, at some point, the principal has to make a decision for that. I don't know all the literature in the English language, but there is a wonderful book about reinventing organisations that is examined with some examples. It comes to the same conclusion as many Dutch authors, which is that at some point you still need a hierarchical person at the top to say, "Okay, let's go there in this way". Or, "Let's find some way to give space to this development". But it starts often with people, functional professionals, who give this person at the top the food for thought by engaging them in conversations.

Speaker: I was just thinking about what was said. I definitely think you would need a buy-in from the principal, or the head, but I was also thinking about the parents. And also about the kids. How will it be beneficial and impactful to the children? And at what age will you actually start? It may be easy to do this at high school. But when you start with elementary school – do you start with preschoolers? Would you start with middle schoolers? I think there is a bigger picture, and it's definitely a conversation that should be had.

Postscript

The authors' reflections, written some months after the conference

In our article, 'Dialogue in Teacher Training at the University Level', we identified six 'pattern breaks' emerging from an online dialogue with students.

The small-group dialogue at the conference underlined the importance of dialogue for the education system. And it confirmed that we underestimate the great influence of the conversational routines we were socialised into. We have continued to think about this topic and especially the pattern breaks with our students during the last two semesters. Two of them seem to be especially important to them: The slowing down, and the pauses in the conversation (*pattern break four*). Also, the students continue to confirm how difficult it is for them not to look for a supposedly correct answer before they speak (*pattern break one*).

In a recent dialogue class a new question arose: *Why do we see the blind spots in other people's conversational behaviour? And why don't we see our own blind spots?* Why it is so difficult to become aware of our own blind spots can be explained with Bohm's differentiation between the observer and the observed (Bohm 1996: Chapter 5).

We see a new pattern break here:

Pattern Break Seven: Becoming Aware of One's Own Blind Spots

Bohm uses the distinction between the observer and the observed to make it clear that each of our observations also generates the observed through our assumptions:

> In a way, we are looking *through* our assumptions; the assumptions could be said to be an observer in a sense. (Bohm 1996: 71)

Accordingly, each of us sees differently. When we try to track down our own assumptions, again we can only do that through assumptions. One's own assumptions are therefore most difficult to access for the observer because what he or she is looking for is hidden within him- or herself:

> Hide them in the looker, and the looker will never find them. (Bohm 1996: 72)

A question we are now exploring: What are the prerequisites for a dialogue (within the process but also within oneself and the participants) that support one in becoming aware of one's own blind spots?

Overcoming Challenges to Dialogue in Professional Higher Education

Timo Nevalainen

Higher education, a context that often promotes open thinking, synthesis of ideas and collaboration as an ideal, is itself rife with fragmentation. This becomes apparent in many ways: through often-conflicting institutionalised habits and practices, mental models, formal and informal relationships (such as between directors, managers, lecturers and students), unevenly distributed participation, a weakened sense of agency and conflicting goals.

I believe that dialogue can play a key part in countering this fragmentation. In this paper I will attempt to combine insights from different theories of dialogue and my own experience in professional higher education to illustrate the important role of dialogue in the context of higher education. I will also include a brief exploration of beliefs that may support dialogical practice in professional higher education, as well those that may work against it. For some readers this may sound rather theoretical and conceptual. Still, through examples rooted in experience and practice, we will see how the implicit theories that educators hold have wide-ranging consequences for their educational practices.

Besides sharing perspectives from different dialogical traditions, I will draw on my own experiences and observations in my workplace, TAMK Proakatemia, which is an entrepreneurship education unit in Tampere University of Applied Sciences in Finland. I'll offer examples from working as a coach for team entrepreneur students, as well as from training teaching staff in universities on dialogical team coaching.

Many Dialogical Traditions

One can approach dialogical education in many different ways, each rooted in seemingly different philosophical traditions and communities of dialogical practice. I will draw on examples from four dialogical traditions: 1) Bohm Dialogue, which draws from the work of physicist David Bohm and his colleagues, and which has guided the dialogic work of management consultants and organisational development specialists; 2) the pragmatic philosophy of John Dewey, which has provided a foundation for dialogical practice within the democratic education movement; 3) the dialogic ideas of critical pedagogue and educational philosopher Paulo Freire; and 4) Martin Buber's dialogical, philosophical anthropology. While sourced in different traditions of thought and practice, and based on different interests of their initial proponents, these movements appear to share some aspects of their ethos, their reasoning and their concept of being human:

- **Ontology (the nature of being)**: The world and our awareness of it are conceived as a systemic process involving responsible agency.
- **Holistic and situated notion of human being**s: Human beings are to be understood as whole beings rather than as a collection of parts, and they are fundamentally 'situated' (deriving meaning through context), as they share the world with others.
- **Responsibility over encounters with the other(s) and communication.**
- **Knowledge as a process developed in generative dialogue**: Treating each other as human beings, colleagues in the shared endeavour of developing awareness of the situation.
- **Respect for difference and uniqueness of the others and their perspectives.**
- **A relational notion of self and knowledge**: both self and knowledge are conceived of as open to influence and development through mutual participation in dialogue.

Different traditions of dialogue emphasise different points and principles, but what they appear to have in common are active resistance to society's tendency towards division and fragmentation, and treating dialogue as a *discipline* that requires active deliberation and participation. More specifically, what they seem to hold in common is a view of consciousness as a process that is inherent in the way human beings are in the world with others, and dialogue as a means of exploring and countering forms of division, fragmentation and conflict within the process of consciousness and healing the symptoms caused by them.

In all of the above-mentioned descriptions, engaging in dialogue means actively and deliberately resisting the tendency towards division and fragmentation. Where these philosophies seem to differ, however, is in their view of what constitutes human consciousness within the world that we share with others and, consequently, the divisions, fragmentation or conflict within it. For all of them, to engage in dialogue seems to mean directing the conscious attention back towards itself, exploring how consciousness becomes constituted as a process; how it becomes divided, fragmented or conflicted with itself, and then countering this fragmentation by listening with conscious awareness and *suspending*. (Here I use *suspending* in both the sense of delaying our assumptions and evaluations, and also offering them, together with our conflicted habits of thought, in the open so that others can inquire into them.) In the field of education, a particular challenge to dialogue comes from the largely unchallenged idea that a main part of a teacher's expertise consists of his or her ability to evaluate *others'* ideas and performance!

John Dewey

For John Dewey, the main cause of what he terms 'moral confusion' lies in our *incoherent consciousness, which itself is built on conflicting habits and impulses*. The concepts of habit and impulse are central to Dewey's pragmatic philosophy of mind, which has later become, alongside the study of consciousness and direct experience, one of the cornerstones of more recent thinking about how we humans interact with and shape our environments. For Dewey, habits are neither simple, routine nor automatic. They are the complex patterns of interaction between living beings and the world – the ways of organising of an organism – that make up its whole way of being. In the case of human beings, our way of being, including what we call conscious awareness, is made of these patterns of interaction and their continuous reorganising in relation to the environment and different kinds of impulses.

What is often forgotten in relation to the concept of habit is that many of our habitual tendencies are culturally shared rather than individual. While they make it possible for us to function in the world and communicate with each other, it can be difficult to become aware of the multitude of intertwining habits or change any one of them individually. Even if one habit meets with a strong impulse to change, it can still be held in place by other, even stronger habits that depend on it. For Dewey and other philosophers and cognitive scientists, the most effective way to change habits is to change the environment where they function.

As in Bohm Dialogue, where *dialogue* means shared inquiry into the quality of awareness, democratic dialogue through the lens of Dewey's concept of habit could mean inquiry into our habits and impulses. We can do this in order to gain awareness of the ways our habitual routines interact and influence us, and how they constitute the whole of (mostly shared) consciousness and habitual action in the world. For Dewey, what determines intelligence and morality is the complexity and integration of different, potentially conflicting habits and impulses that cause them to be continuously reorganised.

Implications for Education

When new students come to Proakatemia they have already become habituated in their role as students through at least 12 years of formal education. The idea that they should be the primary agents in their own learning process, as well as that of their peers in the team and the community, is often weaker than their habits related to the role of a passive recipient of instruction. However, this situation is slowly becoming better in Finland, as educators from primary schools to high schools are adopting more dialogic and active modes of learning and teaching. At first the team coach is likely to hear requests for 'lectures' or direct advice, which need to be resisted. When the old habits of mind have relaxed (usually after three to six months), giving a short lecture every now and then will no longer encourage the students to revert back to passive recipients of information.

Paulo Freire

In Brazilian educator Paulo Freire's work, fragmentation in consciousness is a result of a division between political consciousness and a sense of agency, which in itself is a result of uncritical and unreflective education and practices that have turned education into indoctrination. In this approach, the key practice is 'depositing' information in the form of facts and procedures into individual learner's minds. Freire attempts to counter this process of indoctrination through advocating dialogic education for critical thinking, which begins by taking seriously the participants' everyday experience and struggles and builds on what is relevant for them in their current situation.

Implications for Education

The learning community in Proakatemia is led by the team entrepreneur students and team coaches together. The leadership board of Proakatemia that makes all the decisions on how the school community is run (including the schedules for training sessions and shared goals for the community) consists of one team entrepreneur from each team and one representative from the team coach team as a facilitator. The leadership board is itself led by a team entrepreneur student from the second- or third-year team, hired in the role of an assistant coach by the university. The assistant coach often has a comparable, but more important role to that of the head coach (the leader of the staff members in a coaching team) in the school community. The head coach and the assistant coach work as a close-knit team in facilitating the direction of the community.

Martin Buber

For existentialist philosopher Martin Buber, the primary form of fragmentation to be resisted is *the division within how we experience the Other in a relationship*. His most widely known concepts probably are what he calls the 'basic words': the *I-Thou* and *I-It* of relationship. For Buber, these signify two fundamentally different ways of relating that, in turn, determines the way in which we exist in the world.

If a human being can exist only in relationship, the *I* in the *I-Thou* relationship is, for Buber, existentially different from the *I* in *I-It* relationship. The major difference between these ways of being and relating is that, in the *I-Thou* relationship, the Other is encountered as a whole in its totality. This is reflected in Buber's lines (1923/1996):

> *When I confront a human being as my You and speak the basic word* I-You *to him, then he is no thing among things nor does he consist of things. He is no longer He or She, limited by other Hes*

and Shes, a dot in the world grid of space and time, nor a condition that can be experienced and described, a loose bundle of named qualities. Neighborless and seamless, he is You and fills the firmament. Not as if there were nothing but he; but everything else lives in his light.

Even as a melody is not composed of tones, nor a verse of words, nor a statue of lines – one must pull and tear to turn a unity into a multiplicity – so it is with the human being to whom I say You. *I can abstract from him the color of his hair or the color of his speech or the color of his graciousness; I have to do this again and again; but immediately he is no longer You. . . .*

As long as the firmament of the You is spread over me, the tempests of causality cower at my heels, and the whirl of doom congeals.

The human being to whom I say You *I do not experience. But I stand in relation to him, in the sacred basic word. Only when I step out of this do I experience him again. Experience is remoteness from You.*

In the *I-It* relationship there is no encounter as a whole, but rather fragmented experiencing and analysis; it is a reduction of the Other into qualities that define *It* and its usefulness to us. What is important for educators to note, especially within formal institutions, is that Buber says that one cannot remain in the mode of the *I-Thou* encounter indefinitely, as it is impossible to function forever in it, but what one can do is to always retain it as a *potentiality*, even in the most formal institutional contexts. For Buber, maintaining some the 'tone' of the *I-Thou* encounter and holding it up as a possibility may even partially serve to 'defragment' the relationship within institutional encounters in the *I-It* mode.

Implications for Education

In Proakatemia each team entrepreneur student is treated as a uniquely valuable human being first and as a student only second. The relationships between the team entrepreneurs and the team coaches are often collegial rather than hierarchical. The coaches need to have some authority in order to maintain the dialogic space when necessary (the team entrepreneurs also help in this!) and to assist the team entrepreneurs in solving possible relationship conflicts within the teams. This authority, however, is not based on treating the students as objects of educational interventions but always treating them as the subjects of their own futures and the shared future of the community.

Based on the above elaborations, I am suggesting that if we are to counter fragmentation of consciousness within education, be it a result of our conflicting habits, division within how we experience the Other, or division within our political consciousness and agency, we need to establish dialogic education as a discipline that can be consciously trained and practised together by educators and students. This will necessitate establishing certain kinds of spaces and relationships within educational institutions.

Obstacles to Dialogic Education

Our established notions about the world and human beings in it, about knowledge and learning can, if left unexamined, play against dialogue in educational contexts in many different ways.

Without personal experience of dialogue, or the experience of what David Bohm, in a term derived from Patrick de Maré, called *impersonal fellowship*, an educator attempting to understand dialogue by reading theoretical texts or experiential accounts will flounder. This is especially true where there are differences of opinion and worldviews, and within the depth of emerging knowledge and learning that is both intensely personal and obviously collective.

Anyone who encounters dialogue in theory, without being able to connect it with personal experience, will be at loss in evaluating its usefulness in education. This was exactly the reason why in Proakatemia we decided to emphasise the experiential aspect of dialogue in the team coaching courses we give to teachers in universities and high schools. When teachers gain a positive experience of dialogue as really listening and being listened to, both by colleagues and coaches, and of delaying of assumptions and evaluations and bringing them into open, many of these teachers are likely to be drawn towards that experience in their own work with students.

Even if I am always likely to emphasise the experiential aspect of dialogue, without having an understanding of the ethical, ontological and theoretical background of dialogue, it can become a frustrating exercise for a Dialogue Practitioner to try to 'explain' dialogue to colleagues or managers as anything other than a supplemental method or tool with limited use in professional higher education. Indeed, within professional higher education in Finland, I often come across the term *dialogue,* used to describe a method or approach to encountering clients, patients or students in social services, healthcare or education – or, more recently, customers in the service-based business. Even this limited, instrumental use of dialogue can lead more people to take an interest in dialogical approaches, but I will later in this paper suggest an experiential alternative to starting by treating dialogue as merely an instrument fit only to some very specific practical situations.

Three Different Approaches to Dialogic Education

Drawing a parallel with sustainability education as outlined by Stephen Stirling, I will elaborate on three different approaches to dialogic education and give examples based on my own experiences in TAMK Proakatemia. These three approaches can be described as follows:

1. Education *about* dialogue (learning about the theory and benefits of dialogue)

2. Education *for* dialogue (using dialogue as a means to provide better service encounters in the future)
3. Education *as* dialogue (engaging in the practice of dialogue)

While the traditional approach in higher education would be to first give people enough information that would, in theory, at least, allow them to engage in independent practice, I would rather suggest an experiential approach that may pose a more direct and concrete challenge to the established beliefs of the students.

During my career as a teacher I have met a number of people, both students and teachers, who have been sceptical about dialogue and group work in general. Their scepticism often seems to be based on their own negative experiences at school or at their workplaces. Indeed, before my own intensely dialogical teacher training, I was profoundly sceptical towards both dialogue and teamwork. Many of my own experiences of group work at school had been suboptimal (to put it mildly), and spaces for dialogue were practically non-existent. A small factory town in the middle of an economic recession in the late 80s and early 90s was not conducive to dialogic classrooms, where the students would somehow magically take responsibility over the quality of their interactions with others.

However, based on my later experience, I found that it is possible for a competent enough Dialogue Practitioner, perhaps aided by one or two colleagues who already have had some experience in dialogue circles, to set a space where the established beliefs of the participants can be challenged through taking part in a dialogue rather than through theoretical explanation or by treating dialogue as merely a method for improving encounters in service professions.

Education *about* dialogue is bound to lead to situations where dialogue remains a purely theoretical possibility. Education *for* dialogue will lead, in the best of cases, to a situation where dialogue becomes a future possibility (but is most likely to remain as such). Only education *as* dialogue allows for the serious development of dialogue as a discipline. Preliminary practice can begin long before anyone has mentioned has the term, and no opportunity for conscious practice need be wasted.

There is a major difficulty involved in how knowledge itself is viewed in education. This is something I gradually grasped after grappling with the difficulty of university teachers to understand how dialogue could possibly work in their classes. The teachers of natural scientific subjects and mathematics seemed especially resistant to considering the possibility that dialogue might be useful in their work: *How could anyone without specialised knowledge of the topic at hand bring anything useful to our conversation?* Then I came across Donald Schön's notion of different kinds of knowledge (1991):

1. Knowledge as objective facts, rules and procedures that can be possessed and disseminated by an expert (usually through books or lectures)
2. Knowledge as cognitive processes of an individual that can be trained and evaluated by experts

3. Knowledge as reflection-in-action that cannot be separated from action, but which instead requires us to take the action and reflection within it seriously – not only as a source of knowledge but also in a way in which knowledge gains its relevancy

These views of knowledge are complementary, but they still involve conceptual problems and misunderstandings. For example, the first view of knowledge as outlined above is not, strictly speaking, about knowledge but rather it is about *information*, which may or may not be relevant for the students in what they are trying to accomplish. Knowledge as information about facts, rules and procedures will never constitute knowledge if it remains uncoupled from goals and actions of the students. In much of education, especially in universities, it is assumed that this information either becomes knowledge for immediate use (assuming that the students are already involved in some action where the information is useful and relevant), or that it remains in some sort of stored format in their brains. This assumption is based on unfounded beliefs about human memory and cognition, and which were already challenged by Paulo Freire in the early 1970s.

The second view of knowledge is more useful, as it takes the process-nature of knowledge seriously; however, it remains too focused on the cognitive *processing* of an individual. That is, as with the idea of the human mind as an information storage system, the idea of the human mind (or brain) as a sort of individual information processing faculty has also been contested (Noë, 2010). Where humans may appear to process information, it is perhaps not the individual brain but rather the intertwined, individual and shared collective (cultural) habits (including, for example, language) that do the heavy lifting. These processes are in constant connection with the environment, including the various technical aids such as notebooks, computers and smartphones that we have developed.

Finally, if we take the last view seriously, it will lead us to rethink how we can together develop our skills related to knowledge as a process. I have attempted to clarify this process through three different illustrations of how we understand knowledge.

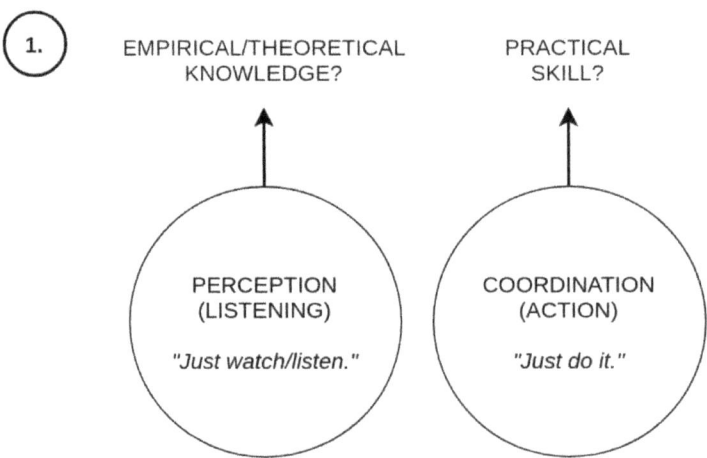

Knowledge and skill as separated *results from a fragmented process*

The first – and, I would argue, still the most common situation within higher education – is one in which perception as a way of acquiring information (as knowledge) is thought of as strictly separate from coordination of action. The action may still be expected to be 'informed' by theory, but the two are trained, managed and evaluated separately both in time and in space. Thus we see the separation of readings and lab courses, as well as the division of lecture halls and labs. The focus on action is often thought to compromise the rationality of the theory, and the theory is seen as unnecessarily slowing down and confusing effective action.

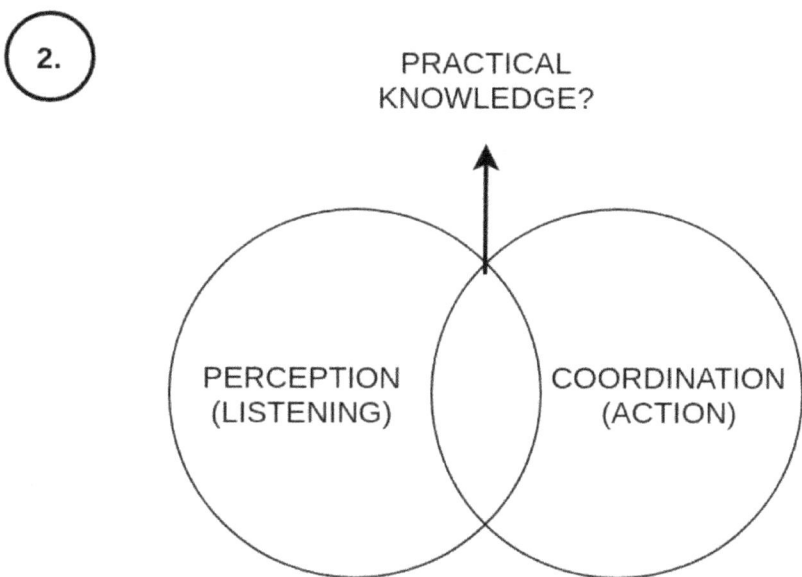

Knowledge as *a result from* a reflective process, proprioception as alternating between perception and coordination

The second model of how knowledge comes about is more common in professional higher education, such as in Finnish universities for applied sciences. In this model, knowledge acquisition through listening and reading and action alternate, often at such a pace that they overlap, giving rise to knowledge that cannot be clearly separated from action. Even if the acts of perception and coordination alternate, they are still seen as fundamentally different activities that sometimes coincide to produce practical, action-oriented and action-tied knowledge.

The third model of knowledge as a process requires conscious direction on part of the individuals engaging in it. The capacity of individuals for this kind of direction is not often innate and requires careful guidance from and collaborative effort with others who are willing to support them and work on it themselves.

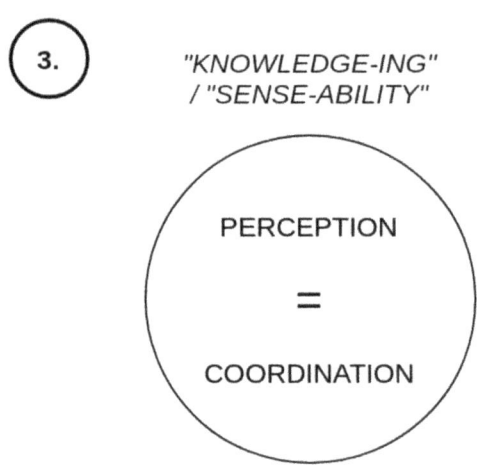

Knowledge itself as a *dialogic and proprioceptive* process

The third model depicts knowledge as a process that comes about when perception and coordination are made to coincide, not accidentally but deliberately. This idea may seem strange initially, but once we start thinking of situations where we learned something individually or collectively, it begins to look like this might well be the most common path to real learning and improvement in our capability of action.

To illustrate with perhaps the easiest, even somewhat naïve example for an average person, would be first standing on one foot. It is relatively straightforward to balance oneself (*coordination*) when one has a clear view of the surroundings (*perception*) and can feel the ground under the foot. (In fact, what one feels is not only the ground but how one's weight is continually rebalancing on the sole of the foot.) Now try closing both of your eyes, thus shutting out part of your capacity for perceiving the environment. The results will likely be profoundly different! What this simplistic example attempts to make clear is that our capacity for coordination (such as balancing on one foot) is effectively the same as our capacity for perception (perceiving our relationship with the environment).

As another example, a team that is struggling to build coherent goals and actions will fare much better if, instead of trying to coerce every member to work for some predetermined goal in a pre-established way, it focuses on building a shared understanding of the situation through dialogue. When the situation is clear for everyone and the team has a clear idea of the individual strengths and weaknesses of all of its members, the right path of action will usually be self-evident to everyone and their motivations aligned.

For working teams that are struggling to build trust and dialogic relationships, it is quite common for all team members to seemingly agree on some suboptimal way forward, and to appear willing to continue to that direction. (In popular psychology, this phenomenon is known as the 'Abilene-paradox', in which a group of people end up going in a direction that no one wanted.) The most drastic example of this kind of thinking would be the collective agreement to dismantle the team; in Proakatemia-equivalent terms this effectively would mean that everyone collectively fails the degree program. No cohort within Proakatemia over the last 15 years has failed entirely, but many of the teams still go through moments when the question of dismantling the team hangs in the air. This seeming agreement is caused by the inability of the team to engage in open, trust-based dialogue on what they want. The leaders of the team, usually assisted by the team coach, can often disarm the volatile situation by going deeper into what each individual team member wishes and expects from others and of the team, and what they are willing to invest of themselves in order to make it happen. Without this kind of dialogue, the teams would not likely be able to engage their deeper wishes (and resentments) in a way that would allow them to continue and often strengthen in the process.

Another example from the Chinese practice method of *taiji*, push-hands, is a way of perceiving, through the palm of the hand, the subtle movement within the balanced structure of a sparring partner. By being sensitive to this balance it becomes possible to blend with the movement and use any small amount of force exerted by the partner to push him or her out of balance. This exercise is first and foremost an exercise of listening and perceiving, and only secondarily an exercise of the careful application of force. If the application of force is attempted by tensing the muscles of the back, shoulders or arms, it will effectively shut off the fine perception of the movement of the other. The effective level of listening needs to be such that one can clearly feel the training partner's breathing in and out and heart beating but, at the same time he or she needs to be aware of their own structure and balance as a continuously shifting process. This requires awareness not only of own body but also of the surrounding environment.

Thoughtful Wrongdoing

The belief is very generally held that only if we are told what to do in order to correct the wrong way of doing something, we can do it, and that if we feel we are doing it, all is well. All my experience, however, goes to shew that this belief is a delusion.

– FM Alexander (1885-1932)

One practice which examines proprioception, or 'awareness of awareness' in detail in the context of body-mind-environment is the Alexander technique, a deliberate and disciplined way of mindful learning which is often associated with more efficient ways of using voice or moving one's body, but which can help in making any practice more mindful and efficient. The core concept in the Alexander technique is 'conscious control of the individual' or 'use of the Self', which means being aware of the way we direct ourselves in relation to any external situation or internal state, and learning how we can guide our reactions, choices and actions in a more intelligent way.

Another core concept of the Alexander technique is 'inhibition', which is related to both the concept of *suspending* (of assumptions) and *proprioception* ('directing awareness to the process of consciousness') in Bohmian terms. In the Alexander technique it means inhibiting our habitual responses in a given situation and making a free conscious decision to direct attention and action instead.

This may sound simple, but in practice many of our habits, whether collective or individual, are almost entirely unconscious. We are scarcely aware of acting them out when we do. The most prominent example in the Alexander technique is the way in which we stand – or attempt to stand – straight. (Most people are wholly unaware of how to accomplish this but, instead, end up shortening themselves by tensing their back). Through the Alexander technique we can learn to stand or walk without unnecessarily tensing the muscles in our whole body (in Alexander's terms, 'shortening the stature'). Indeed, even if we learn to correctly use one previously habituated part of the body, the new pattern will end up producing conflicting feelings in all the other parts, because of their habituation to inappropriate use. As Alexander put it,

> *If a part [of the body] directly employed in the activity is being used in a comparatively new way which is still unfamiliar, the stimulus to use this part in the new way is weak in comparison with the stimulus to use the other parts of the organism, which are being indirectly employed in the activity, in the old habitual way.* (Ibid.)

It should perhaps be noted that I use the terms *habit* and *habituation* in much the same sense as John Dewey, referring not only to simple, routine behaviours but also to habits as the primary units of consciousness (alongside the stimuli that engage the habits). For Dewey, the fragmentation of consciousness results from conflicts between habits. Habits can here mean both individual ways of behaving and thinking ('stream of consciousness', in William James's thinking, is itself a result of habits conflicting with one another and external stimuli), as well as collective and cultural conglomerations of habits, or practices.

Drawing an analogy to dialogue in an educational context, a teacher willing to use more dialogic teaching practices must be ready to accept some discomfort. This is due to the conflict between what she is trying to achieve and the existing practices of the educational institution, often carried over generations. Indeed, as the process of habituation includes all participants in the institutional context (colleagues, directors, the students, even the parents), the teacher must be willing to trust the process of dialogue even more than her own inevitable feelings of discomfort when the new practice clashes with the prevalent ways of talking and thinking, acting and relating. These prevalent cognitive, material and relational practices are themselves a result of decades, if not centuries of institutional habituation. Practicing dialogue in their domain is bound to feel wrong initially, giving rise to many kinds of feelings of unfamiliarity, discomfort and uncertainty. Again, Alexander says it well:

> *Obviously, any new use must feel different from the old, and if the old use felt right, the new use was bound to feel wrong.* (Ibid.)

To give another example, education in schools is commonly based on an idea of a teacher as a 'possessor' of knowledge whose job is to disseminate this commodity to the students via instruction. This knowledge is often taken to mean 'shareable information' consisting of facts and procedures which the teacher is expected to possess and transmit, and the students receive and internalise. These facts and procedures – and their correctness – is conceived as both relatively static and independent of the participants' situation. Now consider that if a teacher wants to start working from a different, more active concept of knowledge as a process that involves co-construction and dialogue, she will face institutional structures based on a habituated concept of knowledge which will not yield easily to what she is trying to achieve. Indeed the teacher, especially if alone, will come to feel that her idea of education must be wrong, as it is in constant conflict with the reality of the school. Even those students who come to share her practice of dialogue will experience problems in their other encounters with the habituated practices of the institution. It will not be automatically easy to switch from dialogic co-construction of new knowledge and shared awareness to the docile following of lectures and the established processes that clearly lead away from dialogue rather than towards it.

Thus, in the beginning, a separate, shared safe space for disciplined practice of dialogue is needed, and the whole environment of that space has to make it obvious that this space is intended for a different kind of practice than what normally goes on within the school. Indeed, the space must facilitate dialogic practice not only for the students but also for the teacher. Even she is in constant danger of submitting to the prevalent non-dialogic practices that afford a sense of familiarity and certainty where dialogic education cannot.

References
Alexander, F. M. (2001). *The Use of the Self*. London: Orion Publishing Group.
Buber, M. (1971). *I And Thou* (W. Kaufmann, Trans.; 1st Touchstone Ed edition). New York: Touchstone.
Frankl, V. E.. (2004). *Man's Search For Meaning: The Classic Tribute to Hope from the Holocaust* (New Ed. edition). London: Rider.
Freire, P. (1996). *Pedagogy of the Oppressed*. London: Penguin Group.
Dewey, J. (2012). *Human Nature and Conduct: An Introduction to Social Psychology*. http://www.gutenberg.org/ebooks/41386
Noë, A. (2010). *Out of Our Heads* (First edition). New York: Hill & Wang.
Schon, D. A. (1990). *Educating the Reflective Practitioner: Toward a New Design for Teaching and Learning in the Professions* (First edition). San Francisco: Jossey-Bass.

Conference Session Extracts

From a conversation with participants considering the paper with Timo Nevalainen

Timo: Okay. What happened when I asked you to think very hard about something? What kind of body reaction do you get when you are asked to think very hard, and have this expectation that you will be asked to say something very soon? How did the pressure feel?

Speaker: Fear about being seen. I began to think of the places where I have experienced education. I was imagining the places and my feeling was the memory of the competition involved in almost every aspect of education.

Speaker: I was narrowed down a little bit and focused. Normally when I want to learn something I'm opening up, but you asked me to be very strict on this. So I narrowed down. I don't like so much what I found.

Timo: This is this also what I tell teachers when they feel nervous. They clench up a bit, they start frowning and the field of vision goes narrow. When I open it up I can feel that the muscles all over are relaxing. I believe that thinking is a whole lot more embodied than we might realise.

Speaker: Hey, can I just say how delighted I am that you have brought these other traditions of dialogue into a discourse? I'm intrigued by the way in which you have demonstrated in your paper, how the traditions come together in the way they perceive the world.

Speaker: I thought you were wonderfully clear about how we are inherently relational. We don't start as separate. We start as inherently relational. The relation is primary. You were clear about that.

Speaker: What is apparent from both what you've written, Timo, and what you talked about Daniella, is there's a deep tradition of a dialogic thinking in relation to education. I wasn't aware of that.

Speaker: I've got a question. I do know a little bit about Paulo Freire. I am curious to find out more about what he stands for and what you alluded to about being teacher-centred or student-centred in a classroom.

Timo: In dialogic education we let ourselves be affected as well, so it's a two-way learning process or a mutual process – instead of the positing of information.

This idea of dialogic education goes against the mainstream of educational psychology, which says that memory is a kind of warehouse where we store bits of information and the mind is something that processes those bits of information.

Speaker: It's hard to break those traditions that we have followed from a very young age. It's a little fearful for the teacher to enter into dialogue because I'm supposed to know everything and share it with you.

Timo: We are in constant engagement with the world. We can't exist and we can't think . . . there is no consciousness or awareness without our engagement with the world. So, there is no learning without engagement either. I don't know how else it would work.

Speaker: I work with the Department of Corrections, and within that context there has to be control and there has to be public safety, and of course that's first and foremost in our system. But within that context, we operate as an educational entity and our goal is very much to engage in this dialogue in education. So it's very relevant. The things that we're talking about here are things that we as educators have been trying to incorporate into that environment.

Speaker: Yeah. I would like to follow what James said. I do not believe we could have accomplished what we bring into our classrooms with our staff on a regular basis without the dialogue. I think the foundation has been our ability to dialogue.

Speaker: I would say that is correct. Thanks to Director Clarke, we spread it out to all of our staff, then to the offenders, and now we see it going out to some of the other public safety agencies and some of the court systems. I guess you start small and it expands. Maybe to offenders families. And it's all about a culture shift. Not just one particular aspect, it's about a cultural shift.

Speaker: How do you disseminate success? How do you get other potential adopters to take on some of these approaches? In the context of corrections, my understanding is that Virginia has the lowest level of recidivism in the United States, but other states are not exactly crawling all over Virginia, coming to see what it is that you're doing that is distinctive that leads to that lower level of reoffending.

Speaker: If the world needs dialogue, which I believe it does, how do you get the world to embrace more dialogue? What is it that we can do? In Virginia you've got Harold Clarke who had this idea. He made it happen in the context of the organisation and, no doubt, overcame lots of resistance to make it happen. So you had this kind of senior sponsor who really believed in it and sort of made it happen.

Speaker: In the US organisations are mostly interested in the quick fix. Peter Senge talks about it in *The Fifth Discipline*. When you choose a quick fix, it just leads you right back into the same problem.

Speaker: I think you're right. I think that is the only way that something like this works through the relationship through human contact. It's antithetical to the power dynamics that are inherent in the general structure that we live in.

Speaker: The key question remains. If future teachers don't know how to communicate dialogically, how are they supposed to communicate in that way with their students?

Postscript
The author's reflections, written some months after the conference

My paper was intended to facilitate dialogue and to cross conceptual gaps between apparently different approaches to dialogue. As we look at the theory and practice of dialogue from different perspectives, we will inevitably see the reality, including dialogue, unfold in different ways for each of us. These different-looking realities easily translate to different methodologies and approaches with a different focus. In the paper, I drew on my own experiences in the field of education, where different approaches to dialogue aim to help the participants grasp the fragmented state of educational practices and the fragmented consciousness that this state of mind is furthering and, hopefully, overcome it together.

Dialogue is crucial in this process of perceiving and overcoming fragmentation in education. Its most apparent contribution is in collectively making sense of the shared situation and enabling the formation of collective will to coherent action. More importantly, dialogue opens a space for recognising the unique value of each participant to the whole and the collective consciousness which, in turn, opens the whole architecture of educational practice for creative rethinking. This rethinking can encompass the ways we talk to each other about the world we share, how this enables us to think about our shared world in new ways, recognise each other's humanity and uniqueness, relate to each other in terms of power and solidarity, and care for each other.

It includes our shared material surroundings, environment and resources, other living beings, artefacts and inanimate things. Without dialogue, there is a danger that we remain blind to fragmentation and the fatal lack of care and responsibility it entails.

In the session we first explored how we tend, because of how many of us are schooled, to embody thinking as a narrowing or tightening of presence and focus. Some of the participants noted how this is antithetical to the more open focus that is needed in order to engage in dialogue. This idea of concentration as 'tightening up' is only one of the ways schooling can prevent people from being able to engage in dialogue. Another is the hierarchical power relations, already noted by David Bohm and Paulo Freire, that can restrict the ways we can relate to each other. Also, our desire for quick fixes, like the wish of a teacher that the student immediately 'learns' what the teacher is explaining, can be detrimental to the possibility of dialogue that does not rely on the students "storing" information handed out by the teacher. Rather, dialogue is characterised by mutual collegial exploration of experience, thought and consciousness.

Section Two

Shaping Corrections Through Dialogue

Can Corrections be shaped through Dialogue? If so, then an assurance starts to emerge that any sector of human endeavour could be shaped by Dialogue! In this section we look at ways that Corrections is already being shaped by Dialogue. Two of the papers are by Jane Ball, a significant authority and skilled practitioner in this field, and the third is by Peter Garrett, her business partner and colleague. Between them they have led this field internationally for several decades.

Jane developed an innovative Dialogue system for high-repeat offenders in the south of England called Threshold Dialogue. The 'threshold' was the prison gate. Three of the interlinked Dialogues she describes were in prisons and three in their local release community. Offenders progressed through the Dialogue settings that were co-facilitated – in and out of the prisons – by pairings of officers from the prisons, the police, probation, the local council and various other treatment and support agencies. These organisations provided the supporting infrastructure, because individually and collectively they valued the opportunity enabled by Threshold Dialogue. On an ongoing basis they could access, engage, inform, learn from, support and challenge the offenders in their care. The very candid Dialogues generated a common understanding and progress in a typically fragmented situation.

Peter Garrett shows how Dialogue can be incorporated into the decision-making process with significant benefits. The scope of this paper is wider than Corrections, but it is included here because the Working Dialogue pattern was designed, tested and proven in this sector and is a standard business practice in many prisons and probation and parole offices. The steps are ideally suited to structured organisations like local government, where fragmentation is inevitable. The challenge is how to reduce the distance between decision-makers and those impacted by their decisions. The Working Dialogue brings everyone (or representations of the subgroups) together to consider the matter and co-create the decision – but without interfering with already-defined organisational responsibilities or accountabilities. This is a remarkable step in shaping the culture.

In her second paper Jane Ball explores the underlying dialogic concept that enabled the Threshold Dialogue and other related initiatives to be so successful — namely the Offender Resettlement Journey (ORJ). She considers the multifaceted awareness and skills needed to facilitate an event that starts to integrate any fragmented criminal justice system. The integrating thread is the journey of the offender, who is effectively the client. Every agency supports this in some way, from the police and courts through the jails, prisons and various community support and treatment organisations. Their combined effectiveness is measured as the recidivism rate. Rather than working separately with limited awareness of each other, the ORJ events brings them into interaction with one another as they focus their attention on the human successes and failures of the offenders and their families.

– P.G.

Threshold Dialogue to Change a System

Jane Ball

How do I live a better life and how do I do a better job? Threshold Dialogue, a structured dialogue programme designed to bring together people involved in the criminal justice system in the UK – high-repeat offenders, police officers, prison staff, local government officers and politicians, housing and employment staff and many others – provided a forum specifically to consider these questions. The common goal of all these participants was to improve resettlement of offenders and thereby reduce recidivism. This was achieved in Threshold Dialogue because everyone who was involved changed – not only the offenders but also practitioners – and, with it, the services and the way agencies worked together as a system changed. We focused on preparing for and making transitions, marked by crossing the threshold from one physical environment to another, especially from prison to the community. The experience was enriching for everyone involved. Over a five-year period we considered real and current issues; people in the Dialogues sought to understand themselves and each other, and thought together about the choices and decisions each of us had to make.

This paper describes the generative development of Threshold Dialogue, through which change embedded itself in the system and had wide-ranging impact. Changes were made in ways we did not imagine when we began. The generative process worked like water finding its way through the land, creating rivers and streams where there were only channels and furrows. It was very different from a project with a five-year implementation plan, like building a motorway to a predetermined destination.

I led the process with Peter Garrett, working with colleagues in Prison Dialogue at different stages, and many people from Bournemouth and Dorset who took part and affected the emerging work. The quotes, taken from the many records and reports in the Prison Dialogue, and bringing in their words, are featured below in italics.

Our Program Origins

Threshold Dialogue was originated by Prison Dialogue to support the successful resettlement of high-repeat offenders stuck in a revolving door between prison and the community. Typically, these men and women have chronically unstable lives, are addicted to drugs or alcohol, suffer poor health, and have no home. They commit minor crimes, spend perhaps six months in prison, and reoffend soon after they are released. This is a human tragedy for the individuals and a collective crisis for the criminal justice system. In 2006, 61,000 adults in England and Wales were sentenced to terms of imprisonment of less than 12 months (meaning 6 months served in prison), and around 60 per cent of those were convicted of at least one offence in the year after release. Not much has changed: in 2018, 63% sentenced to less than a year reoffended within 12 months.

The criminal justice system is complex and the agencies that affect each other often act as if they are independent. In addition, individuals, groups and organisations within the wider community – local government, shop owners, private accommodation landlords, neighbours – who affect and are affected by this situation are completely excluded from any conversation about resettlement service and policy development.

Over a five-year period, we achieved:

- Recognition of Dialogue as a mode of engagement that made a difference to the way people were thinking, and specifically to offenders' behaviour, based on the experience of hundreds of Threshold Dialogue sessions.
- An established network of Threshold Dialogues in six different prison and community locations along the offenders' journey, to support their transition across a range of 'thresholds'.
- Development of theory and language about the offender journey, providing different ways to think about how to intervene in the crises that accompany the cycles of reoffending: Crisis of Release, Crisis of Entry and Re-entry, and Line of Sight, each described below.
- Progress in staff practices, and everyday on-the-ground partnership between different professions and agencies.
- Service improvements and innovations based on what was learnt from Threshold Dialogue.
- Integrated local multiagency ownership at a strategic and operational level, and day-to-day in a local Threshold Dialogue facilitation team.

What is a Threshold Dialogue and How Does it Work?

Picture a room, perhaps the multifaith room in a prison. There is a circle of chairs in which 25 people are seated: a police officer and a prison officer identifiable by their uniform; a few people in civilian clothes, including a probation officer and a housing support worker; a woman in a suit who is a magistrate; and a larger number of men in the T-shirts and sweatpants of prison clothing.

The session begins with a check-in – a pertinent question is posed by the facilitator and each person takes a turn to answer. As they do, the group becomes more attentive and focused. Some of the participants are there most weeks – the offenders, our core group of police or prison officers, or housing workers – but there may be guests too, invited along because there is something of importance the group has asked to consider. If the question is employment-related, such as, "How do I get a job with a criminal record?" we might be joined by staff from the employment advice centre or training college, or a local employer. The check-in question might be "What was your first job?" or "Describe your first day at work". We discover that some of the offenders have never had a job, or their first job was given to them by one of the officers in the room, who made them the wing cleaner, or that the prison officer started out at 16 in the army. Given their experience, or lack of experience, how *do* the prisoners get a job when they are released? Where do they start? How do they think about what they would like to do, or what they could do? The Dialogue develops and, in a flow, moves from formal information about the system and what different services have to offer, to frustrations (perhaps masking a feeling of hopelessness) about the reality of the situation and what 'should' be provided; from ideas about the steps people could take, to personal stories, dreams and desires: "If only John had joined the army at 16 his life might have turned out differently", and "Why don't they let ex-offenders join the army, where they could contribute and benefit from the institutionalised life and structured, disciplined work?"

The next week the guest might be a someone from the family courts, and we may be thinking about relationships and how offenders can stay in touch with their children. In another session we might be talking about the impact of crime on the lives of so many people, or what goes through someone's mind when, after nine missed calls from their mentor or probation officer, the phone is ringing again and they choose to press busy – triggering a series of events they know too well.

If anyone starts to complain about a service that is not represented, the facilitator encourages them to take responsibility for their own actions – even if *they* did that, what could *you* have done differently? For example, a comment that probation officers never stay in touch with offenders when they are in prison, and what a difference it would make if they did, almost triggers a whole-group barrage of complaints – politely called *whinging* – about probation, with people egging each other on. Then someone asks, "Did *you* stay in touch with your probation officer? Have you thought about writing to them?" And the discourse changes to a focus on *me* rather than *them*. Soon afterward a probation officer is invited to a session to talk about their work, and the group explores what a partnership between a probation officer and their client might be like and what impact the partnership would have on successful resettlement – they learn to work **with** each other rather than trying to do things **to** or **for** others.

I think it is an opportunity for agencies to better understand what offenders are saying about the system and where they think changes could be made. But it's also about offenders and ex-offenders understanding what agencies are there to do and dispel some of those myths that build up, particularly in prisons, around what people can and can't do, or why certain decisions are made.

– Local government manager

In the Dialogue all participants learn how to be authentic, to listen to each other and stand in each other's shoes. No teaching is required. As well as benefitting from practical information, people develop impersonal relationships, close but not familiar and based on respect for each other's situation. They support and challenge one another and begin to change their thinking and attitude. This might be staff reassessing how they do their work or an offender reflecting about their behaviour and attitude. The Dialogue provides a forum to think about both everyday decisions and profound, life-changing decisions. Offenders begin to generate and sustain their own motivation, sense of self-worth and willpower to change as they assume responsibility for their own emotions, actions, choices and direction in life.

I've tried it before! Get a nice flat – not enough. Decent income, a good relationship and kids – not enough. You think those are going to be what keeps you clean, but it's still not enough. I'm hearing you talk about demons and I'm the same as you. Maybe it's time to realise that the real issues lie with me, not with all the other things.

– Offender

It helps me in my job. When you look at defendants now you read their files from probation and you think, 'yeah, I understand that now'. And that's great, because I can help my other colleagues on the bench and give them more understanding of people's background, people's lives.

– Magistrate

It Started with a Single Dialogue in a Prison

Her Majesty's Prison (HMP) Dorchester in the south of England was a local prison (like a jail in the US system), serving the courts by keeping in-custody offenders on remand or recently sentenced, along with some who were serving short sentences. With my colleagues in Prison Dialogue, I had supported the remarkable performance improvement at this prison over a three-year period – a story in itself. This saw the prison rise in ranking from 135th of 136 to 35th in the Weighted Scorecard League Table of prisons in England and Wales. Everything from the security audit to tests measuring the quality of prison life improved, and the prison was recognised nationally as achieving an extraordinary shift in the prisoners' custodial experience. Staff satisfaction scores were also high – so high, in fact, that the Governor-in-charge was contacted by the survey team to find out on behalf of the Prisons Board what had been happening at HMP Dorchester.

Despite their outstanding operational improvements, HMP Dorchester still had a reconviction rate of 74.7%, the worst in England and Wales. This was in part a consequence of the nature of their prisoner population. However, rather than accepting the situation as inevitable, the leadership was ready to engage with the community and improve their impact on reducing reoffending.

Staff at HMP Dorchester were used to seeing the same men come through their doors time and time again, and different generations of the same local families. These were persistent and prolific offenders, but their crimes were not serious – few ever served a long enough sentence to benefit from meaningful intervention, and the local prisons were not funded or expected to provide treatment or offending-behaviour programmes. Many of the men experienced problems with drugs and alcohol, mental health or homelessness; they had little experience of regular work and were trapped in this revolving door.

National policy provided an opportunity to address this local need. Local Criminal Justice Boards were established at executive officer level under a national government directive to improve 'joined-up' work in the criminal justice system. They were tasked with addressing harm caused by Prolific and other Priority Offenders (known as PPOs) and other High-Repeat Offenders (HROs). PPOs were generally defined as those who had been sanctioned for 16 or more offences. The national policy requirement was an incentive for the other agencies within Dorset Criminal Justice Board (DCJB) to follow the lead of the prison, and the influential statutory partners of police, probation and local government were enlisted.

DCJB decided to focus the initiative on offenders from Bournemouth, where most of the area's PPOs came from. Bournemouth is a seaside town on the south coast of England. Like many seaside resorts in the UK, the rise in foreign travel in the 1970s and 80s had decimated the holiday industry. Hotels were replaced with drug rehabilitation centres – ideally suited to the multi-occupancy buildings and communal spaces. Along with the community of residential drug rehab centres came a significant chaotic, drug-addicted PPO population.

Under the name *Bournemouth Threshold Dialogue,* colleagues and I designed, convened and facilitated a one-year programme of weekly Dialogue sessions for PPOs. Offenders and the agencies involved in resettlement and crime reduction came together in these Dialogues to talk and think about their resettlement. The Dialogues developed along the lines I have described above. Having run Dialogues in prison for many years, we were not surprised by the positive impact on participants.

The structure of the Threshold Dialogue system was innovative, and it was key to making a sustained difference to PPOs. A Dialogue was held every Tuesday afternoon in HMP Dorchester and every Tuesday evening in Bournemouth town centre – you could attend a Dialogue in prison one week, in the community the next, and in prison again the next! This started to create a sense of routine within people's chaotic lives, and the benefits of the Dialogue experienced in prison did not have to stop when they were released – which was often when things got really difficult.

The same staff came to all of the sessions in prison and in the community, maintaining continuity and building relationships across the threshold. Before Threshold Dialogue, you would never see a police officer in HMP Dorchester except for a formal interview – and if they were seen, prisoners would shout and kick the doors to their cells. The first time two police officers came into Dorchester with me the prison staff were so concerned they escorted us to the meeting room through the back corridors to avoid being seen.

In the other direction, prison officers attended Dialogues in the community, and some prisoners were granted temporary release to attend (escorted there and back by an officer). In the community Dialogue they could establish relationships with probation and agency staff who would be supervising and supporting them and the police who would be 'keeping their eye on them'.

The Prison Gate Was Becoming More Transparent

Talking at length and in depth with offenders about their experiences stuck in the 'revolving door', swinging in and out of prison, we realised some generic features of their journey that, if the journey was to be successful, they had to think about. A **Crisis of Release** – an emotional, mental and physical crisis – occurs for prisoners as their release date approaches and when they leave the prison. We observed and heard about the detrimental effect of incarceration on their independence. Prisoners lose the freedom to make decisions about many things, including when to eat, when to shower, what to wear, how to behave. They follow a day of core activities and their behaviour is controlled by schemes of punishment (losing privileges such as visits or TV) and reward. This custodial regime becomes a 'comfort zone' for many, and they are used to putting aside thoughts of the future in favour of day-to-day issues, immediate need and satisfaction. On release, as soon as they step across the threshold of the prison gate, offenders have to think for themselves and manage their own lives – even with supervision and strict licence conditions. We talked often about the challenges of negotiating sudden freedom, lack of structure and containment.

There is also a **Crisis of Entry/Re-entry** suffered as people anticipate going to prison – however many times they have made that journey before. Some of the experiences were easy to understand, such as feeling the stress of leaving loved ones. PPOs also had what one described as a 'f★★★-it button' – if they knew they were going back to prison anyway, they would commit another offence, or wreck their accommodation, or fight a police officer. Of course this only made things worse. More vulnerable people might panic, behave erratically, overdose or self-harm. Once in prison there is a lot to digest as the regrets hit home, detox from drugs or alcohol begins and people worry about their belongings that have been lost or held by the police.

The Dialogues on each side of the prison gate provided space and time for the men to talk and think about these crises, to recover and learn from what had happened, or prepare to manage, rather than suffer, the crisis. As a result, they could cross the 'threshold' more successfully.

Building on the subject of preparation, we developed a concept we called the **Line of Sight** and used this to help offenders and staff to think realistically and generatively about the present and the future. The idea likened the offender's journey to driving on a motorway – if you know where you are and have a clear line of sight, you can see the road and signposts ahead, you can travel well and safely to your destination. If the signposts are obscured, there is a lorry in your way, or an accident in your path, you may miss a turn, or even come off the road. We proposed offenders needed some vision of where they wanted to get to in life and a clear line of sight of the path to get there. This meant seeing and understanding well ahead what they needed to do, and the choices, compromises and challenges they might face – why they had to stay in a hostel rather than with their girlfriend, how and when would that chang . . . and do you have to get clean of substance abuse before you can hold down a job, or do you get a job to keep you busy and motivated to help you get clean?

To reinforce the foundation for Threshold Dialogue, we maintained extensive records about the impact of the work, commissioned an external qualitative evaluation by Coventry University, and reported to the Criminal Justice Board. We were also Team Award Winners in the category 'Partnership of the Year' in the Dorset Justice Awards.

This has been about broadening my understanding of the work I do. My job satisfaction has increased and I've seen it benefit previously sceptical and resistant colleagues. Our work can't and shouldn't end at the prison gates. We can be so much more than just turnkeys.

– Prison officer

When I first came out of prison it seemed like I was bouncing between different agencies. It didn't seem like they were talking to each other and it was frustrating because I didn't understand how the process worked.

– Ex-offender

Extending a Community-Led Partnership

Our reflections on the first year of Threshold Dialogue, the enthusiasm from local agencies based on successful outcomes, and awareness of the extent of needs led to a series of productive developments, as I will outline next.

A Threshold Dialogue Network: By following the journey of the Threshold Dialogue participants, we found even short-sentenced PPOs and HROs were moved regularly to nearby HMP Guys Marsh, a prison set up for sentenced prisoners to engage in purposeful work, training, education and programmes. As our aim was to provide continuous engagement through the offender's journey, Threshold Dialogue was introduced at HMP Guys Marsh and later at Her Majesty's Young Offenders Institution Portland to engage with youth from Bournemouth. Over time Dialogue sessions in the community were placed at three different sites: Dorset Lodge, a supported Housing Unit that offered accommodation to prisoners on release; St Paul's Hostel, a direct-access night shelter and day centre for people whose lives were more chaotic; and in a community centre in the middle of a more stable residential area in Poole. Each location supported a different transition across a different threshold, and each transition brought its own crisis – the move from a supported hostel to independent accommodation was as great a challenge to many as leaving prison. The reality of increased responsibility is balanced against the hope of a different way of life in housing, employment and relationships.

For a couple of years I left my house at 5:30 am every Tuesday to travel to HMP Guys Marsh for the morning Dialogue, on to HMP Dorchester for the afternoon, on to Bournemouth in the evening and home around 11pm!

More people were drawn to be involved, supporting different phases of the journey at different locations. Police, probation, and prisons were joined by local government-elected representatives and staff, drug and alcohol services, accommodation providers, magistrates and court officials, landlords, employers, staff from social security, employment advice, and training centres.

The people who are coming in are often amazed by the rapport they get going with some of the service users. People obviously have their stereotypes, and when the barriers are dropped and people are genuinely engaging on the level that everyone's comfortable at, I think the flow of information is a lot better; it's heard and it's received. That information's been there previously but they've not been able to get hold of it, so obviously the environment the dialogue creates is conducive to getting information.

– Housing prison liaison worker

Establishing community ownership: Based on our experience of running Dialogue groups and interventions from Prison Dialogue since 1993, we knew that Threshold Dialogue would need to be owned by local agencies and embedded in the normal work routines of their staff in order to be sustained. Without that, Prison Dialogue would be looking for commissioners and funding, and running the programme from the outside, indefinitely.

We began to think differently. We had been working from the perspective of the prison, which was where we began, and found it was more productive to look from the perspective of the community. Communities forget about their residents when they are in prison – they might even be hoping that they won't come back. However, based on their experience in Threshold Dialogue, the police were getting more interested in engaging with offenders and building the relationships required for effective community policing while the prisoners were literally a captive audience. We decided Threshold Dialogue would be led by community agencies and began to recruit other partners with that in mind. This also made sense, given the extending network. We were able to engage local government staff and politicians more strongly. The combination of a clear logic of the value of Threshold Dialogue (offender and staff development, cost effectiveness, service improvements as described in this chapter) and a profound experience when people attended the Dialogue, was compelling.

The public perception is the key thing in Bournemouth. It's no good just sitting back and hoping they'll go away. But they're not going to go away. They are part of our community and they have got their problems, and I'm sure 90% of them don't particularly want their problems. So I think the rest of society does have a duty to try and help wherever possible to try and get these people back on the straight and narrow.

– Elected councillor, Bournemouth

If they're going to move on they need to feel that they've got some relationship with that community that doesn't involve criminality.

– Local government manager, Safer and Stronger Communities team

Three-tier structure for sustainable partnership: Sustainability would require more than the spirit of local ownership; an integrated governance structure was necessary to provide leadership, strategic direction, and operational management of Threshold Dialogue across this open, multiagency system. Working with executive officers from each agency, we created a Governance Board for statutory partners (police, prisons, probation and local government), chaired by a high-ranking local police officer. At this level Threshold Dialogue extended beyond Bournemouth to include the county of Dorset. The Governance Board's agreed role was reducing recidivism and increasing the successful resettlement through developing and maintaining a Dorset Threshold Dialogue network.

An Operations group was also established for all partner agencies, including relevant charitable and private-sector organisations, for operational decision-making and resource allocation to support Threshold Dialogue and improve integrated services. The third tier was a multiagency facilitation team.

Through this structure, the integration of different agencies, staff at different levels of seniority, and offenders was possible, creating a widespread common understanding and the opportunity for change in the system. Threshold Dialogue was able to adapt as new needs and opportunities were identified. When the national government required every police force to set up a multiagency Integrated Offender Management Unit to work with persistent offenders 'through-the-gate', the Dorset team worked with Threshold Dialogue. An innovative Line of Sight Project, providing private rented housing with employment advice and support to prisoners immediately on release, was initiated by group of employment and housing agencies from Threshold Dialogue.

We are one of a dozen or so partners (from the community) who came together on the back of the phrase 'line of sight' to look at a way of reaching people 'on the other side of the wall' . . . we had one important principle that underpinned it: we didn't have a single extra penny to spend. This particular project wouldn't have happened but for dialogue.
– Housing manager, Bournemouth Borough Council

Developing a local facilitation team: This was probably the most challenging part of the new structure. On the one hand, facilitation was far beyond the skills and confidence of many of the agency staff. On the other, some of my colleagues thought you needed years of development and practice to become a Dialogue facilitator. I did not agree. I believed that, with the right pattern and basic training, anyone could facilitate and achieve a 'more dialogic' outcome, and with reflection and support they would learn by doing.

We identified the first cohort of facilitators from local agencies – police officers, prison officers, drug counsellors, housing support workers, probation officers. They were all very experienced and recommended by their supervisors. One was also recommended by the offenders. "You need to get that Robocop in here!" they had said. I found that Robocop had been officially commended for several years as the police officer with the highest rate of arrest in the county. He was a straight-talking policeman with years of experience. He saw the people he arrested go through court, into prison and out some months later only to reoffend again. "We're just not getting anywhere", he said when he joined the team. He soon became one of the most popular facilitators and a big advocate for Threshold Dialogues

The facilitators were to work in pairs from different agencies, and they would not facilitate the session in their workplace. This meant, for example, a police officer and drug counsellor would facilitate in the prison. We designed a pattern of activity – what had to happen before, during and after the Dialogue, including how to work as a facilitation team and report on the session. Peter and I ran a facilitation training programme, introducing this pattern, along with Dialogue Practice Skills that would enable them to get all of the participants engaged and into Dialogue.

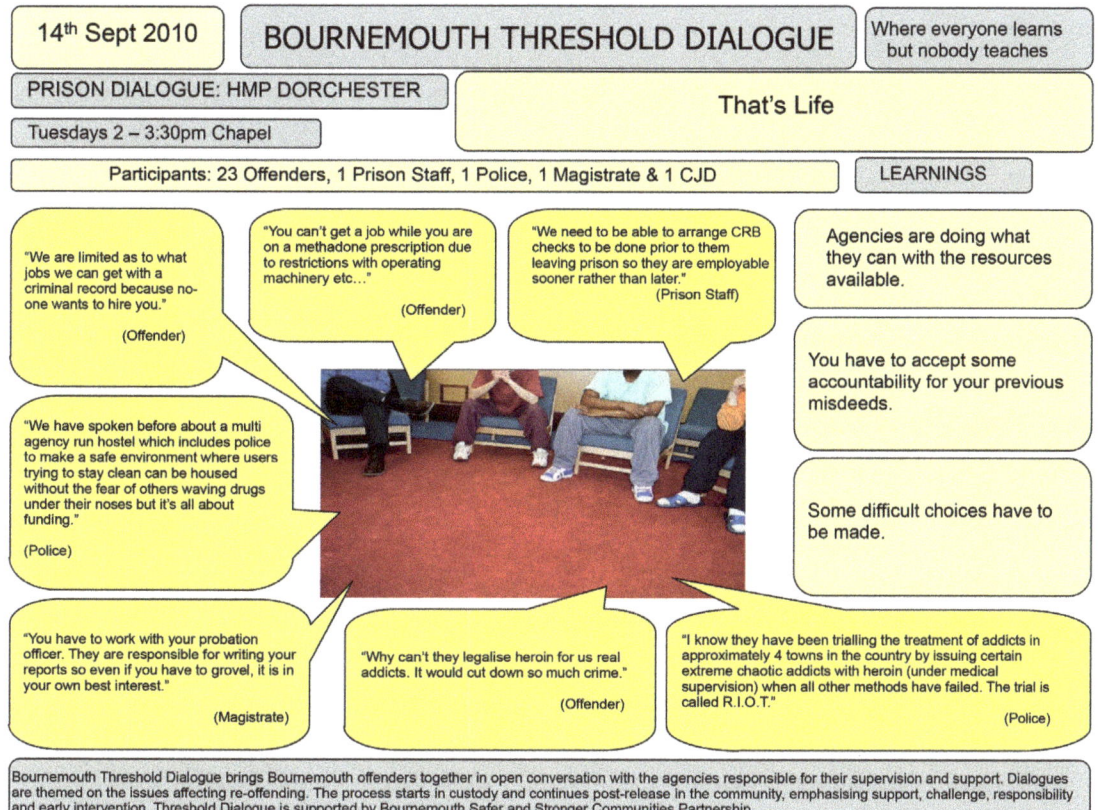

The session report was crucial to their skill development. To write the report the facilitator had to notice what was happening – they had to listen to be able to quote what was said, understand and reflect to know what people were learning, and see the common meaning emerging to name an overall theme (as you can see in the image below). Early on, one police officer remarked he had tried so hard to remember what he thought was a good quote that he missed what was said for the next 10 minutes and in the end had to give up! I suggested he concentrate on listening and see what he could remember at the end. He took my advice and of course found he could recall many significant comments. As facilitators learnt how to complete the session reports, they developed skills and understood more about what was happening and what they were aiming to achieve. As the team began to lead sessions, I was alongside to coach them through pre-session briefings and a post-session debrief, and to help out as they gained confidence.

Over two years an effective multiagency team of Threshold Dialogue Facilitators was established to take on facilitation at the six Threshold Dialogue sites. We trained 55 facilitators, including three ex-offenders.

The multiagency partnership provided strength through diversity of experience, skills, reputation and relationship. The common experience and purpose and the process of Dialogue that does not require consensus or agreement allowed the team to operate effectively together, while subject to their own agency policies, procedures, and line-management supervision.

Performance measures to 'do your day job better': To embed Threshold Dialogue in the normal work routines of agency staff we made the case that it would help them to 'do their day job better'. Meta-analysis has been used to show the impact of offending-behaviour programmes on reoffending, but we were operating far from the scale required to prove such outcomes. I thought it was more realistic to provide output measures. With the help of the Operations group we identified 'hours of engagement with offenders' as an output measure that was relevant to every agency. The police recognise that engagement with local offenders is an effective way to improve community policing, providing relationship building and intelligence. A police officer could achieve over 20 hours of high-quality engagement with local offenders in a 90-minute Dialogue with 15 prisoners. The same principle applied to every agency.

> *In my day-to-day work on the beat . . . [Dialogue] has proved invaluable in opening doors that would otherwise have been firmly shut, breaking down barriers with offenders and their families in the community where I work.*
> — Police officer

> *Of the guys in the session in the prison, five of them were clients of mine, from families I'm working with; people who I need to engage with and are hard to reach within the community.*
> — Family intervention worker

> *His response to police was very, very different. Whereas [before] he would kick off big-time, the last time I had to personally arrest him for breaching his recall and he just sat patiently waiting for the car to arrive. There was no fighting, no one had to take time off because they were injured.*
> — Police officer

We wrote "Threshold Dialogue: A Proposal" to describe the potential of this approach to resettlement and reducing reoffending.

Our Exit Strategy

Everything was in place for Dorset Threshold Dialogue to continue without Prison Dialogue, apart from ongoing facilitator development. When we needed to take the final step away, our exit strategy took two parts.

First, we conducted interviews with major partners – members of the Governance Board and Operations group, facilitators, and other participants. I video recorded their descriptions of the impact Threshold Dialogue had had on them and their work. Not only did this gather evaluation stories for our records but also, as they spoke, they realised for themselves what had been achieved and how they had changed.

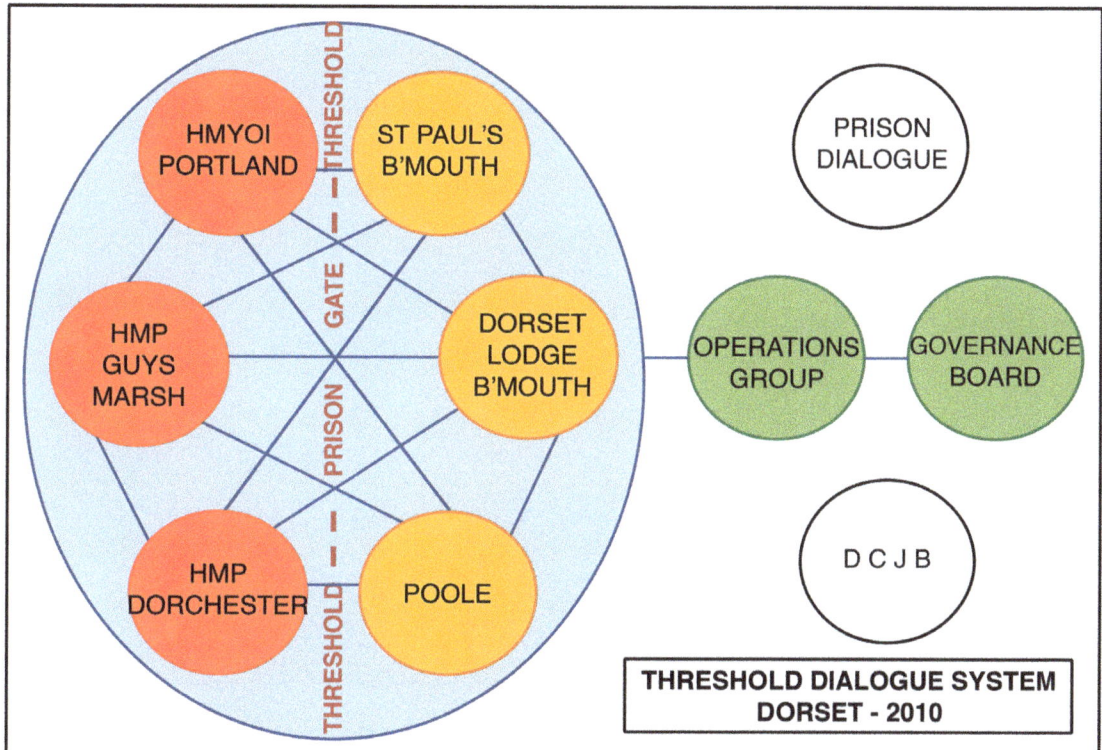

Fig. 2 represented by around 50 people. The graphic above shows who was there and how they were connected to the whole system (Fig 2).

Secondly, we initiated, convened and facilitated a Line of Sight Workshop for the Threshold Dialogue Governance Board in partnership with the Dorset Reducing Reoffending Strategy Board. All the major partners, including some ex-offenders and current prisoners (escorted out of the prison for the day) took part. The Threshold Dialogue system was in the room,

The event included a review of the previous five years, an opportunity to recognise what had been achieved, and we acknowledged the leadership and contribution of many people. This was followed by a consideration of the current situation – where much had improved, but also where were there still gaps.

We explored this from the perspective of the ex-offenders, who had first-hand experience of where the system succeeded and failed. Peter and I facilitated an Offender Resettlement process, in which we heard directly from some of the ex-offenders.

The agencies were spatialised, seated around the room according to their position along the line of sight from prison to independence (Fig. 3), represented by the Threshold Dialogue that had been meeting regularly in a residential area of the town of Poole.

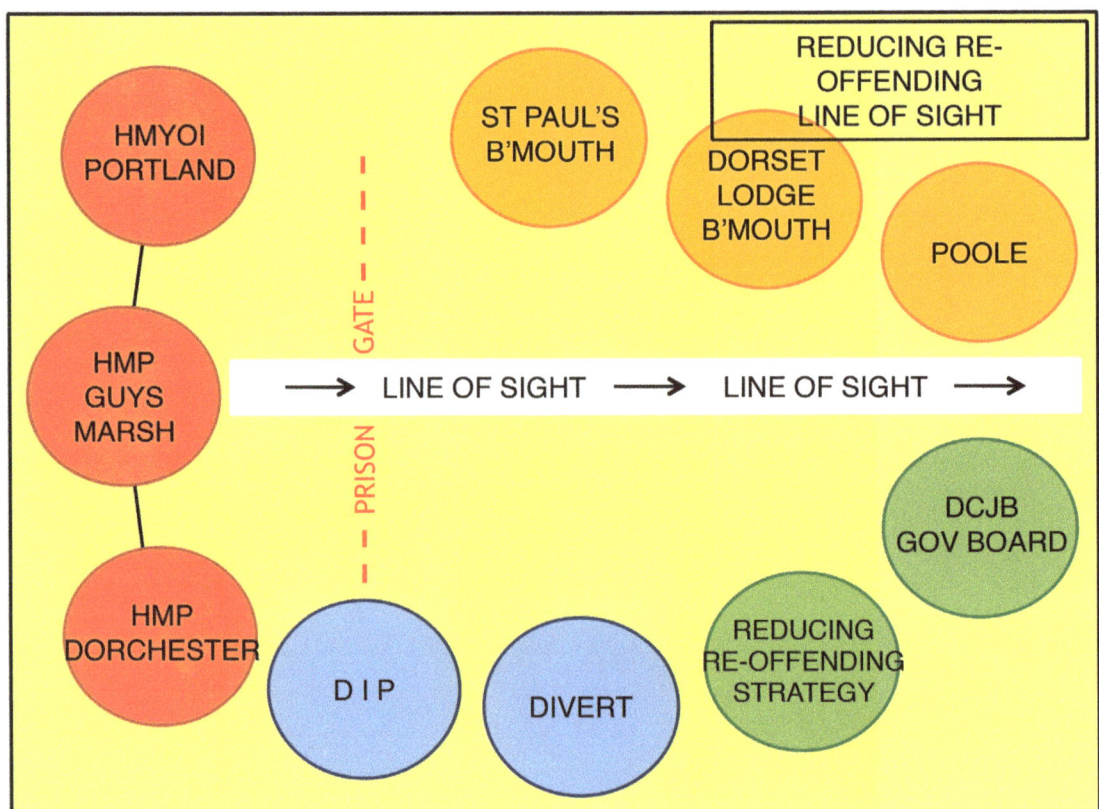

The ex-offenders who shared their stories were heard by everyone as they talked to me or Peter, and we walked together along the line of sight: into prison, over the prison gate on release (more than once), tracking their experiences chronologically. As each person relived their experiences, we could all see and hear the practical reality of their life, the emotional roller coaster and the thinking that trapped them and released them. This was a reminder of the impact of talking directly to offenders, which was experienced every week in Threshold Dialogue. A final process gathered impressions and ideas from everyone in the room, to be integrated in the Reducing Reoffending strategy for the county. So much understanding was shared through the day.

The event was also a ceremonial handover. It was the first time every level had been present in the room together – Criminal Justice Board and the newly formed Reducing Reoffending Strategy Board, Governance Board, Operations group, facilitators, other agency participants from across the six locations, prisoners and ex-offenders – and for such a profound experience.

Peter and I spoke explicitly of our departure and handed over the baton to the Assistant

Chief Constable of Dorset Police, who announced that the Governance Board would be integrated into the statutory Dorset Reducing Reoffending Strategy Board.

Reflections

Threshold Dialogue was a success and made a great difference to the lives of many people, both the offenders and staff who came together week after week in Dialogue. The closure marked the end of an eight-year chapter in my life working first with HMP Dorchester, then with the prison and community. Language and images that carry ideas are important for this work. When I began working with HMP Dorchester the failing prison, we helped the leadership articulate a simple strategy and vision in four words *Comply – Perform – Serve – Shine*. To *Shine* was to be a beacon, seen from afar and influencing those beyond the prison gates. We certainly achieved that.

My development was learning to work in an open system. The transformation at HMP Dorchester, and other successful work I had been a part of, was achieved in a closed system, partnering with one leader for whom everyone ultimately worked. When that leader said people had to attend the Dialogue, they did – which happened in the early days at Dorchester, to the surprise of staff who found themselves sitting in a circle with 20 prisoners! Threshold Dialogue was an open-system partnership. Each partner agency had a different reporting line, a different leader, a different role in the community, different policies and procedures. Yet they worked together to bring about change.

To achieve this we had to identify and establish a partnership with someone who was willing to stand up as a leader among their peers (first the prison Governor-in-charge, then the police superintendent), with vision, enthusiasm and energy to attract others. We had to help people find their connection to the common purpose, engaging their hearts and minds, finding the desire to make a difference to the lives of offenders, to better themselves and improve the system in which they worked. We also had to enable each agency and individual to meet their own interests, and better those interests – fulfilling a new national requirement, meeting targets, finding more effective and safer ways to work and improving services without more resources.

The potential of a generative process was also important to discover. In the richness of common understanding we could recognise needs and opportunities as they emerged and integrate them into the process, creating results I would never have thought possible.

Conference Session Extracts

From a conversation with participants considering the paper with Jane Ball

Speaker: Jane, I read your paper last night. I actually worked in the prison system as an HIV test counsellor many years ago. One of the issues about recidivism at that time is why they keep going back. In your paper it was revealing that it's the structure that they don't have outside of the system, that kind of draws them back. As I think about working with families who are trying to reunite with their relatives who are in prison, I was curious to know how, or have you thought about using a Threshold Dialogue in a family context, as they re-enter back into the community? Because many families have really gotten burned out with recidivism as they keep going back and forth. I think that your paper really gave a clear understanding about why that is. So I'm just curious to hear more about that, and helping them in their families with the re-entry as a part of the process to help them come back into the community.

Speaker: In our small group, where the consensus was that we can participate, we can be active as a dialogic organisation, not just getting buy-in from community stakeholders but by being able to pull us all together as different agencies – because a lot of times we're talking, but we're talking different languages. So what came up was the idea that there is somebody or some group to pull all of this together under one umbrella.

Speaker: One of the things that I found really valuable in this conversation was the idea that in order to buy in sponsorship, you really need to make sure that this work was not seen as extra work, but really aligned with helping everyone do their day job better. Another aspect was this moment where the dialogue just clicked for them and they felt like, Oh, this is something new. This is something really valuable that enables me to do my job better. I'm curious to hear what the mechanisms are for that, and if we would be able to articulate better, we could probably more efficiently create buy-in.

Speaker: One of the things that I'm just wondering . . . The Virginia Department of Corrections are doing a great job, I think with dialogue. There's always room for improvement, things change, so you need to go back and review and revise and edit, you know. Maybe some of these things have been done. My concern more is with the community partners and getting them to buy in. I'm just wondering if there is some type of word matrix or some type of time study that could be created to have on hand when we try to get our community partners to become more involved in dialogue.

Speaker: In our group we asked a similar question about how you get the stakeholders, such as our local jails, our judges and district attorneys more involved, especially when dealing with female offenders, as well as with mental health offenders and sex offenders. That's one of the problems the department faces on a daily basis. And I think if they had the opportunity to see what we see during the Offender Resettlement Journeys, that people would be more inclined to be involved and to know that it has an impact on our communities once offenders are released.

Speaker: One of the things that I've found in the community is we tend to talk. We used to talk *at* people rather than *with* people. Even before I became a Dialogue Practitioner, but I'd had my basic training, I began to use basic dialogue principles in our family reunification seminars that we do in the community. We have had 40 or more people in the dialogue circle, and we remain in the circle during the whole event. Instead of talking about things that would make the family members feel like that they are on probation when their loved one gets released, we wanted to hear their concerns. Their concerns are not as surprising as what you might think. They have a lot of feelings that need to be shared. They have a lot of fear, especially with family members of people that have severe addictions. They're scared. What do I do if nothing changes when the loved one comes home? The loved one is still incarcerated when we hold these seminars, but there are returning citizens or probationers or parolees in the circle. I invite people from a different ongoing support group that I run to be a part of that circle. So we also have treatment providers, we have resource providers and I've tried to get law enforcement involved. They're always invited, as are people from institutions.

The point I would want to make with this is that when someone comes from the prison to sit in this circle in the community, we started that threshold process. We've got a long ways to go to be as excellent as you, Jane, with all the work you've done, but we've got a start and I'm going to keep moving in that direction. Things are even more important than we were doing before the Covid, and we just might need to find a way to do them in a different way. Thank you so much – I really enjoyed reading your paper.

Speaker: One of the things we're doing in the division of administration in the Department of Corrections is, we partnered internally with the division of programs, education, and re-entry to talk about how to train offenders while they're incarcerated. I'll use one of my units as an example. One of the units that I supervise is infrastructure and environmental management, and we train offenders to run wastewater treatment plants. And on the outside, they're very high paying jobs.

We talked about we make sure those people leave with the exact certifications reflected on their records so they can take those out to job interviews. That grew into including small diversity businesses that we invited into our circle. They're helping with this population to make sure they understand and get trained at how to register as small businesses. Minority business owners are eligible to bid on contracts and to engage in business here in Virginia. So, we started out internally and, like you were saying, it just naturally grew to include an outside group.

Postscript
The author's reflections, written some months after the conference

I was encouraged by the response to my paper and the work I had done in Threshold Dialogue. Writing about a five-year programme that had so many strands felt complex and at times difficult to articulate. I was delighted to hear how inspired people were, and their practical questions and ideas about what they could do. I was surprised to hear the many ways in which they were applying Dialogue and bringing people together around common practical issues. Based on what was said and comments in the online chat, they started to see how they could take another step and grow an initiative, including more perspectives and adapting to needs. It started to sound simple.

There were lots of questions about how to engage stakeholders. People were noticing Professional Dialogue is not only about how you talk with others, but with whom you talk. Many of the participants worked in corrections and were unsure about how to engage community agencies and how to keep them involved.

I had named the principle of working *with* people, rather than doing things *to* or *for* them. I realise that working *with* tends to be used in relation how people who have more power work *with* people who have less power. However, it is a principle across the board. The challenge for many is, How do I work *with* someone who has more power than me? How do I work *with* a judge, or sheriff, so the work makes sense to them and is of benefit to all? Engaging with everyone as a peer in a sustained way is necessary for convening, just as it is for facilitation (a subject I address in my second conference paper, *Live Facilitation to Awaken the Offender Resettlement Journey*). As a Dialogic Organisation, Virginia Department of Corrections has addressed this internally; however, the communication constraints of status and hierarchy still exist in places outside of the agency and I realise this is a new challenge for them.

Finally, I was left thinking about a thought-provoking question placed in the chat that we did not have time to explore in the session. Chukwu-Emeka Chikezie from Sierra Leone asked, "With the adaptive, generative model you used, did you start with a grand vision and roadmap or was it radically responsive and demand-driven and opportunistic?" I believe reducing crime is a necessity rather than a vision, and I am learning that is where I often begin.

Dialogue within Decision-Making

Peter Garrett

This is a companion paper expanding the consideration begun by Harold Clarke and Whitney Barton in their paper, "Putting Dialogue to Work in the Virginia Department of Corrections," that was considered at our 2019 conference. That paper described the value of the Working Dialogue as a business practice for the management of organisational change, and gives specific case studies to substantiate this. In this paper I want to explain the thinking that led to the original design of the Working Dialogue by me and Jane Ball with a small team from Virginia. The pattern involves a sequence of Dialogues with a fixed group of people in one room together, and results in a collective view about a plan of action. So it requires *in-the-room* Dialogue skills. Each Working Dialogue is also intended to be an *intervention* in the way things are currently working, so this requires further skills along with the careful placing of the Working Dialogue at the point of intervention in order to yield the most value with the right grouping of people. It is intended for use in every business unit across a large state agency, and is therefore intended to be *systemic*. This third level requires architectural thinking in the design process, as outlined in this paper.

I believe it is timely to explore the relationship between Dialogue and decision-making. Given the general levels of complexity and ambiguity we experience in society, if the world needs Dialogue, *we* surely need Dialogue to influence the quality of collectively made decisions! So I track the key factors that, if left unaddressed, would prevent us from making a difference in the world in this regard. Dialogue in the room was our starting point with David Bohm, with the theme of addressing fragmentation in consciousness and hence in the world. As we stepped into the world after his death, we had to address how decisions are made in organisations, and the decision-making process itself. The Working Dialogue is a prime example of doing just that. I believe this will be of interest to those practitioners wanting to expand their reach beyond their starting point of Dialogue 'in the room'. Those who already use Working Dialogues in their workplace will benefit from understanding the thinking behind this pattern; this will enable them to be more effective in how they sponsor, facilitate and participate in Working Dialogues. The third and smallest grouping is those who are embarking on systemic Dialogue work and are interested in the architectural thinking required to do this well at scale.

From Dialogue in the 1980s to Dialogue in the 2020s

I believe that there has been considerable confusion amongst Dialogue Practitioners over the years about the relationship between Dialogue and decision-making. Many claim the fundamental features of Dialogue are that it has no agenda and is not a decision-making activity. If this were the case, it would not be viable to bring Dialogue into organisations, since those working in them are employed to make decisions every day, and they are accountable for those decisions. Given the proliferation of organisations, this would result in the marginalisation of Dialogue, leaving it unrelated to everyday working life. In the 20th century almost every aspect of our lives is enabled or defined by organisations – from hospital births and deaths to our food, clothing, housing, transport, education, leisure and so on. I do not see how we can ignore the pervasive presence of organisations in how we proceed.

From our earliest Dialogues with David Bohm in the 1980s, we took a transparent position on decision-making. We considered Dialogue to be a way of establishing a common meaning amongst a group of people. *Dia* means 'through' (as in 'diameter', which is a line through the middle of a circle) and *logos* is 'the word', or 'meaning'. This shared meaning came about through establishing a common content in the conscious awareness of all the participants in the Dialogue, by participants 'suspending' or revealing their experience in the moment. With that shared understanding, people do not need to be told what to do because it is self-evident to them. It could be called 'common sense'. Each decides what to do for themselves, based on a common understanding. The analogy of the hunter-gatherer tribe, like the Kalahari Bushmen, who lived in small social groupings of 15 to 30 people, illustrated well this way of living. They spent the smaller part of their day finding food and most of it talking together. We speculated about what organisations would be like were employees to be in a similar position of holding a common understanding and a shared content in consciousness. We related Dialogue to decision-making from the outset, and I still hold that perspective.

The hunter-gatherer society was sustainable for hundreds of millennia, but even if we in the current era wanted to, we have to accept that we could not revert to that way of life. The overall population is too great, and consequently we spend most of our days working for our livelihood. We live in a technologically driven society, in the midst of myriad perspectives and conditioning. In comparison to the hunter-gatherers whose environment was simply the undeveloped local ecology, we are both highly coordinated and fragmented. What is the relevance of Dialogue now, given the situation in which we find ourselves?

There is a simple path that runs from the early form of Dialogue that several of us developed with David Bohm prior to his death in 1992, to the Professional Dialogue that many of us now practice. That early work was an enquiry into the pervasive fragmentation in human consciousness that leads to endless counterproductive decisions with unintended consequences. The challenging complexity is that the resulting problems, are in turn, 'fixed' by the people using similarly fragmented thought – which leads to further proliferation of the problems in different forms. Quicksand may be a good metaphor for the many seemingly insoluble challenges we face, including the ecological crisis, loss of species and global warming.

This path crossed over three significant 'mountain ridges' after David's death. They relate to *time, power* and *decision-making*. Without crossing over these three passes, I believe that students and practitioners who only read about our early practice (which some now call Bohm Dialogue), will be held in theoretical and practical abeyance, unable to get traction in the world to make a difference – our primary intention from the outset. Our society is sorely in need of relief from a litany of insoluble problems and, in many ways, (but by no means all) our culture is more fragmented than it was when David was alive.

Time as a Context for Decision-Making

First, let's consider *time*. There are many ways of conceiving of time, and I have outlined my thinking about this in A *Dialogic Model of Time* (2006). The most relevant notion for this consideration is the distinction between *seasonal* time and *chronological* time. Seasonal time is centred on the earth. It is dependent on the rotations of the earth around the sun, and of the moon around the earth. These annual, monthly and daily cycles determine opportune timings for things to happen. Migrating birds sense when to arrive and depart, and the sap rises and falls with the summer and winter weather, just as the tides rise and fall with the waxing and waning of the moon, and flowers open and close with the rising and setting of the sun. This seasonal time features strongly in agriculture, as it does in human relationships. As people establish a common meaning and a common content of consciousness it clearly has a flow, an unfolding cycle that opens and closes potential opportunities. The art of Dialogue is to be sensitive to this changing field of potential as one participates in the flow, thereby finding the timing that meets the moment. It is not by chance that many languages have the same word for time and the weather, such as *le temps* in French.

In contrast, chronological time is centred on technology and is man-made. It is derived from the clock, providing divisions of time established by the rotation of the earth around the sun. Chronological time emerged in Europe in the 1700s with the town clocks (each of which determined their own approximate time), eventually being standardised to enable the reliable scheduling of transport by coach and horses. By 1884 Greenwich Mean Time was defined along with the 24 time zones, and technological coordination became possible. We are so used to chronological time now that we hardly notice its pervasive influence. I can arrange to meet you at the entrance to the Louvre in Paris at 11:30am on 23 January, and we can do so successfully even though I may live in London and you in Rio de Janeiro. We are accomplished in the use of chronological time. We create timelines that include arbitrary deadlines (not lifelines) that may be unrelated to the rhythms in our bodies, lives or surroundings. Such timing turns our thinking inside out. We think we are caught in 'rush hour' traffic, when clearly it would be better called 'slow hour', except that our inner experience is one of rushing and being frustrated by not getting there easily. Note the exhausting experience of sitting for two hours in a stationary aircraft on an airport runway – as against the next six hours in the same seat crossing the Atlantic.

What does this have to do with Dialogue? Understanding the source of fragmentation in human consciousness, which is where we began, requires stepping out of the external fixation of chronological time and slowing down sufficiently to become familiar with how consciousness works. There is an ebb and flow in thinking, which acts at a different speed and with a different sensitivity from memory-derived thought. Past-thinking is fast, automatic and reactionary. It is carried forward from a past experience and situation that may or may not be relevant in the present one. Hence the fragmented experience, one that is lessened as we bring our thoughts and feeling into the present situation. So – clearly Dialogue occurs in seasonal time, not chronological time? No. It may have been so for hunter-gatherers, but we are unable to step out of a civilisation and society that is based on chronological time. To my dismay, even sleeping out at night in the remotest Iranian desert and far from the nearest evidence of civilisation, I spotted the regular flashing of light from a satellite passing overhead in the starry sky. So in my thinking, every Dialogue is a compromise, or an amalgamation of the two kinds of time. Within a chronological time period (perhaps 90 minutes reserved on our calendars) we can create the space for seasonal time and thinking, or even for a sense of timelessness out of which generative thinking emerges. Then we probably dive back into chronological time as we attend to responsibilities and decisions elsewhere.

Achieving Dialogue in the world requires a set of skills which might seem alien to some practitioners. These skills include the ability to 'paint the painting on the size of canvas available', time-wise, by starting and ending at the predetermined hour; learning to help people to get engaged with one another (without which they cannot form a common meaning); guiding people to think together, rather than resisting and asserting by thinking separately; enabling the transition into understanding one another; and, most importantly, leaving the time and space for the emergence of the still-forming thinking that is unique to this moment. With these kinds of skills it is possible to step into the workplace to enable productive Dialogue, as we have done in prisons, industrial plants, board rooms, universities, fire stations, banks and rural agricultural settings in the so-called Third World. Real Dialogue is about rubbing shoulders with people who have to make decisions that affect themselves and others, and enhancing this process by gathering them into a common understanding of what each of them is doing and may need to do.

The Impact of Power on Decision-Making

Next, *power*. Why do we need to understand power to bring Dialogue into the world? By *power* I mean authority: the power of attributed authority that is, for example, fundamental to organisations. In my mind, differences of power and authority are a root cause of violation and fragmentation. Dialogue is essentially concerned with managing power differences in a generative and productive way. There are some ways we are all equal, perhaps as human beings in the eyes of God, but in many ways we are not and cannot be equal in power. This has been the case since hunter-gatherer days and remains the case today. Our skills, experience, wealth, state of health, education, social position, dependencies, gender, age and a long list of other factors may determine who has power and authority in any situation. In my thinking it would not be possible to bring Dialogue into the world and into the workplace if we were not conversant with how to manage power.

Power differences are most evident in organisations. There are many ways to understand the structures and processes embodied in organisations, but a few simple notions will help us here. As I outlined in my paper ('Engaging Fragmentation, Subcultures and Organisational Power', written for the 2018 *The World Needs Dialogue!* Academy conference), organisations predominately are methodically ordered power structures with delegated decision-making authority and accountability. The owners or shareholders delegate authority to the executives by assigning the authority or right to make certain levels of decision. They, in turn, delegate parts of their decision-making power and responsibility to others in the organisation. That is the nature of a typical organisation. This delegation follows two distinct lines: hierarchical power lines (vertical) and functional power lines (lateral). The vertical power lines are the chain of command, whilst the lateral power lines are the functions that may run across all the power lines, like finances, human resources, legal and regulatory expertise. The problem of fragmentation arises because the vertical power lines tend to break into competing silos. Also, there is a tension between the lateral power lines that use central control to try to standardise everything, and the vertical power lines thrive on customising their activities according to local opportunity or need.

But worst of all, everyone concentrates on their own specialised delegated responsibilities and pays less attention to those outside their

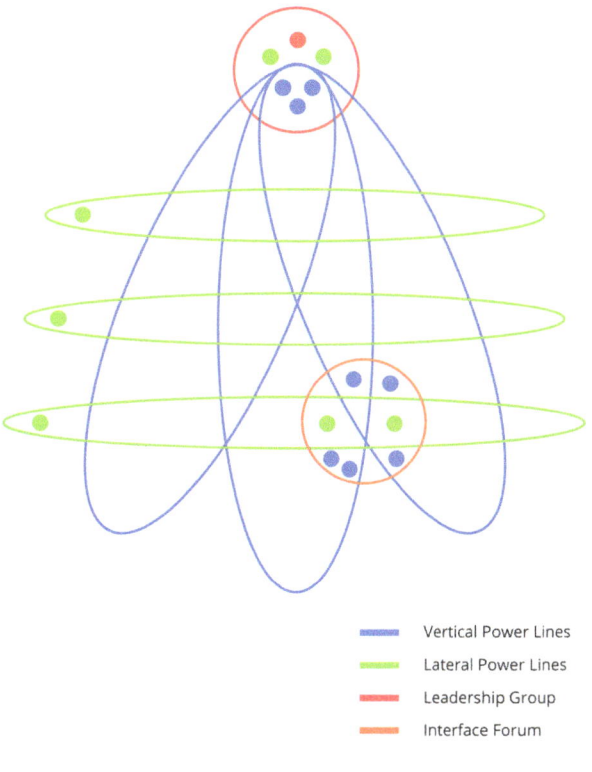

ORGANISATIONAL POWER LINES

— Vertical Power Lines
— Lateral Power Lines
— Leadership Group
— Interface Forum

© Dialogue Associates, 2007

immediate contacts in the power lines. People are still making decisions that affect one another, but from a localised area of knowledge and a broader ignorance. Counterproductive decisions abound, impacting one another, creating unintended consequences that originate from often unseen sources. This results in discrete self-contained subcultural groupings. If one can locate a Dialogue in that fragmented situation, bringing interdependent people into a consideration of how they are managing their interdependencies, then it quickly becomes evident to them that they appreciate and need Dialogue. They want a common understanding and a common content of what to take into account as they make decisions largely independently of one another.

Essentially these Dialogues themselves are power centres. They bring together individuals from different vertical and lateral power lines to find a common understanding of how to proceed. Then each takes that common understanding back into their part of the organisation. The power centre may involve a one-off Dialogue, or the organisational structure may require regular Dialogues at a particular power centre to align different and changing needs and interests.

We have created both many times, and with great effectiveness, which I outline in some detail in my 2018 paper. In brief, one example is an ongoing monthly forum we set up for management, unions and skilled technicians within an oil refinery and chemical plant that transformed years of ugly contention. Another is the resolution of a long-running dispute between business units in the US, the UK and China that affected three hierarchical levels of management and threatened people's jobs. People might have called it a wicked problem, but the dialogic resolution was swift and long-lasting. Similarly Jane Ball and I created the architecture for power centres that straddled the prison gate when we were working with high-repeat offenders who were in and out of prison so often they were receiving no therapeutic treatment. The resulting Threshold Dialogue involved staff from prisons, police, courts, local government and hostels along with treatment counsellors working both within several prisons and outside in the local community. It was remarkably effective.

Decision-Making and a Common Understanding

What about *decision-making* itself? The original Dialogues with David Bohm assumed that a common understanding amongst a group of people, and a common content of consciousness which naturally unfolded to deepen that understanding, would lead to a kind of common-sense basis for each to act in accordance with others. It also yielded a sense of impersonal fellowship as people sought to understand each other rather than prove they were right. There was a disposition to the enquiry that was, and still is, important. This dialogic stance involves authenticity and respect, based on the understanding that things are as they are for a reason, and that reason may not yet be evident to us all. If we understand the factors being managed by those involved in any situation, then it becomes clearer how to incorporate and address them in different ways for common benefit. These Dialogues were gatherings of individuals, mainly academics, who had a common concern about the well-being of society given its fragmented state. As we took this Dialogic approach into organisations, we found a different configuration. People employed there had a common organisational history and purpose, although they held many different opinions about them. We immediately encountered the challenges I have been considering regarding time and power. Those working in organisations pride themselves on getting the job done well and generally they value efficiency and achievement. Utilising plans and timelines, they use chronological time to achieve things and are impatient for results. The pace depends on the ambitiousness of the leadership, management and supervisors, but generally time and attention are a scarcer commodity than other resources. As a result, a mindset can easily be established where decisions are made at speed by those higher in the chain of command and those with the most expertise in the functions.

This approach has the potential benefit of speed (assuming the leadership are not a constraining 'bottleneck') and the handicap of ignorance about the implication for others who are not involved in the thinking. The decisions are based on the available knowledge and understanding – but the interpretation of data and information is different at every level of the organisation. Although the overview held at the executive level is essential, so too is the local perspective. That local knowledge is at the level of implementation, without which nothing gets done. The fragmentation arises from differences between intention, decision and impact. Well intentioned people make decisions without realising the impact they may be having on those affected by that decision. As a result, organisations are often fast moving and highly inefficient. This is embodied in the employee attitude of 'tell me what to do and I will do it' which demonstrates loyalty and hard work, combined with the unintelligent abandoning of their valuable local knowledge.

The key is to bring the decision-maker and those impacted by the decision into closer or direct relationship with one another. That is the essence of the power centres. If we find ourselves talking about 'them', and 'they' are not in the room, then we have a problem of fragmentation, and this will affect the quality and sustainability of our decisions.

The Systemic Design of a Working Dialogue

It was an interesting challenge to design a business practice for dialogic decision-making in a large state agency. The agency was the largest employer in the state and had a high turnover of staff. How would we (Jane and I) manage the issues of time, power and decision-making in a dialogic way? We drew together a small team of Dialogue Practitioners that represented the main vertical power lines (the delivery channels) and lateral power lines (the functions) and used them as a participatory sounding board. The staff of 13,000 members had been exposed to Dialogue skills, and the infrastructure of 250 Dialogue Practitioners were both in place to enable this to become a required business practice. We intended the pattern to be used to resolve issues and to develop opportunities at operational practice, policy and strategic levels. The Dialogue Practitioners in the design team helped to set up and facilitate the first pilots (that helped us to adapt the design in a number of ways).

First, I had to accept that at the outset staff members may not hold a dialogic stance and would use whatever pattern we designed with a normal business mentality. We needed something that would improve general management decision-making and could easily evolve into a dialogic process. We could see that whenever a problem presented itself, they tended quickly to identify a couple of options, choose one and act. This could be called a 'fire-fighting' mentality. So at least to improve that way of reaching decisions, we wanted to include a sequence of three parts: a) the current situation (how is it working now?), b) what do we want? (where do we want to be in the end?) and c) how can we get from a) to b) (what is a good plan?). Although this could take us in the right direction, there is nothing inherently dialogic in this three-part process to reaching a decision. It is simply good management and we knew it would help the decision-making process in the agency to adopt this. Also, the agency is a 'closed' organisation that likes structured steps that can be accomplished, and be seen to be accomplished, in a measured way. So this would be attractive. I recognised that it was essential to respect the hierarchical power structure, and we were at pains not to propose a consensus or voting model that could cut across the existing well-defined accountabilities.

The next step was to address the fragmentation in the decision-making process by bringing those authorised to make decisions into direct conversation with the people who would be affected by those decisions. What we proposed was different from consultation or gathering data to inform a later decision to be made elsewhere. The group gathered would actually design the plan and take accountability themselves for its implementation. This was no longer a matter of 'tell me what to do and I will do it', but rather it involved drawing on the local knowledge and know-how as well as that of those with expertise, authority and overview from other parts of the organisation. Given the cost of time to gather the right people, we ensured the set-up phase included a determination of the cost/benefit value of the Working Dialogue – is it worth doing? If there is enough potential value in addressing and resolving a particular challenge or issue, then let's identify who needs to be involved and get everyone around the same table. Of course, the cost for such meetings has been significantly reduced with the advent of Covid-19 and the wider use of audiovisual online systems that are ideal for a pattern like a Working Dialogue.

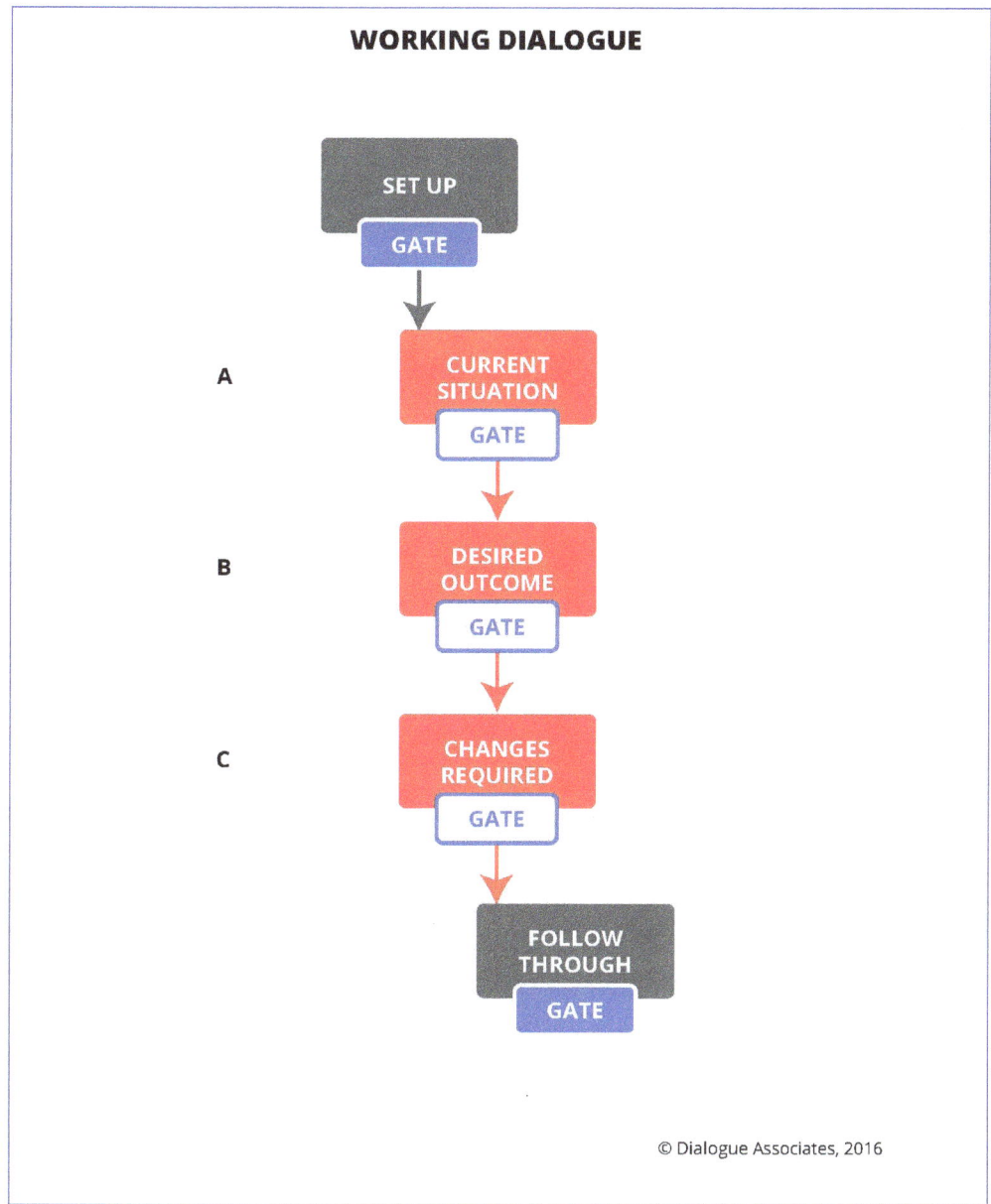

We wanted to address the cultivation of Dialogue in the Working Dialogue. We had the advantage that participants would all be familiar with the dialogic skills, given the trainings that had been provided. It is also the case, however, that using those skills does not mean you are necessarily in Dialogue and thinking together to understand one another's perspective. One can be authentic and listen respectfully in a debate where you are trying to win, as well as in a Dialogue. This is a common misconception of course – we believe we are in Dialogue because we are using dialogic skills. That is a good start, but more is required – the primary interest of trying to understand each other as well as ourselves. So we introduced a specific role for a Dialogue Practitioner to play in the Working Dialogue. This would help participants to use dialogic skills, and they would use their facilitation skills to shift the mode of conversation from monologue, debate or discussion into Dialogue when the timing was right. We went further and required the Dialogue Practitioners to work from the outset with a 'sponsor' (the executive or manager who was sponsoring the Working Dialogue, and who was responsible for the outcome). The two of them would think together during the set-up phase: they would consider the issue, the value of resolving it, who would need to be involved and what invitation should be issued to the proposed participants. We were starting to build the dialogic stance into the process through the Dialogue Practitioner.

Then we took a further step that makes all the difference: we introduced a 'gate' between each of the phases. The gate is a short set of questions that have to be answered successfully to proceed to the next phase. The questions at each gate were simple and direct. To pass the set-up gate, the sponsor and Dialogue Practitioner had to feel comfortable answering the questions positively, such as: Is it worth doing? Have we included everybody (or representatives of everyone) affected by the issue? And so on. If these could not be confirmed then they could not proceed to the next phase. Later, once the group was gathered and considering the current state (how does it work now?) they had to confirm that everyone affected by the decision was present or represented in the Working Dialogue, and that they all felt their perspective was understood by others in the room. This was achieving a common understanding. It did not mean that people had their way, simply that their perspective and situation was understood and being taken into account by everyone else present. If not, the group could not pass through the gate into the next phase. This proved quite liberating for those who had felt misunderstood and therefore unappreciated, but also led to better-informed logic in the later planning.

The Dialogue Practitioner contracted with the group to be the custodian of the gates, so it was he or she that assessed the participants' success in answering the gate questions, and their collective readiness to pass through each gate, not the sponsor. As one senior executive said at the time, "Wow, in the past I have driven right through an awful lot of those gates!" The Dialogue Practitioners had a challenge on their hands too. They had to create a summary of the current situation (how the issue or problem works now) on a single sheet of flip chart paper. That meant perhaps five to seven bullet points. It was the same requirement for the next phase when they would determine the desired outcome. Those without the skill to see the key statements ended up with 10 or 12 sheets of flip chart paper with scores of bullet points. That meant they had not achieved a common understanding but had simply created a list of different perspectives that remained largely unresolved. This skill to précis the many words spoken into the essential points is necessary for good intervention work, and that is what we were inviting and training the Dialogue Practitioners to do.

Next, we return to the matter of *time*. The shift of emphasis on chronological time was to be managed through the gates. The gates meant the process would take as long as it takes. The time set aside for the first phase may or may not be adequate to achieve a common understanding. If it proved to be inadequate, then they would have to extend the meeting, or adjourn and meet again with the same participants at a later date. This enhances the value of the Dialogue skills, of course, because people come to realise that giving attention through respect and careful listening, and explaining one's own perspective honestly and clearly, saves time! So then participants start to lean in the direction of encouraging the use of the skills to aid their progress. Some Working Dialogues can be completed in a day, and the most complex statewide ones involving many interested parties could run over a year or more.

Did some of the more forceful executives sometimes 'call rank' and overrule the process to get the result they wanted anyway? Yes, of course. Did some of the Dialogue Practitioners fudge things to get through a gate, or still have six flip charts rather than six points for participants to agree? No doubt they sometimes did. But still, they were in a better decision-making process, one that was more inclusive and more thorough than would have been the case otherwise. And over time they would start to learn that it is easier and faster working dialogically. I should emphasise that we were aiming for a shift across the whole organisation, in all business units, and not just with small pockets of willing Sponsors. Their executive directive, that we supported, required every business unit (of which there were around 140) to do one Working Dialogue every quarter. We were *using* the culture ("tell me what to do") to *change* the culture, which is a powerful way to achieve across-the-board change.

The planning phase also had different features from what people had anticipated. So many good plans are never implemented because some of those responsible for specific tasks do not deliver them. A good plan on its own is rarely good enough. We ensured that the plan for the Working Dialogue not only stated what would be delivered by when, but it included who was responsible – and that responsible person had to be in the room. They could delegate their responsibility to another, but they still held the accountability for the delivery. This closed a significant gap through which many plans had fallen in the past. Also, the plan had to state a review date and who needed to attend the review.

This review was the fifth and final phase. The idea here was to learn from successes and failures. If the Working Dialogue failed, was it the plan that was inadequate (and if so, why?) or was it a failure of delivery (and if so, why?). That meant people could be coached or held to account depending on the situation. When the plan succeeded, it was a fine opportunity to acknowledge those involved and to build their confidence about how to address issues well. It would not be long before more junior employees requested a Working Dialogue, as they realised it would get to the bottom of seemingly intractable problems, some of which had been stuck for a long time.

Working Dialogues in Practice

I encourage you to read Harold Clarke and Whitney Barton's paper for the 2019 Academy conference titled "Putting Dialogue to Work in the Virginia Department of Corrections", (see references) detailing their experience of the introduction of Working Dialogues into their state agency. The case studies they include cover operational issues, such as the balancing of workloads, drug testing systems and the optimisation of offender movements. I recommend reading their paper in conjunction with this one to get a feel for the practical use of Dialogue in an organisation.

Let's revisit the question some may ask, posed at the beginning of this paper: "That is all fine, but where is the Dialogue? What you have described does not sound like the agenda-free enquiry that David Bohm advocated". The answer depends on the purpose and nature of Dialogue as you understand it. In our work with David Bohm we wanted to establish a common meaning or understanding to deal with the fragmented state of human consciousness that we saw as the cause of so much counterproductive damage in the world. In the Working Dialogue we see a common understanding established in each of the five phases. And all five phases together constitute a decision-making process that is thorough and sustainable. Each phase may involve a mixture of monologues, debates and Dialogue, as was definitely the case in our sessions with Bohm. In the case of the Working Dialogues, over time the structure and process lead participants into a dialogic disposition, with the Dialogue Practitioners judiciously holding the gates in a way that helps the overall development process.

Closing Reflections

It is worth noting that the Working Dialogue pattern can be used to turn issues and problems into creative opportunities. It is conducive to people learning how to use Dialogue to tackle more complex multistakeholder issues. Facilitated well, Working Dialogues are likely to cultivate open Dialogue as a way of doing business. This is how the muscle is developed to tackle larger and tougher issues. Already the Virginia Department of Corrections, for example, has taken Working Dialogues into the community to work with other agencies such as the courts, police, treatment centres and so on to tackle social problems of mutual concern. A huge next step would be the use of Working Dialogues in determining policy, which in turns drives the allocation of resources and measures of success. And then – who knows the limits of where this simple but thorough pattern may prove useful?

References
Bohm, D. (1985) *Unfolding Meaning – A Weekend of Dialogue with David Bohm*. Mickleton, England: Foundation House Publications.
Bohm, D,. Factor D. & Garrett P. (1991). "Dialogue – A Proposal". Available at: http://www.dialogue-associates.com/files/files/DIALOGUE%20A%20PROPOSAL%2026-3-14(2).pdf
Bohm, D. (1996). *On Dialogue*. Abingdon, UK: Routledge.

Clarke, H. & Barton, W. (2020). "Putting Dialogue to Work in the Virginia Department of Corrections", in *The World Needs Dialogue! Two: Setting the Bearings*. Chipping Campden: Dialogue Publications.

Garrett, P. (2006). "A Dialogic Model of Time". Available at: https://www.dialogue-associates.com/files/files/A%20DIALOGIC%20MODEL%20OF%20TIME%2024-1-14.pdf

Garrett, P. (2018). "Engaging Fragmentation, Subcultures and Organisational Power", in *The World Needs Dialogue! One: Gathering the Field*. Chipping Campden: Dialogue Publications.

Conference Session Extracts

From a conversation with participants considering the paper with Peter Garrett

Speaker: The demand is still there for Working Dialogues. There are always questions that need answers and things that need to be changed. We've had two or three dialogues recently, but that is a reduced number since the Covid-19 pandemic. What has not changed is people's understanding and desire because we've continued to have issues we've needed to address. We hear people from different levels of the department say, "Hey, maybe that's a working dialogue. Maybe we should use a Working Dialogue". We require everybody to get trained and it has helped us with the language. There is a common understanding. You can go into a prison on one side of the state or to a probation office on the other side, and everybody understands the same language.

Speaker: I guess there must be a whole family of Working Dialogues under the title 'What's the new normal given the pandemic?' I was part of the 'new normal' task force that was convened in Virginia to look at every aspect. We were dealing with work issues and offender work issues. Many people don't have cameras, and we want to have all the voices involved. Safety has been the biggest problem. We have no shortage of need. As a matter of fact, we probably have more because of Covid-19.

Speaker: To me, there's something about being inclusive of people to get the job done. You could get the job done without the Working Dialogue and make the decision anyway and do it. So this is about caring. People have to understand how to make good decisions, and how the process works so that they naturally think a bit more clearly when they make their own decisions.

Speaker: What do you think of the three skills that are really important for a sponsor?

Speaker: Identifying who needs to be there. And making sure that the problem is identified, so that when people are invited to come they know what they're coming to discuss, and making sure it's clear and concise. And we talked about checking your ego at the door. The sponsor needs to make sure they don't come in with predetermined decisions which shut the process down. People will simply not communicate. They're not going to share in that setting. You have to be able to suspend the judgement and allow people to work through the process. And if you can't suspend the judgement, then you might be in the wrong position. A healthy challenge to everyone.

Speaker: One of the skills is being able to develop rapport with people. In my role I have to figure everything out amongst 15 or so prisons. That's a tall challenge to try to meet the needs of individuals and the institution. So I have always really tried to focus on developing good rapport with staff so they're able to have conversations with you and tell you if there's concerns that I need to address.

Speaker: Being a new supervisor, I think that skill is trust. I think people have to trust you. I think the second thing is that you build trust by showing consistent behaviour, and I think also empowering others. Then I would say being a sponsor to any dialogue, you would need to show courage. In taking a risk to sponsor a dialogue you're showing courage in leading others.

Speaker: Your staff really have the working knowledge and the technical knowledge to find a lot of the solutions to what you are working on anyway. So leaning on the local experts is the way to get from A to Z. You're basically letting them define the solution, because they really have the answers.

Speaker: I totally agree with what was just said. It's not something that comes naturally, because a lot of leaders believe they need to have the answers and the solutions because of their position. So when they come into the room, often the conversation stops and people look towards them for the answers. I think to be a good sponsor and a successful sponsor we need to have the ability to recognise that there's a problem, something that needs addressing. Then to understand that there is value in hearing the voices of others and genuinely inviting others to participate in the process. It is not something that comes naturally because a lot of leaders think it is their position to solve the problem because generally that is how they got promoted to the position they're in.

Speaker: I think reflection and inquiry are the two main components. The practitioner has to take a lot of information and simplify it down to a few bullet points. There's a skill to taking half an hour's conversation and reducing it to three main points.

Speaker: The Dialogue Practitioner has to have the confidence to be able to stop a Working Dialogue if it's not going the way it should go, if fidelity isn't there. If you violate the rules, then people lose trust in the process.

Speaker: I don't think it's been said, but neutrality. Focusing on the process as opposed to being part of it and trying to insert themselves. Sometimes it's nice to have somebody who's completely uninvolved with what's going on, who has that perspective, that unbiased perspective, to hold the process. But also to say, "Maria, I am going to oppose you". In a respectful way, "Maria, I understand your enthusiasm to get it done, but can we slow down a bit and just make sure we've got all the input we need?" That that can be quite difficult, with some of the people we work with at times. So, there's the skill of being able to deal with more senior people in a respectful way. But equally, at the same time not losing the rigor of the process, and not compromising it.

Speaker: Neutrality. It's a tricky concept, but we need a distance between providing empathy and still being impartial.

Speaker: Curiosity. And I think a good participant is one who voices without pretense, just putting it out clearly and straightforwardly, orally. Along with that, they genuinely have to want an outcome that's beneficial to everyone. I think there is a need for respect and a curiosity. Trying to understand why they think something different. What's behind it? What do they see that you don't see? It's surprising with a group. If you allow the process to start to work with people, something emerges, which is actually pretty straightforward. And usually it's only about letting the group find its own life. I think the dialogic practices of Voice – Authenticity – Listening, Respect and Suspension are the critical ones. But also the move, follow, oppose and bystand . . . and just simple inquiry.

Postscript

The author's reflections, written some months after the conference

I was encouraged by this session. My paper, made available to everyone before the conference, was about the Working Dialogue. In the session itself many of the participants had experience of participating in Working Dialogues, particularly sponsoring or facilitating them. The Working Dialogues clearly work, there is ongoing demand for more and it is rewarding to see this dialogic pattern being formally recognised as a business practice. Following the conference, my thoughts have centred on the value of embedding the Working Dialogue in an organisation.

One of the conference participants had pointed out that you build trust – and the consequent good flow of information through an organisation – by consistent behaviour. Well, the Working Dialogue is a structured pattern for consistent behaviour in addressing multistakeholder challenges. Thereby it has the potential to deepen the staff's trust in the workings of the organisation that employs them. The pattern provides the assurance that there is a way of addressing complex problematic issues. This is important for the culture of the organisation. Otherwise, dysfunctional patterns will simply remain stuck and reluctantly accepted as 'nobody likes it but that's how it is around here'. Now stories are shared about how 'it used to be like that until we had the Working Dialogue'.

Also, the Working Dialogue improves the overall quality of decision-making. There is a clearer definition of who will make the decision, and why they have made it. If the sponsor needs to do so, then they must participate in the Working Dialogue. If not, he or she can delegate that responsibility to those in the Working Dialogue and accept their decision. Either way, there is a structured and recorded method to solve problems – and to realise opportunities that might otherwise be missed.

At the same time as addressing the challenge at hand, the Working Dialogue provides participants with a practice-based training for decision-making to use in other situations. Junior staff members learn about rigorous decision-making. Supervisors and leaders benefit too. Thinking on their own they make poorer decisions than when they think with others before deciding how to proceed. The Working Dialogue takes some of the pressure off the leader having to make and be accountable for all the answers. It shares this responsibility. Because the participants' views have been incorporated, they understand and are more likely to own the outcome.

Live Facilitation of the Offender Resettlement Journey

Jane Ball

This paper is intended as a companion to my reprinted 2018 paper (next chapter), in which I outline why the Offender Resettlement Journey (ORJ) is important, how an ORJ process works, and what we might learn about some of our underlying concepts about the archetypal journey in practice. I believe it is a useful resource for anyone working in the criminal justice or correctional system.

I wrote that paper through the lens of my own 20-year journey through my Dialogue Practitioner experience and work in the criminal justice system. It outlined how Peter Garrett, my colleague and business partner and I, had generated such a distinctive way to bring a system together and how I had developed the skills and understanding for this work through first-hand experience and learning.

In this paper I want to provide some additional reflections for practitioners about the facilitation of the ORJ by taking you 'live' into the immediate experience as it is being facilitated. Where the 2018 version gave an overview of the context for and construction of the ORJ, in this briefer paper I give something of a more visceral sense of impact it has on participants, whether they be walking the symbolic journey or witnessing it. For simplicity I will use the label *offender* here to distinguish the man or woman whose story of their journey is being told, from the many other characters to name. When we are together, I would simply use their preferred name.

The Description of an Experience is Very Different from an Experience

What if we did not have time to organise a complex ORJ event, and instead ran a multiagency meeting to *talk* about the offender's Resettlement Journey or consult with offenders? The meeting might include descriptions and stories about what happens and how things could be better. Well-facilitated, the meeting would encourage authenticity and thorough explanations about what lies ahead, listening and a desire to understand different perspectives, providing depth of understanding. It would draw out memories, and those memories would include layers of analysis, self-justification, blame, guilt, and interpretation. An ORJ takes this further, because it does more than prompt memories – the ORJ *is* an experience as well as being *about* an experience. The spatialisation provides a symbolic journey that is visceral, emotional, and intellectual, just as the offender's journey is visceral, emotional, and intellectual.

If you have ever been to a school reunion, you might have experienced what I am describing. Some years back I went to a college reunion, held at our old college building. I found myself, a 40-something professional, with people I had not seen for 20 years, behaving together like we did as 19-year old students. No one told me to do that, and I did not plan to do that. The invitation did not say come to relive your youth for an evening, but that is what happened. We found ourselves unconsciously assuming roles that seemed every bit as real as the ones we played in the everyday 'modern' versions of ourselves. When we were 'in role', we were the stars and even villains in a unique play we somehow created together.

With more conscious intent, this is why I ran through a mock ORJ at the Academy of Professional Dialogue conference in 2018, with the participants playing the role of prison warden, police officer, probation officer, an offender, and their mother. The impact on many of the participants was sincere, and intense for some. The creative act of taking on a role, finding a personal connection to the part they were playing, and to the relationship with other people who were playing different roles, conveyed more than the words on the page or my description.

This is why the ORJ stimulates such excitement, passion and interest.

The ORJ wakes us up and reaches parts of our common experience and humanity that other events do not. The urge to participate – one that people feel, but can be deadened by the routine or frustrations of daily work – re-emerges in the constructive environment of the ORJ. This enlivens the system as well as individuals.

What Makes a Good ORJ Facilitator?

The facilitator must be able to manage the live, spontaneous expression and engagement between people as they express fears, excitement, exhilaration, disappointment, shame, loss and annoyance. It means to facilitate, for example, what is said between a mother who watched her son as he was sentenced to a long term of imprisonment, and the son who feared for his mother's health when he was in prison – rather than facilitating an exchange between people who have different views about how to help prisoners maintain family ties.

The facilitator's role, as the accompanying 2018 paper describes, starts with helping the man or woman, offender or ex-offender, to tell their story authentically in front of an audience of 40 to 80 people, many of whom have played a significant part in their life. The audience may include their juvenile probation officer, the arresting police officer, admissions corrections officer, their wife or father. Easily and quickly the facilitator builds the rapport to stand alongside the offender and enable them to find the confidence to speak up. They find the relevant chapters and incidents in the story to help guide the process of learning and development for everyone. This requires some understanding of key events and turning points of the archetypal journey: receiving sentence, the first night in custody, the last day in prison, crossing the imagined prison gate, the first minutes and hours out of prison – and the profound personal experiences of the individual. You will realise how reluctant the storyteller is to cross the duct-tape line that symbolises the prison gate. The walk and movement from community to the prison, to higher levels of security and back again, awakens the experience. As a facilitator walking alongside them you can feel their tension and relief physically in their body, and you help them to put that into words.

How many things can you be aware of at one time? Even as you are deep into the story, you have one eye on timing. This is not just a logistical necessity; it is an essential skill. It is respectful to the storyteller, so they can work their way from the desperate phases of their life to the prospect of a positive outcome. It is also respectful to the whole system and the part that everyone plays, so that every phase of the journey can benefit from this unique form of scrutiny.

The facilitator is part of the storytelling too. While I am guiding someone on their journey, I notice what I am thinking and feeling, discern what is relevant and how I can bring this out. I feel the sadness, such as when I hear about the children who are left behind to be looked after by their grandmother. I am not debilitated by it, and neither do I ignore it. I use my personal response to decide what to say or ask next. I might ask if the storyteller wants to say more or not, knowing that to do so might be a real victory for them, and that my job is not to push them to say more than they want to. Equally, rather than be carried away by the excitement of success for someone who has, for example, left prison and started a business, I check for the reality of sustaining that success.

To feel into the life of another person with respect is a delicate process. I look for opportunities for the storyteller to grow and benefit from the experience – to realise something about themselves, be it from direct feedback from people, realising themselves how far they have come or letting a loved one who has accompanied them understand their story.

The ORJ is also complex to facilitate, because while you are talking to the offender you are also talking to the 'audience', and they are also players in this story – from the daughter to the judge, the correctional officer to the probation officer. As I walk and talk, I am aware of the staff and what the words of the story might mean to them. At times I stop and ask if anyone knows the offender, to open up the possibility for an exchange between them. This introduces feedback to the offender, perhaps a reminder about aspects of their story they have forgotten or skipped over. Staff are also interested to hear how they and their colleagues are seen. They may also want to add their thoughts to what is being said about the system – perhaps the lack of healthcare or education or holding prisoners so far away from family.

As facilitator, I am also aware of the leadership in the room, and what they might be thinking and feeling as the stories bring out what is and is not working in their agency. They may look for an opportunity to speak as well. In my experience some leaders have to work hard not to explain or justify why things are the way they are, and to accept the offender's story of their experience. While the urge to defend the agency is understandable, the risk is that their words will deter the offender or staff from speaking up further – now or later. The facilitator has to balance the power difference and not silence the leadership. Coaching leadership is key to achieving this, both in preparation and 'live', when the dynamic comes up.

There is often a family member in the audience too. Sometimes they come to offer support, other times to hear the stories they have never heard from their loved one. Recently a man brought his 16-year-old daughter with him to an ORJ. As a young child she believed she was visiting her father at his university when she was taken to see him in prison. The distance between the offender and their loved ones in the room, as they walk across the gate into prison, is obvious. As you look back with the offender and point out the distance, you have an opportunity to acknowledge the family member and, reading their reaction, invite them to make a comment and perhaps ask more. Usually, my co-facilitator will sit with the family member. The relative is potentially vulnerable, and the co-facilitator can work with them to bring out their story. It is not always needed, as sometimes they are jumping up to speak.

Beyond the room is a larger context that adds weight to some aspects of the story, or the words of some of the participants. Knowing, for example, that zero-tolerance attitudes to drug use, the needs and rights of veterans, or victimisation of women are important local issues would lead the facilitator to go into relevant aspects of the story.

The goal is to engage everyone in the story of the ORJ – to elicit and draw on the spontaneous response of everyone present. If everyone recognises their part in the story, they can participate in changing what happens. No one is a spectator at this very personal event; even witnessing the storyteller's progress through the symbolic journey binds people to the process in ways that often are unanticipated and healing for everyone. And, stepping back and seeing this from a larger perspective, a healthy and generative criminal justice system would use the ORJ as a regular and fundamental practice for the improvement and development of facilitation skills in a body of practitioners as they learn to lead the process.

Conference Session Extracts

From a conversation with participants considering the paper with Jane Ball

Speaker: A question for clarification. The individuals in the room may not personally know each offender, each inmate that is walking through their journey. So if the people in the room don't personally know them, what are some things to do to focus on keeping the dialogue going?

Jane: Well, really it's my conversation with the inmate that is the primary thing. Everybody is listening and they will be thinking about the many inmates they have met and managed.

Speaker: So it's not necessary the people are all connected with each other. They are representative voices of the system?

Jane: Yes. The story is absolutely true for the offender involved, but that doesn't mean that this is what happens for everybody. It will still make you think of people you've known like her, or maybe things you've heard other people talking about. It will stimulate memories, and we need to be able to talk about them. So it's a personal story, but it's also representative.

Speaker: You are talking about how the prison people react during the Offender Resettlement Journey, but the bigger work for the prison people is the after work. Afterwards we meet in small groups, and that's where you effect the changes you get from the Resettlement Journey. You go back and you create work groups and you work on those specific things that you found. Some of those may be low-hanging fruit, but then some of them may involve external stakeholders and be much more complex.

Jane: So what do you think are the opportunities and challenges for you around facilitating an ORJ?

Speaker: I think for me as the facilitator it would be about how to keep your own emotions in check. You can get a guy with a tattoo on his face, you know. He turns up looking like this. You start to walk and talk with him and then his vulnerability really shows. Yeah. I think that because of the nature of our work in corrections and concerns about fraternization with the offenders, I think that could potentially be a barrier to how that rapport is developed in that initial phase. As the facilitator, being able to overcome those concerns, and maintain professionalism and your emotions and all of that. But I think that that's what makes it so impactful at the same time. So I guess the challenge is really finding the right balance. And the other thing is the challenge for people in positions of authority, depending how the story comes out. Some of the seniors in probation, maybe thinking, you know, that's not what it's like. We provide a really good service! People can leap to being defensive. Even though we say, look, she was in prison six years ago and we know it's different now. But the urge to defend is quite hard and strong. I think what that means is that you have to be able to talk as a peer to everybody.

Speaker: There was one other question in the chat about the victims, asking if you could clarify the level of any of involvement of the victim. So this is not restorative justice, right? It is not for the offender and the victim – that would be a very different process. But you might have somebody in the ORJ that represents victim agencies, or a volunteer who has themself been a victim. They can bring that voice with that life dynamic. You might find an offender who has never met the victim, and at the end of this kind of offender journey process, they might say, I would really like to do that now.

Speaker: I'm pretty new to the dialogue and the Department of Corrections. I haven't gotten to actually experience an Offender Resettlement Journey. So, I look forward to that. In terms of facilitating, is it usually a single facilitator or is it multiple facilitators, so one can walk with the offender and focus on them and get absorbed in that story?

Jane: You have a co-facilitator who is giving you a little bit of a nudge on the time, and about other perspectives – to draw in other people. That sometimes doesn't happen so naturally. Your co-facilitator might just say, "Well, why don't we hear from the probation staff members?" It would encourage you as the lead facilitator to bring in those other voices when you get absorbed in the story.

Speaker: How far in advance would you recommend reaching out to the person, to speak to them about what's going to be involved on the day?

Jane: Usually about a week, and it's quite a brief conversation. You want enough time that they are settled about it, but you ask them not to prepare. So probably just a week before.

Speaker: The three of us had a nice discussion in our breakout group. We went into the theme of underground power structures. Inevitably in a jail, or in any neighbourhood, you have these underground power structures which can make people hold back from speaking openly.

Jane: I guess it's worth saying that one thing you notice is that awareness is really important for this kind of facilitation. You're aware of the conversation you're having, and you're aware of the rest of the room. You notice body language — you notice somebody rolling their eyes or whatever because they're thinking. You notice sometimes it's an important thing to ask the offender, and other times you notice they hold back. What I aim to do is to name it, and then sometimes it's possible to go into it and to talk about it. You may seem to be cautious about bringing it out, or people are laughing and you can ask what's it's about. Sometimes it feels appropriate to go into it and other times not. Sometimes it really is a question just of the pragmatic because there is no time to go into it.

I guess the real big deal is to get to an aligned, strong purpose that carries the work and creates the safety that is needed so that you could do that together. Because if you do that, it might reveal an uncomfortable truth. One of the things as a facilitator is you have to be able to speak to everybody on the level, be it the offender you're talking to, or the warden or the director, whoever, and be able to say, well, don't be defensive. We need to hear people's experience to learn. And then all of the agencies together can say from what they've heard — the gaps and duplications that they would like to address. The obvious way to do that would be through a Working Dialogue.

Speaker: I just want to say that I did get to experience the walk-through of the Offender Resettlement Journey at the conference a year or so ago, and it was very rewarding. I think it would be an awesome opportunity to be able to walk beside that offender during one of those. And I'll leave it at that. Thank you.

Postscript
The author's reflections, written some months after the conference

2020 was the first year of the Covid-19 pandemic and the first time I had thought seriously about how to work online. Until then, Zoom meetings had been videoconference calls in support of face-to-face work. The Academy's online conference was an opportunity to find out how to achieve engagement and energy, to bring out dynamics and enable live learning in a Zoom room. This session provided an opportunity to see what might be involved in facilitating an Offender Resettlement Journey (ORJ) online, which I had never done, so I introduced a short experimental roleplay of an online ORJ to help participants to understand the process.

Based on this experience, I believe the intimacy of the conversation between the facilitator (me) and the offender (a conference participant) can be developed in this form. Other people who figure in the journey, such as the judge or the prison warden, can be brought into the conversation, adding to the story and changing the dynamic. Technical design and facilitation are required, for example, using the spotlight function on Zoom to show the primary players, adding role alongside your name (Kate Smith – Judge), checking the participant list to see who might want to speak, replacing the visual clues in a real room, etc. The unfolding story can be watched and heard by others, raising their awareness of the offender's journey, the part they play and the impact of the wider system.

However, the system is not able to see itself easily through a list of names and roles. In a full ORJ online, other facilitation patterns would be needed – for example, more explicit use of the journey graphic, ways to reveal the different subgroups that would usually show up naturally in the room, etc. While in-person ORJs will return, other applications will benefit from an online approach – an online Migration Journey could easily include participants from across the world.

As a result of the session, I also thought more about how someone would develop the skills I described – and how would I help them to do so? Structured guidelines are helpful. However, inner work builds the presence and stance required and much of that can only be developed through first-hand experience. A practitioner needs opportunities to do and learn, starting with smaller sessions and growing to work with more stakeholders, more senior people, more challenging stories. They also need coaching, mentoring and a deliberate reflective process to learn and grow from their experiences.

2018 Reprint

Dialogue through the Offender Resettlement Journey

Jane Ball

What is the purpose of the criminal justice system? Is it punishment? Or retribution? Perhaps rehabilitation? Deterrence? Public safety? While there is undoubtedly a little of all of these in practice, rehabilitation is at the heart of modern penal policy in the UK and US systems where I have worked. In my experience the reality of the aspiration to provide rehabilitation (defined as 'the reintegration of a convicted person into society') is hampered by the fragmentation of the criminal justice system that leads different organisations, divisions and people to act in isolation rather than together. The Offender Resettlement Journey (ORJ), created by Peter Garrett and me, is a Dialogic response to integrate the activity of the whole system – including the offender – to achieve the common goal of successful resettlement. The theory and practice of the ORJ is based on knowledge generated over many years of Dialogue with offenders and people who work in the criminal justice system at all levels, alongside our experience of organisational consulting. In this paper I'd like to explore some of the key features of the ORJ, how they developed, and the relevance of the ORJ for effective Professional Dialogue within the Criminal Justice.

My Journey with Dialogue in the Criminal Justice System

Over the last 19 years my work has been based entirely on Dialogue in many fields, both commercial and social, and continuously within the criminal justice system. Over this time I have worked in 15 different prisons in the UK and in six different state and city corrections departments in the US, under the auspices of the charity Prison Dialogue and the consulting business Dialogue Associates. I am director and co-owner of Dialogue Associates with Peter Garrett, who has been my teacher, mentor and colleague continuously throughout this period. We have partnered on many initiatives, co-designed, facilitated and supported each other in the intervening years.

When I started the work was focused on improving the prison, without any additional resourcing or policy changes, through Dialogue and the way that people talked with each other. As we developed partnerships with prison Governors and senior managers, they asked us to use the Dialogues to address specific issues. For example, conflict between a healthcare provider and the prison operation and security staff; the transition from one prison Governor to another; an Equality and Diversity review across prison policy and practice; and union management strategy. Our thinking, practice, and vision also moved from unit-level Dialogues for staff and prisoners to whole-prison transformation, to groups of prisons working together with local communities, to statewide systems. The core of the work has been bringing together people from the different, and relevant, subcultural groups to address individual and collective thinking within the criminal justice system. Things change as a result. The practice, theory and skills have developed through repeated application and practice here, as well as drawing on work in the commercial sector.

Most of the work has involved the engagement of offenders. Time after time, I have seen individuals flourish through the experience, and start to take hold of their own lives, and I've witnessed the awakening of an intelligence in the system that is not often included in decision-making. Why wouldn't the whole criminal justice system provide the conditions for this change to be nurtured in everyone? Why wouldn't it provide a place for a generative, rather than a destructive, relationship between the offender and the system? We have developed the Offender Resettlement Journey through practice over many years, driven by the desire to create such a system – or to provide the conditions for its creation. It is a now a fundamental framework for our Professional Dialogue work in the criminal justice system.

The Offender Resettlement Journey in Theory and Practice

The Offender Resettlement Journey tracks the 'archetypal' path of an offender. It is the journey an offender takes from committing an offence and arrest, through sentencing, incarceration (although not in all cases), supervision by probation agencies in the community, release (from prison or probation commitments) and re-entry into the community, then resettlement – to be independent and law-abiding, and ultimately to make a positive contribution to their community. I have heard many, many stories from offenders over the years, and of course everyone has a unique experience. Despite the variations, we have found core features of the ORJ: common routes, transitions and crises, things that help people to succeed and others that trip them up. Understanding this helps to make those journeys a success in life, and it informs the design and facilitation of ORJ Dialogue interventions. Here are some of the characteristics we have found:

The offender journey is material. That is, the physical experience progresses from court to a prison cell, to a probation hostel, a bedsit, and possibly to home with your family. Your clothing, accommodation, meals – everything – changes. It is relational. As you are incarcerated you say goodbye to your family and friends, and in prison you share a cell with someone you have never met. You live closely with a large group of strangers and have a range of personal and professional relationships. When you return home upon discharge, you try to sever ties with offending 'associates'. The offender journey is *emotional*. It consists of anger, sadness and loss, despair, desperation, hope and expectation. It is *mental*, in that your thinking changes as you learn to navigate a new environment with different rules, norms, processes and ways of working and living. The journey travels from *dependence* – be it on drugs or alcohol, someone to unlock doors, social security or health benefits – to *independence* and, with it, increasing choice about where you live and work and spend your time.

Finally, at its core, this is a journey of *identity*: from offender and prisoner to worker, student, entrepreneur, father, mother, neighbour. (This is why the naming of those who have offended society and its laws is so significant. Are you a *con, inmate, offender, prisoner, man* or *woman*?) The journey may be a one-time passage from arrest to resettlement, or it may repeat and repeat, each time activating the whole cycle, with identity at its centre.

There are some key points in the journey when circumstances change, and care and attention is required to navigate these successfully. As on a road trip, things are different when you depart: you realise the petrol gauge is low, you forgot your bag, can't remember if you locked the back door! and carrying forward, to when you are cruising down the motorway and the only choice is whether to turn the radio on or what speed to drive. They are different again as you arrive – traffic builds up as you reach a major city – and then you are suddenly at a standstill and you don't know why.

As an offender enters the criminal justice system they may be waiting for the police to pick them up, preparing to go to court or be incarcerated, saying goodbye to family, drinking their last can of strong lager, or trying to get hold of drugs that they might try to take in with them. They may know it is coming, or the police break through their front door in the middle of the night. Whatever the specifics, something strong and particular happens at this point. We have called it the *Crisis of Entry*. As the offender's release from prison approaches another crisis arises: the *Crisis of Release*. A new range of questions await: Where will they go? Will old associates be waiting for them? Will they be able to stay clean? What they will do for money? All this, combined with the excitement and anticipation of freedom: choosing what to wear, eating good food, seeing their partner, being with their children . . .

Once across the threshold of the prison gate the reality of coping with those freedoms hits home: Why did the police just stop me? What do I do about the noisy neighbour? What do I tell that employer about where I have been? How do I get to see my probation officer at noon and my drug agency at one in a different town? These are all real challenges that I have heard offenders talk about during Dialogue work, reflecting on what went wrong and sometimes looking ahead to how to manage. These transitions are intentionally named as crises because it is very easy for things to go wrong, and people feel – and are – vulnerable. During research work for the UK Ministry of Justice, offenders described a crisis at the end of their probation supervision in the community, when no one is watching what they are doing any more, there are no routine visits, and no advice or interest. We found that each crisis could be managed best with a 'clear line of sight', a view of the whole journey to resettlement.

With a clear line of sight offenders can see the route ahead, anticipate problems, discover what is required and make better decisions as a result.

Fragmentation in the Criminal Justice System

In my experience most people who work in the criminal justice system are remarkable, dedicated and resourceful individuals. They work hard and achieve what is required of them in demanding conditions. According to where they work they have a different focus: it may be running an orderly regime (lock and unlock prisoners, serve meals, supervise movement around the prison); testing urine for drugs; checking where probationers are living and working; managing the budget; delivering a treatment programme according to set guidelines; tracking of the number of assessments completed within a set timeframe – any one of the hundreds of tasks required to run the system. Staff meet their targets, yet are not routinely expected to consider their impact on the offenders' journey to resettlement, nor to take an interest in what other parts of the system are doing. The education department in one prison where I worked complained repeatedly that offenders couldn't complete their classwork because they were always late for their sessions. This was because they were held up by residential prison staff who made sure that the prisoners had what they were entitled to (breakfast, medication, a chance to raise queries) before they left.

Beyond the prison, fragmentation in the criminal justice system is even more pronounced and difficult to address because it is part of an open system. In an open system, even though the offender may still be under the jurisdiction of the criminal justice system, there is no one person to whom everyone ultimately reports, as there is in even the largest multinational corporation, who can lay out the common purpose and expectations.

Dialogue can support a successful journey to resettlement and provide something of an antidote to fragmentation by providing the opportunity for offenders to talk and think about their situation with the right people who are part of that journey. For example, Dialogue between offenders, family members and probation staff will help people prepare for family life, with the demands that a probation licence dictates. However, the criminal justice system is complex – multiple agencies and many people affect the offender journey. The ORJ reveals the interconnectedness of the agencies, and the departments within agencies, through the perspective of the offender and their common goal of creating successful journeys. Criminal justice staff start to think from an offender's perspective about the current conditions, their role in creating them (whether they are a prison officer, drug counsellor or senior leader), and what they can do to improve those conditions. With that awareness and use of Dialogue skills to talk and think together, everyone can act more intelligently and make better decisions. The awakening in staff in Dialogue groups when they are given a chance to talk and think with offenders and colleagues is inspiring. Some staff respond in action, such as the semi-retired prison officer who galvanised local agencies to come into the prison to offer their services, rather than waiting until prisoners were released. Others notice the quality of the engagement, such as the police officer who told me he talked about things in the Dialogue that he had never spoken about with his wife.

Offender Resettlement Journey Intervention Skills

The ORJ as an intervention requires vision to create an integrating image that reveals the interrelatedness of the system, convening skills to include the right people from the right parts of the system and Dialogue facilitation skills for working with offenders and different agency subcultural groupings. In the pages below I will describe four examples of ORJ work in the criminal justice system that demonstrate these skills and vision in action to begin to address the problem of fragmentation within the criminal justice system. Along with other interventions and experiences not included here, they have been foundational in building the understanding that has underpinned the theory of the ORJ, and in developing the skills and experience required for a Resettlement Journey intervention. Each one is a also valuable Dialogue intervention that could be replicated, with the right support.

Facilitation Skills to Change the Discourse
Staff–Prisoner Dialogue At HMP Blakenhurst

Context
This was one of my first experiences of Dialogue work in a prison. In 1998 Prison Dialogue had been awarded the contract to run monthly two-day Dialogue groups at HMP Blakenhurst, a private prison in the Midlands region of England. I joined in 1999 and facilitated Dialogues between prisoners, staff and managers there for up to four days a month until 2003. Though the Governor-in-charge of the prison at the time was interested in the potential of Dialogue to improve the prison environment, it was only the requirement for the prison to run non-accredited programmes that enabled us to be there.

The Work
The aim of the work was to improve relationships between the subgroups of prisoners, staff and managers, and hence their experience living and working in the prison. Therefore, the Dialogue groups were roughly structured to represent a microcosm of the prison. Up to 20 prisoners from each of the four housing units, two uniformed staff and one prison senior manager (different each time) participated. It was socio-therapeutic in that people could work out issues in the social dynamic of the group. At times they gave and received direct feedback from other people, and they learnt about themselves by listening to others. As one prisoner noted after the sessions, "Hearing ourselves speak has helped us understand ourselves and others".

We met for two full days each time and talked together without a set agenda, allowing the theme to emerge from the group. The first challenge was that some people – offenders, staff and managers alike – didn't want to be there at all. A check-in, in which each person was invited to speak in turn, got everyone engaged immediately, listening, talking, thinking about what they would say, interested in other people, and usually having some fun. A check-out at the end of each day allowed the content of the Dialogue to settle and prepared participants to transition to relationships back out on the prison landings.

Once engaged and with the permission of an open agenda, the sessions typically began with prisoners complaining about prison conditions, poor food, lack of rehabilitation, behaviour of some staff, etc., and petitioning staff and managers for improvements. At times facilitation needed to be strong, enabling people both to vociferously put forward their point of view and stop to listen and understand the perspective of others. As all sides offered this to each other they learnt more about why things were the way they were, how things might be improved and (probably less often) what was good about this prison.

We began to deliberately introduce the Dialogic practices in sessions: Voice, Listening, Respect, Suspension. We explained that *Voice* meant to be genuine, not saying one thing in the room and something different outside of the room. *Listening* was to give your attention and try to understand what others were saying and meant. *Respect* was to take the stance that other people thought and did what they did for a reason that made sense to them; even if it was not what you would do, there was a reason for them doing it. *Suspension* was to hold your views openly, and consider why you thought what you did, like a chandelier suspended from the ceiling so that you could see it all of the way round. I learnt about the practices from Peter. His input to the development of these practices was based on his experiences in high-security prisons HMP Whitemoor and HMP Long Lartin, so they were powerful in this context. They made perfect sense to the prisoners and staff, and they easily picked up the practice and the language.

Outcomes and Limitations

Month after month we created a good rapport between staff and prisoners in the Dialogues, even when unpopular staff attended, or housing units sent along their 'baddest' prisoners. Staff and prisoners found they had common interests; that is, prisoners wanted safe prisons just as much as the head of security did, but they lacked the understanding of the others' perspective without Dialogue. The more focused use of the practices deepened the quality of the container. (The *container* is the term Peter introduced to me at that time, which names the quality of atmosphere among people.) I found that the practices created a strong container that was safe enough for people to be more open about themselves. There was energy of genuine engagement and a quality of relationship that was unusual, and a feeling that change was possible. One prison officer named the changing dynamic: "At first I thought it was about inmate-to-officer but was pleased that we were able to speak as person-to-person."

In this container we saw individual offenders transform as they realised themselves in the

Dialogue group. Take 'Eddie' – in the first two or three sessions he attended he sat in the corner, arms folded, head down, refusing the opportunity to speak. I was surprised that he came back. By perhaps his second or third session when he was asked a question he responded with explosive street talk that was hard to even understand. Gradually his words became sentences, and he began to engage more critically in complaints about the prison. Then one day he started to tell his story and described in detail his offence, robbing people at a cashpoint (ATM). He described clearly his sense of hopelessness and inability to see any other way to make a success of himself, and the pleasure of being able to buy the designer clothes he wanted. In time he was able to talk more thoughtfully with others about his upbringing and community, and then to wrestle with questions about his future. There were other individuals like Eddie who came month after month to explore their life, their storyline, in depth. It is surprising how clearly I can recall those people, even after all these years. Eddie and others contributed to the container, and as a result other people could engage with the same questions about themselves, in depth, even if they were only there once. The focus of the Dialogue changed from 'what others should do to make things better for me' to 'what I need to address to improve things for myself'.

As a group I found prisoners more interested in thinking about their journey and resettlement as they found themselves in the safety of the container. As one prisoner put it to his group, "What is more important, that you can't buy tuna on the canteen (prison shop) or that you need to deal with your drug problem so that you don't end up back here again? What would your family want you to be talking about?" Officers who came to the Dialogues saw how they could have an impact on offenders' lives. One officer, after attending a series of Dialogues, chose a new role managing the work groups who tended the grounds of the prison. As he told me, "We have Dialogue every day, and I can see what a difference it makes to [the prisoners], and I love my job again."

The development of individuals and relationships between staff and prisoners was encouraging, but still there was no structure to take what was being learnt in the Dialogue into the wider prison or criminal justice system in a sustainable way. I remember thinking as Eddie was released that he needed to continue this quality of Dialogue in the community, but there was no way for him to so.

Learnings for the ORJ
Through repeated practice I learnt the critical facilitation skills required for this work, the foundation for any ORJ intervention. Most important is the use of – and encouragement for others to use – the Dialogic practices, creating a container that enables a rich authentic enquiry with an offender about their life and circumstances. It leads even the most cynical staff to listen and understand the offenders' experiences, and others to think about how they are leading their own lives. It is an engagement between people, not an interview or assessment, and that requires the facilitator to be equally authentic and willing to talk about their own experiences, thoughts and feelings, appropriately and professionally. "They left their key in the car and went into the shop, that was why I stole it", said a prisoner innocently on

one occasion, as if it was the most obvious thing in the world! I expressed my disbelief in no uncertain terms, and my straightforward, authentic response deepened the quality of Dialogue. The Dialogue facilitation skills also enable an effective conversation between subcultures. Over time, this moves beyond an us-and-them debate to a common enquiry. This is a necessary skill to integrate a fragmented system. A typical example of such a debate occurred between the prisoners and the head of security about security measures in the prison, particularly how family members were searched when they arrived for a visit. Facilitation encouraged them to listen to each other, enquire about each other's views, explain their own side and why they held them. As a result, they discovered their common interest in keeping the prison safe and secure and, beyond that, something of their common humanity.

The developing enquiries in the Blakenhurst Dialogue groups revealed how much more opportunity there was in prison to enable offenders to change their story, and therefore be less likely to reoffend. Many of the offenders had been in prison many times before, and shared their stories of how they came to be back in prison. ("It is like snakes and ladders: it's hard to climb up a ladder, but when you slide down like a snake it is fast", said one prisoner.) These repeating, predictable patterns revealed where the system was and was not working.

Mind the Gap
Resettlement KPI Conference with HMP Blakenhurst, HMP Brockhill and HMP Hewell Grange

Context
While our Dialogue groups in HMP Blakenhurst focused increasingly on the offenders' story of resettlement, HMPS (*Her Majesty's Prison Service* in England and Wales) announced the introduction of key performance indicators (KPIs) relating to resettlement. The measures were the first time in the UK that prisons would be monitored on what was provided to help offenders re-establish themselves in the community after they left the prison. I had worked in two prisons adjacent to HMP Blakenhurst: a women's prison HMP Brockhill, and an open prison (the lowest security level in England and Wales) HMP Hewell Grange, so we took advantage of our relationships there to centre a conference on these three prisons. The aim was to learn more about how criminal justice system could better support the resettlement of offenders – what was working, what was not and how things could be improved.

The Work
For the first session we created a map of the system that highlighted the factors affecting whether an offender was reconvicted or resettled. We played on the iconic wording from the London Underground notice that says 'Mind the Gap' as you get on or off the train, but here The Gap referred to the gap between incarceration as an *offender* and independent life in the community as an *ex-offender*.

As we began our conference, we required every subgroup to be represented at the gathering.

We invited people by name from each agency and, if they didn't reply, we called them until they did. If they were not available we asked them to send an appropriate representative, and we persisted until we had a guarantee that the right person would be there. I still remember Peter calling the Home Office (in the US, something of a combination of the Justice Department and the Department of Homeland Security) to ask them who they would send – and they did send someone! There were 45 participants, including police officers, magistrates, victim representatives, drug treatment counsellors, prison officers, prison managers, voluntary sector support staff, employment service managers, public health and social policy advisors, an academic criminologist, family members, prisoners and ex-prisoners.

The conference was structured around four themed Dialogues: 'Arrest and Conviction', 'Imprisonment', 'Release and Resettlement', and a final reflection on the whole journey. Participants sat in two concentric circles. Participants with direct experience of the theme – the aspect of the journey under consideration – sat in the inner circle and spoke in an open Dialogue. Those in the outer circle listened and added awareness, which they shared in observations at the end. As such, the Imprisonment Dialogue included the prison staff, prisoners, family members, while the police, magistrates, victim support, and the employment service listened from the outer circle.

Outcomes and Limitations

The primary outcome of the conference was learning about the fragmentation and interconnectedness in the criminal justice system (documented in a full report and published at www.prisondialogue.org). Agencies had little awareness of the impact they had on the ability of others to do their work. Drug treatment counsellors described how they could not work effectively in prisons because of lack of cooperation from prison staff who saw them as a burden rather than an asset to the prison, and policy advisors were disconnected from the experience on the ground, and were making uninformed policy decisions. Security staff could undermine prison visits through their attitude to family members, yet resettlement staff were trying to encourage strong family ties in the knowledge they improved chances of successful resettlement. There was little to no understanding between different phases of the journey, apart from the knowledge held by the offenders and their families. The magistrate, who sentenced people to custody, was not interested in what it was like in prison. Police were told that how they made an arrest (always based on a professional risk assessment) affected how the offender thought about Criminal justice agencies, and therefore their attitude to prison staff once they were incarcerated.

As a one-off event, the session generated a high level of awareness and new understanding about the interrelatedness of the criminal justice agencies, the offender and their family. Previously I had not thought of a Dialogue needing to lead to a plan of action, rather that each participant making their own decisions about what they would do as a result of what they had heard and learnt. However, the criminal justice system is large and complex and the individual motivation at the end of the session was unlikely to lead to the policy or practice changes I could see were needed.

114 | Shaping Corrections Through Dialogue

Learnings for the ORJ

The map, graphic and naming (The Gap) provided a strong and clear external display of the system that everyone could see and refer to. We could show *Offender–Ex-Offender* at the heart of the image and depict the relative positioning of the agencies. The concentric circle design of the session reinforced the image. The offenders and ex-offenders were the only people seated in the centre circle for each Dialogue, and it was obvious that they were the only group to have continuous first-hand experience of every phase of the journey.

Participation by all relevant stakeholders is essential. With each perspective brought out by people talking openly about their first-hand experience, the interrelatedness of the system and its impact is clear. As the criminal justice system is an open system – meaning that there is no one person with authority over everyone – it requires skilful convening to achieve this. This includes understanding and mapping the system to identify the relevant agencies or subgroups, sending invitations purposefully to the right people, taking care to explain why it is relevant for them to be there, and following up to secure their participation. In a closed system, with sponsorship at the right level, you can require people to attend. In an open system, where people do not have a common leader, you have to make the case for them to be there.

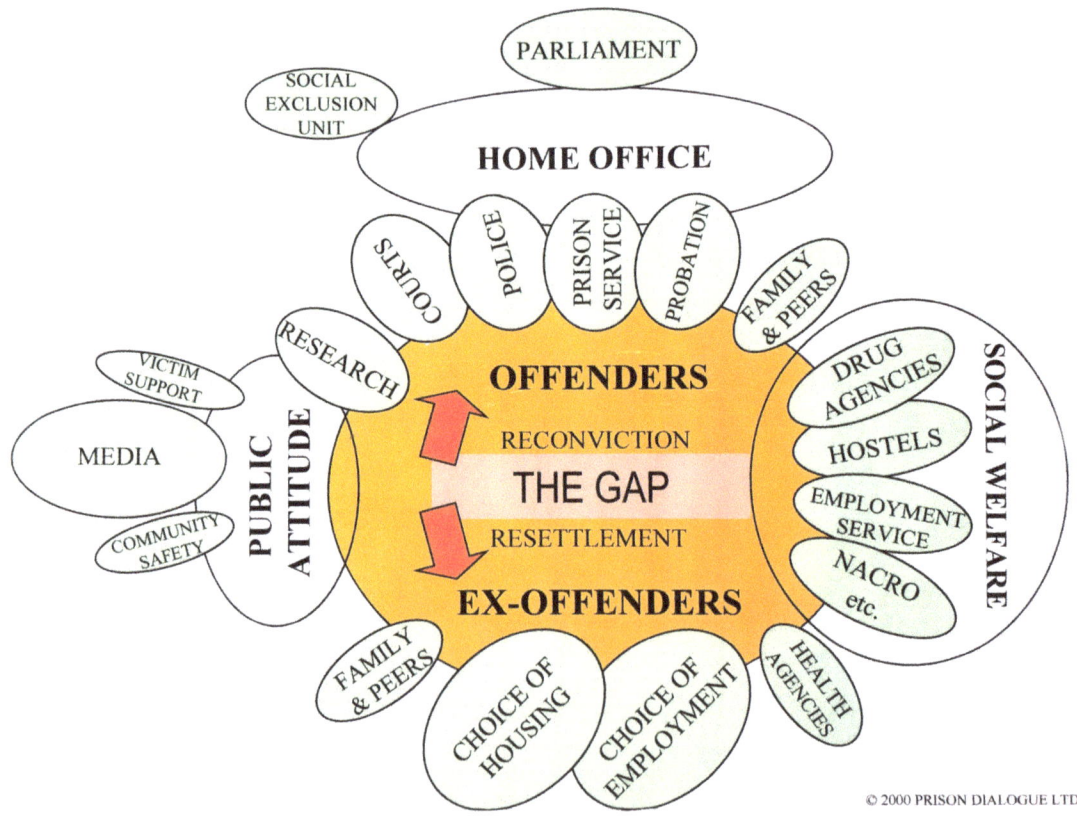

Threshold Dialogue
An Open System Working Together to Improve Resettlement

Context
From 2003 to 2006 Prison Dialogue worked consistently with the Governor (in charge of the prison overall), all of the senior managers and staff at HMP Dorchester in the south of England in support of a prison turnaround. Dialogue was at the heart of the transformation that took the prison from a ranking of 135th of 136 prisons in England and Wales in 2004, to 35th by 2006 – the highest ranking it could achieve for a prison of its type. It also ranked 1st or 2nd in the country across 12 different Measures of Quality of Prison Life (MQPL). The work at the prison was noticed by the Governor, who let us know that "The Director General called me to pass on his personal congratulations for what was seen as an extraordinary shift in the prisoners' custodial experience".

This was only the beginning. The vision went beyond the custodial experience to the creation of a whole-prison approach to resettlement. The Governor wanted the prison to be what was known as a 'beacon establishment', one that shone out among other prisons and had influence beyond the prison walls. Partnering with the prison Governor, we introduced our thinking about the offender journey and developed Threshold Dialogue to operationalise a wider partnership within the criminal justice system to reduce recidivism in the local community.

The Work
Bournemouth Threshold Dialogue was launched in January 2006, and for the next five years I worked to develop a structured Dialogue intervention, designed to address fragmentation in the multiple ways it occurred in this system: between different phases of the journey, particularly prison and the community; between different agencies and between offenders and the agencies; also between line staff (practice), senior managers (procedure) and chief officers (policy). In reality this meant that we created a network of interrelated Dialogue groups at three prisons and three community sites that tracked the offenders' journey in and out of prison.

We did not set it up as a grand design. The network was built over a period of time as we engaged regularly with groups of offenders and discovered what they needed. We knew that offenders experienced a crisis of release that builds up towards the end of their sentence and hits them as they step through the prison gate. The experience of freedom can be unsettling, and there is a lot of pressure to secure accommodation, income and medication, re-engage with family, and avoid past associates. We began in HMP Dorchester with Dialogues focused on preparing for release, and then in the large seaside town of Bournemouth, where many of the offenders lived. The sessions were run on the same day every week within prison and the community – one week a young man would attend a Dialogue in the prison, and on the same day the following week he would be in a Dialogue in the community. This was particularly helpful for the significant group of offenders whose journey took them in and out of prison repeatedly, with sentences too short to receive any interventions in prison. They could continue to engage in the socio-therapeutic intervention of Dialogue regardless.

This was another open-system intervention; therefore, we understood that we would have to establish how Threshold Dialogue met the organisational interests of each and every one of the agencies to secure their participation. It needed to help them be successful in their day job. Every agency accepted that they needed to engage with offenders, but it was difficult to achieve. Few recently released offenders want to be seen talking to the police. It can take hours for a housing worker to see one offender on a prison visit. Threshold Dialogue provided engagement in quantity and quality. In a session with 15 offenders for 90 minutes they achieved 22.5 hours of engagement with offenders from their local community. The impact was significant. For example, police usually got to know offenders when they were arresting them, a time when there was little opportunity to build a relationship. They rearrested people time and time again, and as a result frequently held negative assumptions about offenders. In Threshold Dialogue they could support the offender's thinking about their journey and build mutual understanding and rapport. I knew of a previously violent offender who willingly went to the police station with one of the police officers he had met in the Dialogue when he breached his probation licence. In the past that would have required force, a team of officers and probably some injury. Housing workers who got to know offenders in depth while they were in prison were more able to support them once they were released and dealing with the challenges of communal living.

Prisons, police, local government, housing providers, employment service, and a drug treatment service became primary long-term partners in this intervention. Their staff participated regularly in Dialogues at a number of sites, and some of them trained as facilitators so that the process could be self-sustaining. Facilitators worked in pairs and we created a reporting mechanism to support the development of their facilitation skills. This required them to listen and become more aware of what was happening. After his first session, one officer learnt that if he tried to remember good quotes he wasn't listening, and he couldn't remember what people said. If he just listened, he could recall significant comments easily.

In time there were Threshold Dialogues tracking the offender journey – a local prison which incarcerated offenders serving short sentences, a medium-security prison for those with longer sentences (many of whom started out at the local prison), and a young offenders institution, a night shelter and day centre for those whose lives were more chaotic, a supported housing unit for ex-offenders who were recently released, and at a community hall for people who were living more independently.

We developed the concept of the Line of Sight for the view that offenders have of their Resettlement Journey. We found that many offenders do not have a clear Line of Sight. They cannot see what they must do, either fully or in good enough time to succeed; or they get stuck, with no view of where they are trying to get to, or what they have to do to get there. Threshold Dialogue helped to create a clear Line of Sight for prisoners over their entire journey, with a destination worth aiming and for and manageable steps for each major transition. The participation of agency staff was critical – for example, staff from community agencies came into the prison for a Dialogue about preparing to be in the community.

The Threshold Dialogue system was supported by an Operations group of senior managers and a Governance Board of chief officers from every agency involved. This structure took learning from Threshold Dialogues into management and resourcing of operational services and the development of policy and strategy. After five years we held a Line of Sight event sponsored by the Local Criminal Justice Board to mark our withdrawal and hand over to local ownership. This included use of graphic maps and a spatialised offender walk (described in the following example) to display the system to itself.

Outcomes and Limitations
I witnessed and tracked changes in many individual offenders, including prolific offenders who were stuck in the revolving door of short-term sentences and short-term release who did not reoffend for the duration of our connection with them. Relationships between offenders and staff from every agency developed constructively. Interagency cooperation was more effective, leading to tangible service changes. As a direct result of Threshold Dialogue, a project was set up to provide a package of social security benefit, rent assistance, private-sector accommodation and employment advice for offenders on release. One of the participants, the Manager of Bournemouth Safer and Stronger Communities Team, emphasised the value of Dialogue against this backdrop: "We talk about partnership working a lot, but I think actually what dialogue does is really strengthens some of those partnerships at various different levels – right from the people who are working on the ground, maybe managing offenders or ex-offenders on a day-to-day basis, in hostels, Police Community Support Officers and community workers, but also at a more strategic level: prison Governors; superintendents from the police and community safety managers; probation managers; actually working together and understanding what the system looks like in their local area".

The limitation was the lack of sustainability. Despite the achievements of Threshold Dialogue, including the creation of the local governance structure and facilitation team, it folded once we withdrew. It was disappointing but not surprising. Local leaders (primarily in prisons and police) who had partnered with us to set up the programme had moved on, without establishing the commitment from those who replaced them. Without leadership, participation fell away. HMP Dorchester closed in 2013.

Learnings for the ORJ
Through Threshold Dialogue we learnt about the larger offender journey, between prisons and into the community, and the experience and impact of repeated cycles of reoffending. This included the development of our understanding of and language for the Crisis of Release, Crisis of Entry and Re-entry, and the Line of Sight.

I believe that Threshold Dialogue helps offenders prepare for and successfully make their journey to resettlement and develops the skills of staff to support that journey more effectively. It requires widespread participation from criminal justice agencies – and we found participation can be achieved in an open system where agencies find the value to their individual organisational interests or targets. Even so, you need senior partnership and sponsorship. In an open system you need it across key agencies, from key influencers, and you must work hard to secure the commitment of new leaders.

Offender Resettlement Journey for Organisational Development
A Statewide System

Context
The ORJ can be used at scale for organisational development, as we have shown in a statewide system in the US. This was the first time we named the intervention the Offender Resettlement Journey, and it was a consistent image as Peter and I partnered with the Director and his team to cascade Dialogue skills and practice throughout the agency. The foundation was completely different to anywhere else and, as a result, the potential was more significant. Working steadily with the agency over six years, all of their 12,000 or so employees were introduced to Dialogue skills for engagement and communication, every supervisor exposed to the use of Dialogue skills for management and coaching, and every leader to the use of a Working Dialogue pattern as a business practice for participatory change. The introduction to these skills included an organisational infrastructure to embed the training and practice of Dialogue in a practical way. This whole-system skill-building was cascaded from the Director and Deputies to the Executive team, every Unit Head, every Deputy Unit Head, on down through the ranks.

Intervention Design
The ORJ was introduced at stages alongside the other skills. At the first ORJ we included an ORJ 'Walk' event, held over an afternoon, within a Dialogue Skills Training session with executives and unit heads. In those early days the focus of the cultural change was the communication between ranks, up and down the chain of command in this hierarchical system. The aim of the ORJ was to introduce the idea that you could also think from the point of view of the offender, to understand the system and inform decisions. This was a challenging proposition for some people. It was a 'walk' because we physically walked an offender up and down the room to show their journey through the system from the point they were sentenced, to the current time – I'll outline more about the spatialisation and facilitation below. It was an event because there was no structured follow-up. People were definitely moved and affected. The memories were at times very emotional and, for many of the leadership, a great reminder of the human impact of their work, in that they spent more time with emails and in meetings as a result of the walk. I remember an older warden's touching reaction to being

thanked by an ex-offender for the words of advice he gave him as his counsellor, perhaps 30 years before. The ORJ 'walk' had a personal impact on people, but there was no designed change as a result.

Later, as the Dialogue skills were in broad use across the agency and accepted because of their value, we ran three large-scale, in-depth ORJs to show the potential for organisational development. These ORJs focused on a maximum-security prison, a medium-security prison and a low-security prison in partnership with nearby Community Corrections districts. We worked closely with a steering group for each site so that locally they owned the process (from the research to identify the ORJ through their unit, to giving practical support to the design to the convening and logistics), the organisational learning and the resulting change proposals and implementation.

There were three phases. In the first phase we talked regularly with the local team to understand the flow of offenders into and out of their care and draw the graphic image of the journey centred on their prison. This required data to identify the common journeys and significant points of transition. The enquiry revealed five different archetypal journeys which we named on the graphics and provided useful language to refer five quite distinct experiences.

Local data informed the choice of which journeys it would be helpful to understand, and therefore which offenders, other prisons, probation units or other criminal justice agencies should be invited to the session. Where there were significant drug problems they selected and invited male and female offenders who had been incarcerated for drug-related offences and had been in treatment. Where prisoners we re-released on parole after decades of incarceration, they selected a man who had served nearly 40 years, and where they wanted to learn about the most challenging offenders they selected a man who had been in the highest security conditions and was working his way down the system. Other invitations were also made to specific individuals – not just any probation officer or Sheriff was invited, but rather a probation officer from the office who received most offenders on release from that prison, and the Sheriff who ran the jail that sent more offenders to that prison than any other jail.

Spatialised Facilitation

The second phase was a facilitated event, bringing the system together in one room. These days began with a process of engagement to build the container: first a check-in, then exercises and small-group skilful conversations to introduce and activate the Dialogic practices. One check-in led people to think about their own journey through corrections (when they joined the agency, their first job, next job, when they expect to retire). Questions were posed to give permission to think about how the agency could be improved from a financial, operational and community perspective. The final question was a moral one – if your son, daughter, or some other relative was incarcerated here, would you be happy with the treatment they received?

Next we spatialised where participants were seated in the room. At one end were those who worked in the community, at the other end those who worked in maximum-security prisons. In

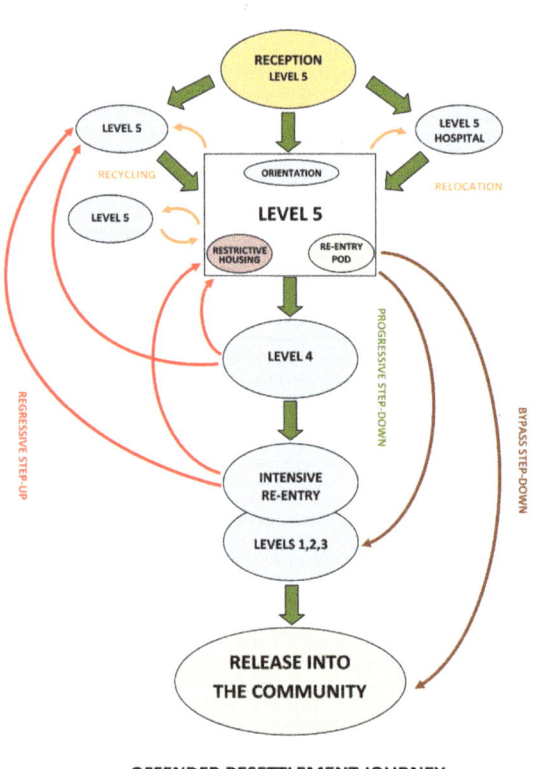

OFFENDER RESETTLEMENT JOURNEY

between were staff from prisons at reducing levels of security until you reached the prison gate – represented by thick silver tape across the floor, or tables or chairs – something that marks a significant change between prison and community. Stepping across that threshold is a distinct and significant change for anyone, and the spatialisation has to represent that. Everyone was seated in a relevant place where there were no observers. Family members sat centrally in the community so they had clear sight of their partner or child as they walked through the system. Then Peter and I took turns facilitating a process for the ex-offender or offender to tell their story from the moment when they were sentenced, beginning with how long they were sentenced for, to set the length of the story. Sometimes they went back before then, and though we assured them they didn't need to name their crime, many of them did. We spoke with them some days beforehand to help them to feel confident in us and comfortable about what would happen,

but not to hear any details of their story. As we walk and talk we want to achieve genuine, spontaneous human engagement, not hear their rehearsed speeches nor our prepared questions. We included other participants as we went, turning to family members, a Sheriff, prison or probation officer or others, to ask what their experience was of the same journey. For example, turning to a mother to ask what they were thinking as their daughter was incarcerated for the first time, to a 'zero-tolerance' judge why he sent someone back to prison, or to prison staff who received the offender as they arrived in a maximum-security prison.

These offender walks were followed by a whole-group Dialogue to digest together what people noticed or learnt about the system by considering it from the point of view of the offender. Next, we facilitated a process of support and challenge to identify and name specific needs and opportunities that could be addressed to improve outcomes, stimulated by the earlier experience. This required focus and persistence, given the emotional as well as intellectual response to what people had seen and heard.

The final phase took each need or opportunity into a proposal and action, using a participative change methodology including engagement of offenders and other stakeholders. The proposals were integrated into the organisations' reporting systems as business improvement projects.

Outcomes and Limitations

The ORJ led to greater awareness and understanding of interdependencies across the system and the benefits of thinking from the offenders' perspective to see how the system works. As a result the agency is looking to embed the ORJ as a regular organisational development process, led by their own staff. On the whole, the proposals that came out of the ORJs were seriously considered and implemented, or rejected with clear feedback. Some simple, practical solutions were introduced (e.g., transferring money to offenders as they arrive in prison, or use of prisoner mentors in prison reception), and others addressed bigger cultural issues that were more difficult to shift, but at least they were being talked about (for example, the practice of moving prisoners with mental health problems to higher-security prisons). They identified opportunities where people recognised common interests and the potential they could achieve together, particularly with willing community partners.

We have not yet developed other practitioners to be able to facilitate an ORJ, with the skills that we have developed over many years of practice. The ORJ pattern is still complex and will need more work to be simplified as a pattern that can be replicated. These steps are important to make the ORJ more widely available.

Learnings for the ORJ

We know the phases required for an ORJ intervention for organisational development, including: research to map the system and understand which journeys will be fruitful to focus on; selection of offenders and other participants; convening; design and spatialisation; facilitation for an authentic, often emotional, experience; and taking that response into proposals and then to action. Each phase requires certain understanding and skills.

Dialogic facilitation skills for an ORJ are notables, and an extension of those we used in prison Dialogues. To manage the event you need to discern how to use the time available to tell the story, and how to pick out the important aspects of this story. Crucially, you need to engage authentically in depth with someone you have just met, enabling them to willingly describe profound, painful and exhilarating personal experiences in front of an audience of 40 to 80 people that includes police, prison staff, judges, priests, and their own mother . . . You must develop the confidence to ask questions that you don't know the answers to, and to respond genuinely when you hear things that affect you. Simultaneously, you have to be aware of and engage the rest of the participants. They will be a diverse group of people, from many agencies and ranks, with different experiences and attitude. You need to use your presence and your own authenticity and invite them into the conversation.

Relevance of and Possibilities for the ORJ

The Offender Resettlement Journey provides theory and practice for the integration of the criminal justice system through the perspective of the continuous journey of the offender. Without this, the criminal justice system is fragmented and different parts act without reference to each other, and without reference to the offenders they mean to help. The integration enables everyone, including offenders, to make better decisions knowing the impact they will have on others. The ORJ could be used widely in the criminal justice system to integrate practice, procedure and policy. It could also be extended to include the journey before arrest to identify preventative opportunities, or journeys that end in prison because there is a growing group of aging prisoners who may die before they are released. The same approach would be relevant in other fields where there is a clear purpose and integrating focus. For example, I designed and facilitated a session for a multinational oil company that was based on the journey of crude oil from extraction to sale, and Peter and I have recently used the Migrant Journey. It may have relevance in education – the child's learning journey, in healthcare – the patient's journey, in social care – the journey of aging. I would welcome others stepping forward to explore these applications.

Section Three

Shaping Social Work Through Dialogue

In this section we consider the critical matter of shaping social services through Dialogue. Nowhere is the fragmentation of families, communities and society encountered more directly, and on a daily basis, than in the social services. Life can be challenging for those who find themselves unable to manage their basic needs for physical and mental health, financial income and accommodation. Being dependent on others can place people at a disabling and painful disadvantage, where it is easy to be overlooked or ignored. The humanising impact of Dialogue can be the decisive factor in the quality of many people's lives. The three different accounts in this section describe the shaping of this sector through Dialogue.

Rebecca Cannara has engaged a handful of the growing numbers of homeless people in California. How can such a healthy economy entertain such a situation? Simply by fragmented awareness. This is essentially a systemic problem, but Rebecca has made a start by gathering a mix of homeless people, housed individuals with experience of homelessness and staff from various support agencies. They began by developing a common understanding of what is needed and what is available. The series of Dialogues she describes were practical yet moving, revealing conversations that have not been had, and untold stories. They describe the immensity of the problem and the starkly different worlds of housed and unhoused people, and those in between, sleeping in a car or on a friend's sofa. She asks people to drop the diminishing term 'the homeless' in favour of 'unhoused neighbours'.

Bernard Le Roux, who lives and works in Sweden, tackles the difficult interface between local government agencies providing care and the families of individuals receiving that care. He describes the mediation he provided where two families believed their autistic adult children were not receiving good care. The organisation's official voice seemed a different language from that of the concerned family members. Bernard prepares the conditions for Dialogue through sensitive engagement and hearing privately what needed to be conveyed by each party to the other. This practice enables them to hear and understand one another. If Dialogue is establishing a common meaning and feeling amongst a group of people, then Bernard makes significant progress addressing a systemic bureaucratic problem. And he arrives at a deeper insight in his postscript.

For the last two decades Lars-Åke Almqvist has been stepping right into care homes in Sweden to work directly with the staff who are responsible for providing residential care to the elderly. His pragmatic and participatory form of Dialogue training engenders collaborative initiatives to improve the workplace. And it pays dividends. For example, he documents three care homes where he had worked, that – at the time of writing – had no cases of Covid-19 during the first half year of the pandemic. This is a remarkable outcome, given nearly half the many deaths in Sweden during this period occurred in residential care homes. Lars is a remarkable figure in this huge field of care for the elderly – one that is likely to affect many of us directly as we draw closer to the ends of our lives – so it is a pleasure to help his valuable work to be known more widely.

– P.G.

Community Dialogues on Homelessness

Rebecca Cannara

In Los Angeles, California, the combination of income inequality, exorbitant prices for homes and rentals, exclusionary neighborhoods and the stigmatization of homelessness have all contributed to a housing crisis that has only been amplified by the Covid-19 pandemic. Persistent cultural norms allow us to distance ourselves from those most marginalized in our communities, resulting in a diffusion of responsibility in affluent areas where homelessness coexists and is at an all-time high. This paper explores the use of a series of dialogues on homelessness in one affluent Los Angeles community to break through stigmatization, and to encourage empathic action toward their unhoused neighbors. Findings include emerging themes from the dialogic process and individual examples of shifts toward empathy and action.

The State of Homelessness in Los Angeles

Los Angeles County has the largest population of unhoused individuals in the United States and, based on 2019 and 2020 pre-pandemic counts, it has been increasing at a rate of 12-13% for the past two years. In 2016 voters earmarked over a billion dollars through the City of Los Angeles' Proposition HHH. In 2017 voters supported countywide measure H, agreeing to send roughly $350 million annually to address housing shortages and homeless services. The Los Angeles Homeless Services Authority (LAHSA) established a centralized entry system to access services, and the county has been identifying locations for permanent and transitional supportive housing. Yet according to the housing coalition Everyone In LA, on any given day, for every 133 people who move out of homelessness, there are another 150 or more who lose their homes. Meanwhile, more than half a million residents are spending 90% of their income on rent, pushing them to the brink of homelessness.[*] Despite voters generously sending a record level of funding to combat homelessness, not one neighborhood has welcomed the housing. Instead many neighbors express hostility, employing age-old tropes about how "the homeless" will bring drugs and violence and will devalue home

---

[*] https://everyoneinla.org/about-us/faq/

prices. However, the opposite is true: additional, new, supportive housing can actually increase home values in a neighborhood.*

In 2020, after much demand at the onset of the Covid-19 pandemic, the state and county established Project Roomkey to leverage empty hotel rooms for unhoused individuals who would be most at risk if they were to contract the virus. At the time of writing, three months after the start of this program, 3,387 rooms have been occupied (out of LA's nearly 100,000 capacity)†, with only 4,968 of the over 60,000 unhoused individuals in the county having been served—falling far short of their countywide goal to house 15,000 individuals.‡ One issue in filling the rooms stems from hostility of neighbors who live in or near the hotels.

Challenging Psychological Distancing

Psychological distancing can be defined as "a cognitive separation between the self and other instances such as persons, events, or times,"§ and may be connected to distancing oneself from another who displays characteristics they fear in themselves.¶

In 2019 local Santa Monica artist Ed Massey erected a statue of what could be seen as a stereotypical homeless man to commemorate his encounter with a man 20 years earlier. Working with his educator-activist brother Ernie, his intention was to get the neighborhood to confront its issues with homelessness.** In his artist's statement, Ed Massey underlined this point:

> *For the vast majority of people going about their daily routines, the homeless are an invisible distraction—humans that many depersonalize, walk by, or put out of mind. Such inattention—and at times contempt—has ensured the continuity of the expanding homeless issue.*

Many neighbors were furious about the statue, as if it were holding up homelessness as something to revere. But one person's comment on the NextDoor app stood out, that they took the statue to be a call for dialogue, given that inequality is such a huge issue in Los Angeles and given Santa Monica's key role in the issue. This is the context that inspired our

---

* https://www.csh.org/2017/02/affordable-supportive-housing-improves-neighborhoods/

† https://www.discoverlosangeles.com/media/facts-about-la

‡ https://la.streetsblog.org/2020/06/19/thousands-housed-in-project-roomkey-in-los-angeles-but-nimbyism-lack-of-permanent-affordable-housing-blunt-progress/.

§ https://link.springer.com/referenceworkentry/10.1007%2F978-94-007-0753-5_2306.

¶ Schimel, Jeff & Pyszczynski, Tom & Greenberg, Jeff & O'Mahen, Heather & Arndt, Jamie. (2000). "Running from the Shadow: Psychological Distancing from Others to Deny Characteristics People Fear in Themselves." *Journal of Personality and Social Psychology*. 78. 446-62. 10.1037//0022-3514.78.3.446.

** https://www.smdp.com/agitating-for-change-through-art/183285.

organization, Universal Human Rights Initiative (UHRI), to pursue community dialogues on homelessness; it motivates our actions and prompts our calls for next steps.

An Equity-Based Dialogic Design

At UHRI we use dialogic models of engagement to provide opportunities for deeper human connection across social and economic barriers. Our goal is to promote human rights and social justice by increasing empathy and inspiring action. We saw dialogue as a potential method to shift people's biases against unhoused individuals so that more neighbors would support providing housing solutions in their immediate communities. In this paper I describe a series of dialogues that emerged after a community exploration of the issue: their format, themes and emerging actions. I employed two key theories to the design of the dialogues. First, dialogue promotes intergroup contact as a means for reducing prejudices. I employed Gordon Allport's four conditions for intergroup contact to reduce prejudice: "1) equal status between the groups in the situation; 2) common goals; 3) no competition between groups; and (4) authority sanction for the contact."* This includes an emphasis from research professors Thomas Pettigrew and Linda Tropp that, to be successful in reducing prejudice, we must provide optimal intergroup contact where the perspectives of those in lower status groups are given equal consideration and voice.† For this reason, I approached the formation of the dialogues through an equity-based design, where the facilitator constantly reflects on her own power in relationship to the theme, invites all stakeholders to participate from the start and continues to reflect on who and what more should be included in the design and implementation of the dialogue.‡

To begin, I first met with various stakeholders about their connection to homelessness in the area and identified that there was a communication gap between service providers and neighbors. At the invitation of the City of Santa Monica staff, we held an open dialogue at a local church in September 2019 with local neighbors, housed and unhoused, local city and county staff, and other service providers in the area. For the first 45 minutes each participant shared why they were attending the dialogue. By the end of that check-in, we established that each participant held a personal connection to homelessness (lived experience, a loved one who was/is homeless, working in the field of homelessness, encountering unhoused individuals in their neighborhood, etc.). We then brainstormed ways to bring the community

---

* From Allport G. W. (1954). *The Nature of Prejudice.* Reading, MA: Addison-Wesley; Pettigrew, T.F. (1971). *Racially Separate or Together?* New York: McGraw-Hill.

† Pettigrew, Thomas F., & Tropp, Linda R. (2000). "Does intergroup contact reduce prejudice: Recent meta-analytic findings." In S. Oskamp (Ed.), *The Claremont Symposium on Applied Social Psychology (Reducing Prejudice and Discrimination)* (p. 93–114). Lawrence Erlbaum Associates Publishers.

‡ https://dschool.stanford.edu/resources/equity-centered-design-framework.

together. During this phase, one of the key themes that stood out was a general lack of awareness of what services and plans were currently in place in LA County. The other key theme was the need to build more human connections across the socioeconomic barriers of homelessness.

The focus of this paper is a primary action that came out of these meetings. This was a series of six monthly dialogues on homelessness, held in partnership with the church that hosted the dialogue described above. This plan was designed to build knowledge about LA homelessness and to encourage more involvement in the issue. Each dialogue was shaped with the equity-based goal to include people who are currently or formerly homeless; other neighbors; the host church's members; and city and county staff and service providers. We also adopted a model of dialogue carried out at the Academy of Professional Dialogue's 2019 conference, where we split the two-hour sessions into information sharing for the first hour and community dialogue for the second hour. Local people with lived experience and/or those who have worked in the field presented during the information-sharing hour. This was followed by a dialogue focused on our personal connection to the information shared. The first three sessions were held January–March 2020 at the church. We provided food and a table with further resources and information. Unfortunately, due to the Covid-19 pandemic, we were not able to meet in person for the final three dialogues and met on Zoom from April–June 2020. While the format maintained the information-sharing and community dialogue, our unhoused participants were not able to join the online sessions, despite attempts to include them.

Our Dialogue Format

For the three in-person dialogues all participants and other speakers sat in one large circle with dialogue tools provided (outlined in Appendix One). Check-ins and check-outs were held for the community dialogue that took place during the second hour. The check-ins consisted of sharing takeaways from the information sharing, and the check-outs highlighted what actions and emotions we were leaving with. Smaller, pair-sharing experiences offered introverted participants a comfortable way to share and provided time for each participant to self-reflect on accountability. The format for the three online dialogues included breakout rooms on Zoom to continue this format and to provide space for smaller group conversations. We introduced some additional guidelines from Weaving Community to support this new format (See Appendix Two).

Additional modifications were made when needed. The information-sharing portion for the youth dialogue was intentionally formatted using a fishbowl setup. The presenters, mostly youth who have experienced homelessness and now work with other youth facing housing insecurity, were placed into a central circle to speak with each other, while all other participants sat in an outer circle to listen. This act of physically centering youth voices allowed us to ensure that they were the focus. We felt the need to do this because some youth were newer to speaking in public, and because there were some participants in the outer circle who were also unhoused, but who participated in the planning and first dialogue of the series and whose voices we hear each time. The fishbowl allowed for a clear way to designate both to the attendees and to the presenters that the focus was truly on the youth experience. The community dialogue returned to the large circle format. In addition, the final dialogue of the series, held online, had only one presenter, James Rojas from PlaceIt.org, who carried out an interactive activity, as will be discussed below.

As a solo facilitator throughout the dialogues, I was aware of the power I held to shape the conversations. The design of information sharing and dialogue as well as the in-person circular format helped to shape a very open conversation. I tended to step back as best I could as facilitator except for one dynamic. Despite efforts to flatten power in the dialogic model, I was very aware of the power dynamic between housed and unhoused residents. I felt responsible for raising the voice of unhoused participants and took the following steps to do so. As mentioned above, I used a fishbowl technique to keep youth voices central in their dialogue. I modelled active listening and making space for our unhoused participants, even if they talked for longer than other participants. I advocated for support for their voices, particularly with a couple of participants who were uncomfortable with the time taken by unhoused participants in the first meeting. I reminded them that the unhoused speakers are the experts in the room, and that their voices are essential. At the same time, because our shared dialogue model and facilitation role is to model listening and making space, over time our unhoused participants internalized the model. By the second and third dialogues they noted when they felt they themselves needed to make space for others to share. The most powerful tool, however, was pair-sharing. Each time participants were asked to turn to the person next to them they broke down social barriers by telling someone whom they didn't know how they were—what they were feeling and thinking about—and by listening actively to the other person. Often this meant housed participants who have never been homeless connecting with other participants who currently were homeless or had been in the past. One participant shared afterward that it was her first time ever talking with someone who is unhoused: "It was very powerful to dialogue with people I may never have opened up to talk with in my daily life. I realize I basically only talk with people similar to me. Getting to the heart of homelessness issues and hearing from the heart of people experiencing homelessness was so needed."

Takeaways and Actions from Each Session

Session One: *General Issues of Homelessness*
(In person, January 2020. Five presenters, 22 participants.)
Presenters: Everyone In (United Way), Casa de la Familia, St. Joseph Center, and The People Concern.

The first session's information-sharing phase featured presentations from county and local service providers focused on homelessness. They shared their insights and held a collective brainstorm that identified the following actions:

- Sharing information about local resources
- Committing to reaching out and asking folks what they need
- A suggestion to give out bus passes if a person isn't comfortable giving money
- Acknowledging that feeling overwhelmed and not knowing where to start can limit our action-taking abilities. Just spreading the word to one other person can be a place to start the domino effect of building empathy and taking action.
- Joining the Homeless Count in March
- Checking the city newsletter for local events to get involved with

After the dialogue we solicited feedback and received the following suggestions, which informed the next five sessions:

- Focus presenters on their overview of their organization, their "ask" and their challenges
- Keep the full hour for action planning
- Offer tangible actions for folks to leave with (maybe from the presenters in advance)
- Find ways to share changes that have happened and successful stories from the previous month
- Contact representatives in government
- Hold a giveaway event quarterly at the church

Between the first and second dialogues I learned of some additional actions that had taken place. One unhoused resident shared by email that he has begun talking to other unhoused folks to invite them to the dialogues and see that there are neighbors who care. A housed neighbor advocated for unhoused neighbors at a library meeting on policing homeless patrons. Offerings of food in plastic bags during a rainy night led to a table at the library to provide donations. And one participant connected with The People Concern about creating a photo project and a garden program in partnership with the city's community gardener.

Session Two: *Youth Experiencing Homelessness*
(In person, February 2020. Eight presenters, 29 participants.)
Presenters: Students4Students, Safe Place for Youth, Mt. Olive Lutheran, LA Homeless Youth Forum (HYFLA), and the UCLA Black Male Institute.

We led with youth sharing their experience navigating the systems set up to support them. A key takeaway for the evening was that housing insecurity disproportionately affects adults and youth of color, and presents intersectional, or multiple-sector, challenges to LGBTQIA+

individuals. Each presenter had a different, personal story, but all shared one theme in common: even though they took ownership in lifting themselves up, they could not do so without the support of an individual who could advocate for them. One of the most meaningful aspects that has emerged in these dialogues is how participants begin to understand such nuanced realities faced by our unhoused neighbors.

During the dialogue, some participants shared actions they had taken over the past month. These ranged from verbal interruptions of bias to specific examples of advocacy. One presenter shared how he formally sits on an advisory board at which he has been pointing out unfair loopholes in the system that even he has benefited from. One unhoused participant had invited a housed participant to the meeting. The housed community member talked about how, after meeting him, they had collaborated to create several websites with clickable links to shelter, food, and other services. Other actions that arose came about through conversations after this dialogue. A local professor was so moved by the youths' stories that she committed to returning to her university to find out what issues her students may be facing that she hadn't been aware of regarding housing and food insecurity, and what her campus is doing or not to support them.

Facilitator note: *I left this evening a bit uncomfortable. We had completed our fourth gathering (the second of the series, but preceded by two meetings), and we had found connection across our social barriers. A few of us continued a conversation in the parking lot, only to say goodnight and send two men back into the streets. I felt hypocritical, like an imposter. What was I doing if this was the outcome month after month? I also received an email from one of the men who felt triggered by the depth of the conversation that focused on how hard the nights are for folks in the street. As he pointed out, the longer you are out in the street, the more severe an effect the situation has on your mental health. He told me to leave him out of the dialogues from now on. And I understood. I felt only an inch of the pain that he was sharing with me, of his personal losses, his disappointments from those who have tried to help before, and his anger at seeing people he cared about fall into drugs and despair. When I processed this with colleagues who have been supporting the dialogues, they advised patience and maintaining open lines of communication. Over time the man came back and has attended each of the in-person dialogues. Our exchange that month pushed me to understand that, in creating connections across these challenging barriers, we must not create false hope. We must honor our limits as individuals and yet continue to follow up with folks most marginalized by society. With this one participant, it has meant not walking away without taking his email and committing to staying connected.*

Session Three: *Storytelling*
(In person, March 2020. Five presenters, 20 participants.)
Presenters: Repair, KTown for All, Invisible People, and an unhoused podcaster and participant.

In our dialogues, we always remind folks that we believe that everyone is an expert in their own experience. So for this session, presenters shared their personal stories of homelessness and action.

We did a *lot* of myth-busting during our dialogue, including a central fallacy that holds that homeless individuals who cannot navigate housing services *have failed*. A key takeaway for the group was that when one person chooses compassion, it can inspire others to do so. As these dialogues continued, we found opportunities to encourage different opinions to emerge. When one activist shared about how unannounced street sweeps destroyed essential medication for one of her unhoused neighbors and led to his decline, an unexpected response emerged in the dialogue. A participant shared that he had been one of those "sweepers" and was moved to hear about how detrimental these sweeps can be. He had seen the sweeps as cleaning up after irresponsible, messy people, but a presenter pointed out that these folks had nowhere else to place their belongings or even to exist, for that matter. He shared a viewpoint that helped the group dig deeper into the nuanced complexities and blind spots of policies and perspectives.

Our group deeply explored the difficult subject of responsibility and accountability: how much responsibility for housing should be shouldered by people in the streets, given all the systemic forces at work that make it impossible to afford basic accommodations? We inquired into the extremes at which we expect people to pay for their mistakes or misfortunes: is not having housing a fair price for these? We discussed looking at housing as a basic human right, no matter what one's path has been. We processed what it means to see someone in the streets and label them as irresponsible, and how it serves to take ourselves out of the equation of accountability. More questions arose than answers: How are solutions working—and where are they not working? Are there funds that aren't going directly to services? Are there vacancies in shelters and other housing that aren't being filled efficiently? Are we finding a way to shift the blame of homelessness from the individual to the society as a whole? What happens after someone returns to housing? What long-term solutions might serve to maintain current housing and prevent future loss of housing?

Session Four: *Local Agencies*
(Online, April 2020. Four presenters, 17 participants.)
Presenters: SHARE! Community Housing, Westside Coalition, Community Corporation of Santa Monica, SoLa Impact.

With the onset of the Covid-19 pandemic and closing of public gatherings, we moved the dialogues to an online format, using Zoom. We incorporated the breakout room feature on Zoom to support the partner and small-group sharing we had been doing in person. Unfortunately our unhoused participants were not able to join us for these remaining three online sessions. In order to focus on questions and themes arising from past dialogues, we invited presenters to speak about current housing solutions and their challenges. With the onset of the pandemic, we also discussed how local housing models respond to a need for adaptive support, development of social networks, and the innovative use of resources.

The critical importance of a variety of social support systems quickly emerged as a key theme of our dialogue. As needs evolve, so should resources and the willingness to innovate and make secure futures possible. Participants expressed wanting to be more involved and wanted to know how to volunteer during challenging times. The dialogue also highlighted how important it is to have this entire network of different providers working together. All of the presenters ended the meeting expressing a desire to collaborate together. Yet, despite an unprecedented public health crisis, there were still negative examples of community pushback. Los Angeles was implementing additional housing programs, such as Project Roomkey and converting recreation centers into shelters. All efforts were met with challenges from neighbors. So the dialogue concluded with the intention to grow our network of compassionate people who will become ambassadors and advocates for supportive housing, in all its forms, in our communities.

Session Five: *Actions During the Pandemic*
(Online, May 2020. Five presenters, 14 participants.)
Presenters: Bet Tzedek legal services, Venice Justice Committee, Services not Sweeps, KTown for All, Streetwatch LA, and Mutual Aid Network LA.

This dialogue made it clear that we have entered unprecedented times and possibilities, and the message from our presenters was loud and clear: there are a lot of ways to help the incredible work being done by local organizations. We heard about legal efforts to protect renters during monumental income loss, the growth of mutual aid networks that provide hygiene and grocery supplies, and community support services. There are now groups that organize undocumented and mixed immigration-status families who are not eligible for government stimulus aid, and other groups who provide support to physically disabled, senior, chronically ill and immune-compromised neighbors. In addition, resources that for years have been requested and denied are suddenly becoming available during the pandemic: funding, loan forgiveness, and supplies. The presenters and group expressed hope that this could speak to a dramatic shift in mindset about who is valued, and that visions of what could be might be taken more seriously. One key aspect about the nuance of advocacy emerged: some of our presenters will not sit at the table with politicians and other governing entities, while others choose to represent marginalized voices that can't get a seat at the table. In the end, the dialogue showed the importance of both types of organizations making these "outside vs. inside" choices and working together.

The presenters provided many tangible actions: street organizers for a legal clinic; collection of PPE (masks, gloves, sanitizer), calls to government representatives, and direct community oversight, such as tracking hotel room occupancy by unhoused folks (Project RoomKey Tracker), and supporting the No Vacancy CA Campaign to push for *all* unhoused individuals to be placed in vacant hotel rooms, rather than just a selection of the most at-risk. There are ways to document and report law enforcement actions against unhoused neighbors and check on the status of handwashing stations and open portable toilets. And while some of our unhoused participants haven't been able to join in the Zoom sessions, we did find out that the church was able to help one of them get housing. We have been in contact with another participant who has been informing unhoused people about accessing government stimulus checks. At the time of writing, he reports that many of these individuals have received their checks.

Session Six: *Envisioning Communities that Center Homelessness*
(Online, June 2020. One presenter, ten participants.)
Presenter: Place It!

Instead of holding another information session, we concluded the series of dialogues with an interactive activity facilitated by the organization Place It! for the first hour and a final dialogue hour afterward. Participants were asked to remember a time in their childhood when they felt truly safe. They shared with the group (using the online chat feature of Zoom) the details of that memory, including the context and feelings involved. All participants shared and we found that each anecdote included warm, positive feelings associated with being in nature and with family and community. Participants were then asked to use any objects around them to create a representation of community that centered itself on the needs of unhoused neighbors and that focused on these key themes around feeling safe. We found that we had each envisioned spaces that helped us to rethink what our communities could look like, based on a significant shift in priorities. Gone were the police stations and government entities, and instead were community gardens and kitchens, cultural centers and housing for all. The architecture and landscape we envisioned suggested an emerging community value of truly supporting our most marginalized members, and what we created looked nothing like our current, segregated neighborhoods and institutions.

By this point, various participants were finding meaningful actions related to what they had learned while participating in all or some of the dialogues. One example to highlight is a participant who had very quietly attended all six sessions. At the end of the dialogues, she reached out to say that, while she has never fundraised before, she really wanted to do something tangible. The current closures of public spaces caused by the pandemic removed the opportunity for unhoused neighbors to gather and charge their devices, which are crucial lines of communication. She researched and fundraised to purchase solar-powered chargers for phones and other digital devices. Within a month, she was able to distribute chargers to over 120 unhoused individuals in the West Los Angeles area, providing over 60 chargers to youth experiencing homelessness, and another 60-plus to individual adults.

Highlighted Themes and Actions

Connection—This was our largest theme. It stood out in small, person-to-person interactions and in the dialogue phase of each session.

- Unhoused participants pointed out the need for more spaces that invite and support those who are unhoused to gather with each other or with housed neighbors in community.
- The possibilities are endless when one person invests in another person. An initial contact at a meeting, or at the library, leads to advocacy, mutual aid, and a shifting of perspectives. Contact is essential in building trust, and it takes a lot of time and patience. Sustained contact proved to be key in supporting unhoused neighbors.
- Each dialogue has exemplified the need for community to keep coming back together, but each presentation has highlighted that sustained contact between those who are housed and unhoused not only combats isolation but builds self-esteem and self-valuation. In my ongoing contact with one of our unhoused participants, he always reminds me that because of the connection that three of us (one city official and two residents) are providing him in person and on email, he's paying it forward in how he connects with folks he encounters who are both housed and unhoused.

Reducing bias—Dialogue participants are prompted to reflect on judgments and assumptions as they arise. Sometimes these aren't apparent to us until after we have shared an opinion, and another participant provides an alternative perspective. Some assumptions that stood out in the dialogue included, but were not limited to:

- **Who experiences homelessness:** When asked to imagine a "homeless person" we often draw on stereotypes that result in a person who looks much like the sculpture described at the start of this paper. However, while many folks in the streets can confirm this stereotype, there are a vastly larger number of folks who are unseen, including families and children who are living in cars, sleeping on couches, and finding other temporary shelters.
- **Myth of meritocracy:** Many believe that our systems are meritocratic, applying equally to all, when so many obstacles are systemically placed in front of people with underrepresented identities such as race/ethnicity, ability status, sexuality, religion and gender identity, to name a few.
- **Mental health myths:** As with housing, at its roots this myth blames an individual for his or her lack of housing, rather than seeing the systemic issues that affect them. While many assume that mental health issues beget homelessness, we learned through dialogue that the opposite is often true: homelessness begets mental health issues and exacerbates them with each day, month and year that an individual or family remains in the streets.
- **Language:** Bias permeates our language and influences our perspectives. "Sweeps" of homeless encampments should be called an unlawful removal of personal property. We use *homeless* as a permanent descriptor, rather than referring to the person first ("people experiencing homelessness" rather than "the homeless"). These labels serve to diminish other people and separate them from ourselves in order to psychologically distance from

them. We also do this with "the poor," "the disabled," and so on. I prefer the term *unhoused neighbors* to challenge our thinking about who we are referring to and the forces acting upon them.

A key feature of dialogue is how participants find that the conversations linger in their minds long after the dialogue ends. This series highlighted the importance of seeing the humanity in everyone in our communities, that action comes from person-to-person connections, that we need to hear each other's stories and see connections of our shared dreams, goals and traumas, and in that way we can envision a way forward together. While participants explored various actions during the dialogue sessions and received emails with dialogue summaries and more suggested actions, many participants shared how the dialogues affected them long after the sessions ended. While I cannot summarize the influence on each participant's day-to-day activity after the dialogues, we can draw from some examples of how actions took shape.

Community-based action—We started the dialogues with top-down support and with high-level organizations helping us to understand the big picture around homelessness, but it was individual participants and activists who inspired us to activate ourselves, our families, and our own community organizations. We recognized the need for more neighbors to join the conversation and to support the large- and small-scale efforts in their communities. This included pushing for more safe parking locations in church parking lots, more acceptance of supportive housing, and a need to get landlords involved in seeing themselves as part of the solution. In particular, we have been asked to invite more landlords to future dialogues, as they are empowered to reduce rents, provide more shared housing, donate space, accept Section 8 Housing Choice vouchers (part of a federal rental assistance program), and commit to truly nondiscriminatory practices. Fostering partnership across organizations, landlords and other individuals is key to providing informed and innovative approaches to housing solutions.

Individual action—Connected to all of the efforts mentioned above were personal commitments to take more action, even when a pandemic made volunteering more of a risk and a challenge. Even those who attended one meeting or only had time to read our email updates were moved toward action. For example, we heard from a professor who participated in one dialogue and read all of the email updates and a director of a local counseling clinic who only read the emails, who both wanted to revisit whether they were doing enough to serve those who experience housing insecurity. As facilitator, I was moved by the SHARE! Housing peer support model and have partnered with a colleague to head up a new peer group for people who have experienced homelessness at some time in their life. Our goal is to introduce the dialogic model, empower peer facilitation and leave the group to run and sustain itself over time. There also was the participant who stayed connected with an unhoused participant, even through his ups and downs. She included him in her yoga classes, connecting him and subsequently countless others to pandemic-related stimulus checks, aiding him in replacing a stolen electric bicycle, and, most importantly, proving that there are people in the world who care—something he is desperately trying to convince others in the streets to believe. And a filmmaker who, once unhoused, is now showing her film in festivals and winning awards.

Conclusion

The final action to mention is for myself and our organization. We are committed to continuing the series, reshaping it as best we can to include all voices—especially those who could not participate in an online format. We have seen that the format of information sharing and community dialogue moves people away from ignorance to awareness, empathy and action. Participants have asked that our learning go even deeper and that we focus next on the root causes of homelessness, systems of inequality, and prevention. We will continue to revisit equity in our design. We need to constantly reflect on each dialogue to make sure that we are noticing whose voices are still missing, pushing to build those bridges so that our dialogues are that much richer. The dialogues played a role in that line of inquiry, always informing who we invited to present next. As facilitator, however, I experience an ongoing internal dialogue about the subjects we still haven't touched on, and who we still haven't included (and why) and whatever more we could be doing. While dialogues on homelessness cannot solve the roots of the problem, they provide the mechanism by which more people can feel their connection to these roots, break down the barriers of distancing between housed and unhoused neighbors and develop a commitment from participants to engage in empathic and actionable responses. This will help us to move from "us-and-them" mindsets to shared community responses. In closing, I leave you with a poem sent from a participant after our second dialogue in the series:

> my bittersweet human experience.
>
> the sweetest sound of angels,
> when 6 or 8 agents of light,
> voices rang out their good nights to me,
> in a parking lot, departing.
> saying goodbye, should always
> be so beautiful.
> i see so much bitter in the world,
> i have great sadness and pity for those who
> would stand in the light, but remain bitter

and in the dark.
to work the light, is hard and scary
cuz then the enemy can see you better.
if you could of heard what i heard during this
groups meeting. so many light knights.
expressing human grace and dignity to and for the lost.
i had forgotten,
many times during the group that bitter was out there in the world.

so i laughed with joy,
and cried for us all as we had to
leave and go back to live in
(The Real World)

mostly though i thank all of you.

—Joe Hawk

References

Allport G. W. (1954). *The Nature of Prejudice*. Reading, MA: Addison-Wesley; Pettigrew, T.F. (1971). *Racially Separate or Together?* New York: McGraw-Hill.

Pettigrew, T. F., & Tropp, L. R. (2000). "Does intergroup contact reduce prejudice: Recent meta-analytic findings." In S. Oskamp (Ed.), *The Claremont Symposium on Applied Social Psychology (Reducing prejudice and discrimination)* (p. 93–114). Lawrence Erlbaum Associates Publishers.

Schimel, J.& Pyszczynski, T. & Greenberg, J. & O'Mahen, H. & Arndt, J. (2000). "Running from the shadow: Psychological distancing from others to deny characteristics people fear in themselves." *Journal of Personality and Social Psychology*. 78. 446-62. 10.1037//0022-3514.78.3.446.

Article references:

https://everyoneinla.org/about-us/faq/

https://www.discoverlosangeles.com/media/facts-about-la

https://la.streetsblog.org/2020/06/19/thousands-housed-in-project-roomkey-in-los-angeles-but-nimbyism-lack-of-permanent-affordable-housing-blunt-progress/

https://www.csh.org/2017/02/affordable-supportive-housing-improves-neighborhoods/

https://link.springer.com/referenceworkentry/10.1007%2F978-94-007-0753-5_2306

https://www.smdp.com/agitating-for-change-through-art/183285

https://dschool.stanford.edu/resources/equity-centered-design-framework

Appendix One

Dialogue tools provided:
   a. Index cards and pens for taking notes
   b. Handouts explaining some basic dialogue tools below:

COMMUNICATION GUIDELINES FOR COURAGEOUS CONVERSATIONS

A -Assume good intent and take Accountability for negative impact
- When someone makes a mistake and offends you, assume that they didn't mean to do it. Remember that they likely have not had the chance yet to learn what you know about this topic/issue/word.
- When you accidentally offend someone else, you have to own the fact that you hurt them, even though you didn't mean to do it. Your good intention doesn't erase your negative impact.

S -Share airtime (take space, make space)
- Make sure that you are hearing from every person in your group, and that a few voices aren't dominating the conversation. Both introverts and extroverts need to challenge themselves to share airtime amongst the group.

P -Practice active listening
- Listen deeply enough to be changed by what you learn. Listen to understand more, not to respond, rebut, or refute.

I -Use "I" statements and speak from your own experience
- Speak for yourself, not for a group. Speak from your own experience instead of generalizing about others in your group, the organization, or other groups ("I" instead of "they," "we," and "you").

R -Respect confidentiality
- Share new lessons that you have learned, but leave the names and personal stories in the room. Dialogue only works when we can build trust and honor confidentiality.*

*Remember that this agreement does not override your duties as a Responsible Employee.

E -Everyone is an expert in their own experience
- Acknowledge, believe, and care about everyone else's experiences, especially when they are different from yours. When you hear something new, instead of doubting, remember that each person is an expert in their own experiences, and not in anyone else's.

Developed by the UCLA Intergroup Relations Program

DIALOGUE BASICS

HOW "DIALOGUE" DIFFERS FROM OTHER FORMS OF COMMUNICATION:

DISCUSSION
Present an idea
Seek answers
Sell, persuade, enlist
Share information
Solve a problem
Give answers Achieve preset goals

DEBATE
Advocate one perspective
Search for flaws in logic
Judge other viewpoints inferior
Stress disagreement
Present a "right" position
Defend one's own position
Win the argument

DIALOGUE
Listen without judgment
Listen with TING
Learn different perspectives
Broaden one's perspective
Find places of agreement
Allow for differences
Bring out areas of ambivalence
Explore thoughts and feelings
Express paradox & ambiguity
Unfold individual meaning
Make the implicit explicit
Articulate the unspoken
Discover collective meaning
Build relationships

ACTIVE LISTENING WITH "LARA"

- **L**isten actively, without interrupting, thinking about body language
- **A**ffirm the feelings behind what you heard
- **R**eflect back the details of what you heard, ask clarifying questions
- **A**dd your perspective

Appendix Two

We also introduced some additional guidelines from Weaving Community to support this new format:

- We will be present and not multitask
- We will avoid assumptions about others and listen first to understand them
- We will give time and encourage all voices, no matter how quiet or different
- We will trust each other to speak honestly
- We will respect each other's fears and vulnerabilities
- We will be patient with those unfamiliar with technology (this came in handy!)

Conference Session Extracts
From a conversation with participants considering the paper with Rebecca Cannara

Speaker: This [homelessness] is a universal issue. It's something that belongs to all of us no matter what, whether it's the men or the ladies. As soon as I go outside, within 300 yards, the only difference between me and the homeless people outside that I meet – the only difference – is the wall. It is the fundamental difference of me having a roof and a wall and them, being human beings on the outside of it. It is such a profound symbol of something that really does belong to everyone.

Rebecca: Thank you so much. Yes. I think that there are so many ways that we can see, when we start to look for it, how are we dehumanizing people in our lives. What does that look like? That is something unfortunately where we can find examples maybe too often, right? Thank you. One other person who would be willing to share something from that came out of their smaller group?

Speaker: Okay, so in our group we had someone who has just received her doctorate. And then me and a few other individuals that also work with the Department of Corrections. In our group we were basically dealing with reflection and understanding how reflection plays a big part in moving the dialogue forward. Also, the matter of not letting our own experiences and emotions cloud things. Not cloud the room first of all, then not cloud their space. Being aware of the atmosphere and being aware of what is being put into the atmosphere—whether it's through what is being said, or the emotions being put out there. And being able to really utilize the bystand—being able to take a step back and really understand how that's going to impact the communication, and impact the dialogue moving forward or being at a standstill altogether.

Speaker: On the equity piece, we all have a role to play. We all bring something to the table and we want to make sure that we have the right people in the room, and the right voices being heard, so that there can be something accomplished. You don't want to have people in a room that are just there but they're not going to do anything, or they're not going to put in their views. So, you want it to be equitable across-the-board, with everybody's voice being heard and the services being put out there to really match the need, so that we can do our piece.

Speaker: Another person from the Department of Corrections here! We talked about how, especially during these Covid times, we're really realizing the impact the different community meetings were having. I think, Rebecca, that you mentioned this as well. We were having these Re-entry Council meetings in our respective areas. We had our community partners from the probation, the prisons and the jails, the police and the courts—all those people meeting together. Personally, I think that we're really seeing the impact of not having those meetings readily available to us. I talked to some people who are clear across the state from me, working in these prisons across the state, who were saying, "We're looking for resources in your area. And, you know, we're really seeing the impact of not having the opportunity to have those meetings in person." Granted, you know, we have this whole digital thing where you can meet over Google Meet, but it's just different, I think. And I feel like our clients, our probationers and our offenders are probably seeing the impact and maybe just not knowing where it's coming from. But also, at the end of the day, I think it comes from community buy-in, because the Department of Corrections or other agencies can want to have more resources all day, every day for our probationers and our offenders. But realistically we need that funding from the government and from the community, and we need our community to want to support us and everything that we want to do too. So, that's why I definitely miss those re-entry meetings and those different community partnerships that I think were a lot stronger prior to the pandemic.

Speaker: One of the pieces that Peter and Jane bring out, and that we have experienced in our dialogue, is that re-entry is like a journey. As we've mentioned before, and as the Chief of probation mentioned, the re-entry piece starts at the sentencing. But it can also be viewed as starting at the arrest where the individual begins their encounter with law enforcement—and how we all have a part in that re-entry process. I just know that while I have a captive audience, it's a three-year Resettlement Journey. I think that our department is doing a good job on talking about some of those topics that are hard to fix, if you will. But I do think that one population that we miss out are our offenders and probationers who are held in the regional jails, just because there we don't have any services. And most of our population is on community side and is held in our regional jails. So while we are making great strides, and you know that the whole purpose of dialogue is that there's never an end to it. You have to continue to want to do things better and do things differently because your situation is always going to change and you need to constantly be evaluating it.

Rebecca: Thank you. I think that last point, this is especially important too, to keep rethinking and rethinking how we bring this, whatever the dialogue can bring forward for us in each of our situations, and to consider who's missing. I think you said the work that was done is in the prisons as opposed to the regional jails. Is that right? Sorry, I may not be using the terms properly.

Speaker: No, that's okay. It's that on the community (probation) side of the house, what we're saying is that most of the people who are released don't serve time in the Department of Corrections. A lot of our individuals, those with shorter sentences, come out of the regional jails. So, unfortunately they're not given the opportunity for programming like we have in the department. In the department we have excellent programming, which is much better, and a good resource.

Speaker: I am with probation in Prince William county, Northern Virginia. There, our district Chief recognized the problem about people being released from the jails without receiving any re-entry services. So she worked closely with our local regional jail, and we developed a re-entry jail program which some of the offenders are going through, and they are getting referred to the same services before they come out of the regional jails and come to us in the department.

Rebecca: Great. Thank you. So there are examples of it already happening. It is just always very impressive to hear the examples of how dialogue has been infused within the Department of Corrections in Virginia. It has definitely inspired me, as I told people in the breakout. It's inspired me to be able to talk to the businesses or the schools or the smaller groups that we work with to say, if they can do it with all those thousands of people in Virginia, this is something we can do in our smaller circles.

Postscript
The author's reflections, written some months after the conference

After presenting my paper last conference on a series of dialogues between housed and unhoused neighbors in Los Angeles, California, USA, and after a year and a half of pandemic, my perspective is cemented in the belief that dialogues that build bridges are essential to promote human (re)connection and to encourage people to take action for people in their communities.

While I always grow personally from a dialogue that I facilitate or participate in, I am deeply grateful for the many new connections I've made from our last two Academy conferences. New dialogues have formed as a result: a post-election series for US-based participants and an international series on homelessness in partnership with Bobby Frazier, Jane Ball and Bernhard Holtrop. We carried out the post-election series for over six months, building powerful connections between women from a variety of backgrounds across the geographic US, and we continue to hold our international dialogues on homelessness, bringing together participants from over five countries. While there has been much common ground and new actions emerging from participants, I find the challenges in providing dialogues on homelessness continuing to be both with logistics and about equity. Logistically, we must find a time that works for our most marginalized participants and consistently show up at that time. And from an equity lens, we must continue to ask: Who is present and who is missing? What barriers have enabled this? What are we doing to alleviate it?

I also experience a slight tension between generative and intergroup dialogue. Both formats intentionally remain very open to whatever arises in the group, but the intergroup dialogue model more often directly names and addresses power dynamics and biases that may be present. At the same time, intergroup dialogue's format may feel too structured for people who are looking for a more generative experience. While this tension exists, I find myself landing in somewhere in the middle at the original format I used for the Los Angeles dialogues on homelessness series: frontloading time to inform the group of new concepts, experiences, and histories, and following that informational portion with time for the dialogue to emerge around what this all means for each participant. In that way, we expand our awareness and circles of empathy while we make space for the dialogic process and for envisioning action.

In my own life, this past year of dialogue has truly influenced me to leave a secure career in online education and commit full time to working on behalf of human rights and dialogue. I now have time and mental space to join committees, provide additional dialogues, and advocate for policy change.

Dialogue and Managing Societal Conflicts

Bernard le Roux

This paper tells the story of a mediation between a local authority and the parents of two autistic adult children. I'll explore the results of the mediation (it was successful for one parent and less so for the other), and will describe its unexpected outcome, a decision by politicians to order a larger public dialogue to improve the way in which the local authority cares for people with disabilities. It is my hope that this story will inspire others to see how dialogue and mediation together can be used to improve both simple and complex problems in the public sector.

On Dialogue and Mediation

Dialogue is the tool that I use when I mediate and when I negotiate. Unfortunately, the word *dialogue* has been used to describe a large variety of conversations. In my view, all conversation is certainly not dialogue. The dialogue I aim for is a conversation where participants are able to move from defensiveness and self-centeredness towards openness, and from confusion to a place of clarity and empowerment. It is a conversation that moves beyond fixed positions, 'going in circles' and deadlock to a conversation that flows. In this paper I use *dialogue* and *mediation* with some overlap. While clearly they are not synonymous – not all mediations are dialogic and vice versa – I believe the principles of good practice apply to both. In this paper I want to demonstrate how a dialogic stance serves in other disciplines, particularly in mediation in this case.

Note: I have used italics in the text to add my reflections to the events I describe.

The Assignment

My involvement in this story began when I received a call asking if I would offer mediation services to help resolve the conflict between the local authority and the parents of the adult children whom I'll call Marcia and Albert (not their real names). I met with a representative for the authority, who explained that the conflict had a long history. The parents were unhappy with the home that cared for their children, and particularly with the manager in charge of the municipality's department for specialised care of people with disabilities. I was told that these two sets of parents were particularly difficult. The account I was given portrayed them as very critical, complaining regularly. They had written to and met with various leaders within the local authority and with council members about the inadequate care provided by the home.

After numerous complaints from the parents, the office dealing with complaints had conducted an inquiry which concluded that the local authority was not at fault. It had consistently followed procedures, and the staff at the home were happy with the leadership and guidance that they received from their superiors. This, of course, did nothing to placate the parents, who continued to complain. It was clear that Marcia and Albert were not well. Politicians on the council finally demanded of officials that something more be done to deal with the conflict. The attempts that had been made to resolve the issue seemed not to have made any difference and it was suggested that an outside mediator be called in.

It is common in Sweden that conflicts between individual citizens and public authorities are dealt with by a combination of inquiry and decision. In the most poorly managed cases the enquiry part is left out and decisions are made from the top without considering the views of the unhappy citizens. Inquiry may consist of meetings to 'listen to views or suggestions' or could involve an expert who advises the leadership on the decisions that need to be made. In cases where the issue involves more people, these consultative meetings are referred to as 'public dialogue'. It is not at all common that mediation is considered as an option. My first thought was that the conflict had either escalated and could no longer be dealt with by the authorities or that this was a particularly enlightened municipality.

Having heard the official version of the story, I accepted the assignment and proposed that I start off by interviewing the involved parties before attempting any kind of mediation to explore a constructive way forward.

Having worked as both a mediator and facilitator of public dialogue, I have learned much through making mistakes. For me, dialogue is the tool I use in public dialogue and in helping others manage their conflicts. One common mistake is to decide on the design of a process before understanding the nature of the problem. The problem is often more complex than the way in which is first presented. It may contain more conflict than meets the eye. Different degrees of complexity and levels of conflict escalation may require differently designed processes. One way of learning more about the problem is to meet with the involved parties before attempting a dialogue. There are a number of reasons for this, which I refer to below.

The Initial Interviews

I booked meetings with the parties directly involved in the dispute: the manager for the homes and the parents. I knew that, unless the conflict was based on a simple misunderstanding, there would probably be other parties involved and more interviews needed.

Meeting with parties before attempting any kind of dialogue is extremely important. I believe strongly that nobody can be forced to participate in a dialogue of this kind. They have to agree to participate and feel safe enough to engage with those they regard as their adversaries in the conflict. Getting people 'into the room' to speak to each other is the first threshold to cross. The prior meetings are essential to establishing trust in the process and in the mediator or facilitator, without which any meaningful dialogue is extremely difficult.

My first interview was with the manager responsible for the homes that care for adults with intellectual disabilities. We met at the council offices. From his perspective, Marica and Albert's parents were unreasonable. They were 'the problem'. He agreed that both Marica and Albert were not well, but attributed this in part to the behaviour of the parents and in part to normal swings in people with autism. He also felt that he was not always supported by his colleagues and superiors in his approach to the situation and bore the brunt of their resentment and anger. He felt that he had dealt with the complaints correctly, had followed all legal requirements for homes of this kind and fulfilled his responsibility as a manager to protect his staff against constant 'criticism and abuse' from these particular parents. I tried to listen with empathy and without judgement and felt genuine compassion for him, as the situation clearly affected him negatively.

My firm's work with larger societal conflicts has taught us that the mediators' or facilitators' attitude is far more important than the skills they employ. The first of these meta-skills or attitudes is being impartial (not taking sides) or remaining 'multi-partial' (being on everybody's side rather than not being on anybody's side and helping them to say what needs to be said). The second, and most important factor, is what we refer to as neutrality. It is similar to the word dialogue, *in that it means different things to different people. For me it implies being empathetically present and non-judgemental at the same time. It is an attitude that is essential in order to establish trust for the process and for the facilitator or mediator. Being empathetically present means that I, as mediator or facilitator, feel what others are feeling and can place myself in their shoes. Being non-judgemental implies that I do not agree or disagree with those I listen to or those who participate in the dialogue. Neutrality is a role that I enter into when facilitating or mediating.*

My next meetings were with the parents, each separately. They chose to meet me at their respective homes. Again, I tried to be present, listen attentively and ask questions without making any kind of judgement. This required me to suspend all that I had heard from the manager about these 'problematic' people. Their stories differed from each other, but there were many similar themes. Both parents accused the manager of being incompetent and saw him as the root cause of the problems that had caused the condition of their children to worsen considerably. I will not go into detail, but the stories I heard about the state of their adult children moved me deeply. They were clearly not well. In addition, the parents felt completely marginalised by the staff of the home and by the leadership in the local authority. Events left them sad, worried and angry. I noted that they chose to speak mostly from their formal position as legal custodians rather than as parents. When I asked about this, they replied that they had no legal rights beyond custodianship as parents, as both Marcia and Albert were adults. The law only allowed legal custodians to engage with the authorities to ensure adequate care for their wards. The manager had been very clear about this and they had little opportunity for contact beyond the formally mandated information and follow-up meetings.

In our experience of working with the authorities on a wide range of issues involving citizens, we have often noted that the relationship is very formal. This is a way for the authorities to avoid getting into the 'messiness' of emotions. Emotional citizens are something that they see as a necessary evil, and one that one has to put up with as an official. That this creates a sense of not being taken seriously and eventually a deep sense of being marginalised, does not seem to play an important role to those who choose formality as their mode of relating. Hearing a person out, nodding sympathetically and saying that one understands does not change the sense of marginalisation experienced. In fact it can lead to a breakdown of trust when a sympathetic response is combined with an attitude of formality.

Needless to say, it took some time for me to understand how both sets of parents viewed the problem. I consistently tried to steer the conversations away from possible solutions. We first needed to understand the nature of the problem. We would hopefully be able to address ways of resolving the problems or improving a fraught situation collectively when we were engaged in a dialogue.

It is very common for us to jump quickly to solutions. It comes from a sense that we know what the problem is and that the solution is simple. This ignores the possibility that the other party or parties may view the problem differently. In this case, after all three interviews, it was clear that each person held very different opinions on what constituted the problem. Both sides appeared to see the other as the problem and disagreed as to whether the care that Marcia and Albert were receiving was adequate. One glimmer of agreement seemed to be that Marcia's and Albert's mental health had deteriorated over the past year.

Yet More Interviews

My conversations with the primary parties in the conflict helped me to identify issues that seemed interwoven with the central disagreement, and other groups of people who were involved. A clear red flag was the manager's statement that he was not being supported by his colleagues in a different department. It became clear that the parents had regular contact with the department that evaluated the support needed by people with intellectual disabilities, and who allocated resources required to meet these needs. The manager's department and the needs assessment department had different views on the level of care that Marcia and Albert were receiving. Also, the staff at the care home were singled out by the parents as unapproachable. This was attributed both by the parents and the manager as a way of protecting the staff against abuse by the parents. The directive had clearly been to formalise all contact with the parents.

A characteristic of complex problems is that one often only discovers the nature of the problem once one starts to work with it. This was a classic case where the conflict was a symptom of a much larger problem.

In my conversations with the staff responsible for assessments and resource allocation, I learned that they were critical of the way in which the manager responsible for the care homes worked. They did not regard the changes that were made in response to their resource assessments for Marcia and Albert as adequate, and they communicated this to the parents. In addition, this department was clear that it supported the involvement of parents (not only as legal custodians) as part of a more inclusive way of caring for people with intellectual disabilities.

Double messages are a common cause of conflict. An individual who says one thing and means another – or acts in a way that indicates that they believe something else – creates confusion and results in the eroding of trust. When an organisation contradicts itself in this way it has the same result. In this case it left the parents confused and angry. In their roles as legal custodians this was evidence that the manager was incompetent and that the local authority was not properly qualified to provide the care that their wards were legally entitled to.

Before I had the opportunity to speak to the staff at the care home, the situation suddenly changed. The head of the department in charge of care for disabled people gave notice that he was stepping down and the manager for the care homes was shifted to the same department as that for need assessment and resource allocation. If this sounds confusing and complicated, it was indeed so. Without getting bogged down in details, the result was that the manager for the care homes now belonged to a new department. He had to adjust to the department's views on adequate and effective care of people with autism and indeed other intellectual disabilities. The care home staff saw this as the leadership giving in to the parents' demands and indicated that they were taking up the problem with their union. Additionally, this was their way of saying that they supported their manager.

Complex problems are characterised by the fact that they are dynamic. Any intervention affects it and results in shifts. These shifts can appear suddenly and unexpectedly. In this case the focus on the problem seemed to shine the light on much more than the interpersonal conflict between individuals. There was clearly a problem within the organisation itself. Upon inquiry, this problem had been glossed over for a considerable period. It had never been addressed directly.

We were now faced with a dilemma. Could we focus on the conflict between the parents and the manager without first dealing with the larger, more fundamental issue of disagreement within organisational on the way that people with disabilities were cared for? Fortunately, this dilemma was partly resolved for us by a clear statement from the head of the social services. She decided that the approach that would be followed for care homes would be one of collaboration with parents and between the different units within the larger organisation. I say 'partly resolved' because, while a top-down decision may clarify an issue, it does not necessarily resolve a deeper ideological conflict.

As a mediator or facilitator, one often needs to be flexible in dealing with complex problems. It may be necessary to limit a dialogue to that which lies within the power of the involved parties to change. In this case, it was the issue of whether a more rational approach and a 'client-centred' approach could be combined, and, if so, how *had to be left until later.*

Besides the interviews I mentioned, I met with the staff, the director of the local authority, the head of social services and with Albert. Although I had visited Marcia, we felt that it was not appropriate to ask her about her situation as she was largely unresponsive to people she didn't know.

Designing the Dialogue

During the preparatory interview phase I asked myself a central question: who needs to speak to whom, and what do they need to speak to each other about? Which conversations were needed and who would be involved in each of these? At this point the issues were clearer. There seemed to be a general agreement regarding the fact that Marcia's and Albert's situation needed to be improved. How could collaboration be achieved in order to improve their situation? The parents would be involved both in their roles as parents and as legal custodians. As parents they had a unique kind of experience to offer and, as legal custodians, they needed to ensure that the level of care given to their wards was sufficient.

Designing a dialogue is important when there are multiple issues and multiple parties involved. Sometimes one needs to negotiate on ground rules or on whom should be present. It is also important for the parties to agree to the appropriateness of the facilitator or mediator. Having gained their trust in the initial conversations, this was no problem. Involving parties in decisions relating to the form, the frame and the content of the dialogue sets the tone for the dialogue itself and clearly defines the role of the facilitator.

I asked the central parties whom they felt needed to be part of the conversations and received suggestions. After verifying that the parties were happy with the way in which the process of addressing issue was proposed – the form of the meetings and the parties involved – we were ready to start the dialogue.

The Dialogue with All Stakeholders

We decided on two separate meetings, one each for Marcia and Albert. The staff from the care home would be present, as well as the nurse and the person responsible for resource allocation, as she had had contact with the parents. The meetings would be held at the council offices. We reserved two hours for the first meeting and allowed for the possibility of follow-up meetings.

The two meetings differed from each other in many respects, each involving parents with different personalities. In both conversations, however, the issue of collaboration was the central focus. The local authority understood that the marginalisation of the parents had contributed to the parents' criticism and protests. The parents recognised that their critical attitude resulted in a defensive attitude amongst those caring for their children. As this was established, the conversation could then focus on how the situation in each case could be improved. In both cases we identified the changes that were necessary and agreed on a way forward for both Marcia and Albert. It was not all plain sailing, however, and there were many fiery exchanges as the willingness to view the other's perspective gave way to defensiveness and criticism.

In facilitating dialogue where tension is present, I use the simple tools of mirroring, summary and deepening questions from the Transformative Mediation approach. In addition, I draw from the approach of Arnold Mindell as translated and simplified by Myra Lewis for group facilitation. The notion that tension arising indicates an issue that is not being addressed adequately, thereby hindering the possibility of speaking about it, inspires our practice.

The two dialogues resulted in two plans of action – one each for Marcia and Albert – based on an intention to collaborate.

In Albert's case the shift was clear, and the plan has resulted in a much-improved situation for him, his family and the co-workers that care for him. The shift during the negotiation of a 'new order' – a new way of collaborating – was enabled because those concerned, and especially Albert's parents, changed the way they thought about the other. They were willing to admit to mistakes and to learn from them. They were willing to make new mistakes and see these as opportunities to refine the effort at collaboration. Albert would move into his own apartment adjacent to a care home and the staff would collaborate with Albert's mother in finding ways that suited his needs of both care and freedom to make his own decisions.

In Marcia's case the result was mixed. Her situation has improved, and she is much happier and healthier than before. There have been highlights and small breakthroughs as greater collaboration has been established. But the ingrained patterns in the relationship between staff and parents resurfaced again after a time. Despite the plan and good intentions, no clear shift had occurred during the dialogue – or if there was, it was only fleeting. The parents have chosen to act from their position as legal custodians and remain critical of the staff. The staff remain wary and suspicious of the parents, and feel that they constantly must remain on the defensive. It is clear that more dialogue is necessary here. But the question that arises is – and this is something we notice in many interactions between the public and the authorities – what does one do if one party refuses (or is unable) to let go of their fixed position?

An Unexpected Outcome

Towards the end of the mediation assignment the head of social services approached me with a request to assist them in an enquiry aiming at improving the care of intellectually disabled people within the municipality. The assignment, initiated by the council, contained a special condition: the enquiry must take the form of a dialogue between all the stakeholders. We have since completed the first phase of this enquiry, an inventory of perspectives through interviews with stakeholders, to determine the nature of the problem.

While it is a story for another paper, I want to mention here an outcome of our mediation / process: it has changed the attitudes of a number of central stakeholders and built a solid basis upon which to build a larger public dialogue process. From experience I know that one cannot take this for granted.

Reflections on Complex Problems

The world can be viewed as a complex network of relationships, in that everything relates to everything else. This is true for society as much as it is for our physical ecosystems. No part exists in isolation.

Problems arise through the way we view this interrelated, interconnected whole – and then, of course, how we act on these thoughts. In particular our insistence on measuring results, on rules and standardised manuals, often gives rise to problems. This is especially true when a situation is part of a larger dynamic whole. Our rational, metrics-based approaches are bound to exclude aspects of the whole.

Marginalisation inevitably leads to tension. If not dealt with, it will escalate into conflict. Conflicts can be constructive if seen as indicators of necessary change within a given system. But if ignored they can also become destructive. Having lived on the mountainside outside of Cape Town, I value fire as a metaphor for conflict. The Cape Fynbos (the natural vegetation that occurs in the Western Cape Province) needs fire from time to time to regenerate itself. Old growth is cleared, and new plants appear. Some seeds even need the fire in order to germinate. Similarly, the heat of conflict, or tension, is useful – if not essential – for the functioning of society. At the same time, it can be destructive. Sometimes it can be prevented. And sometimes we need to accept it as a necessary force.

On the Measurable and the Unknowable

Jonna Bornemark, a Swedish philosopher, has written about the problems that arise when we adhere religiously to the New Public Management approach to organising society. In her book *Det omätbaras renässans : En uppgörelse med pedanternas världsherravälde* [*The Renaissance of the Immeasurable: A Reconciliation with the World Domination of the Pedants*] (Volante, 2018), she highlights the tension between the desire to name, sort and measure and the attitude of embracing the 'immeasurable' – a conflict that she traces back to the Renaissance philosophers Nicolas Cusanus, Giordano Bruno and René Descartes. Her thesis is that we have one-sidedly adhered to the rational (Latin: *ratio*) at the expense of the unknowable and unmeasurable (Latin: *intellectus*), and that we need to find a balance between these seeming opposites.

You may ask why this is important. In my experience, many of the conflicts that arise in society stem from an approach that is rooted firmly in the rational, and that ignores the living, fluid and undefinable aspects of life. This is abstract, so let me illustrate it with an example from the mediation/dialogue story.

The local authority had followed all the laws and prescriptions in their care of Albert and Marcia. They planned. They measured results. Their budgets were in balance. What they failed to take into account, however, were the parents' concerns and their wish to contribute to the care of their adult children. The law does not provide for this; it is, in fact premised on the autonomy of the persons who need to be cared for. The parents, for their part, felt marginalised, ignored and sidelined. They had adapted and acted from their legal custodian status. They argued from a legal perspective that the authorities were not following the law. They gathered evidence. They enlisted legal experts. The manager defended his actions. The relationship became one in which only one side could be right. The rest is history – but it is a history that repeats itself all too often. Nobody wins a war and, sadly, the victims are often others than those who are fighting to be right.

The Thorny Problem of Stubbornly Rational People

Often the openness of one party creates an openness in the other. When people remain stuck in a role or in a clearly adversarial position, however, it is very difficult to enter into dialogue. The challenge is to be able to move out of a particular framework – for example, the legal framework (in the case of Marcia and Albert's parents, the designation of custodians) or that of measuring results – into a broader context where dreams, feelings and wishes can be shared. If one party regards this as a weakness and identifies strongly with a rational approach, unable to move beyond adversity into a shared space of exploration, resolution becomes nearly impossible. This was a factor in the case outlined in this paper. Much is written on how to resolve this deadlock. Usually it involves some kind of compromise or a willingness to delve more deeply into more personal issues that may be obstructing true collaboration.

Final Reflections

As mediator and facilitator, I find that maintaining an attitude of non-judgement, offering an empathetic presence, not excluding issues or people and valuing resistance and tension as indicators of necessary change are central to both dialogue and meditation. The tools I use are helpful but need to be used sparingly – fixed methods or formulaic approaches should, in my view, be avoided. The mediator should be viewed as a co-creative party rather than the leader of the process.

As with each process, there are, upon reflection, areas that could have been done better. As part of my practice I will consider what would have made a difference. At the same time, there are certain parts of the process that worked well and that confirm the practice we have developed in dialogues of all kinds. I hope that this paper has given some insight into how dialogue can be used to resolve conflicts between citizens and authorities, and how a dialogic approach can provide a useful foundation for other disciplines.

Conference Session Extracts

From a conversation with participants considering the paper with Bernard le Roux

Speaker: I didn't think I would enjoy this paper this much, to be completely honest,

but I really did enjoy it. It applies when dealing with any conflict, not just social conflict. It could be any workplace conflict, because we only know some things, then when something is mentioned we get that aha moment. We can be so caught up in policy and procedure that we forget people are human beings and that we do actually need to empathise.

What I shared in my group was that I've been in a foster care system with my biological aunt, but she's my mom. She said to me, the worst thing you can do is to have pity for someone, which is sympathizing, because that doesn't help them. The best thing you can do is understand where they're coming from, how they feel, why they feel that way, so that you can start from the root and help them help everyone arrive at the same place, and to see how they can contribute in this space. And understand that they have the responses and the solutions within themselves. You don't actually have to do anything. You just help them move, which is facilitating the process.

So I enjoyed the paper because it brought that full circle for me. We always say, don't operate from the place of emotion. However, we also should be clear whether or not it is emotion we're operating from, or are we operating from a different relationship with a different situation? For instance, the parents operated from a custodial place. Maybe operating from a parental place would be perceived as operating from emotion, but really that's just a different part of the relationship that they had with the individuals that were being discussed.

And so it's not emotions, it's just that they had a different level of understanding and consciousness about the situation and about how to help those people. They felt marginalized, because they had to stay within this margin that was the policy and a procedure placed by the other side. They felt misunderstood. In our breakout session, I used the word *bilingual* as a parent and the custodian. I'm bilingual, where these people are only speaking one language. To mediate is to translate or to help everyone to speak the same language. Sometimes we don't know how to move between one, two or three languages.

Bernard: Brilliant. Thank you so much. I will remember this bilingual and singular language.

Speaker: In our group, we discussed formality in corrections, from the perspective that it was created to prevent being placed in a position of compromise. When we're empathetic, it is sometimes the gateway to being sympathetic, and thereby you may be placed in a position of compromise and being manipulated. I think that in different levels of corrections there are some aspects of dialogue that we can use, but we have to put certain parameters in place so that we are not compromised – for our own protection and for the protection of the population that were responsible for as well. As they are ready to be released into society, I think we can practice more of the use of dialogue. But quite frankly, for some that have no release dates, there has to be a barrier there in place for protection.

Speaker: Sometimes people misinterpret conflict as always in a negative aspect, when sometimes conflict can be good. It's just like a car battery where you need a positive and a negative to go forward. So it's all about how we handle conflict in the workplace. In my method that I use at the institution, when I got two parties involved, I deal with each one individually, then I bring them both together. Individually you can hear each party better, so when they come together, they can utilise their voice better. But you got to be able to create safe space. That way I want you to listen to what I'm saying, and I want to hear what you're saying. That way, when you get each party in the room, it enhances that level of respect. Sometimes when someone is talking, you want to cut them off, but it's teaching them discipline. Wait a minute. It goes back and forth, back and forth.

Speaker: Thank you for your wonderful paper and this session. Conflicts are a lot of my colleagues' work, and they have become professionals dealing with conflicts. They stay proactive in conflict situations and they are afraid of conflicts. You have to do self-reflection and dialogue with yourself. We can all develop these skills if we want to. These are skills that can be learned.

Speaker: I work with probation, and a lot of times the most escalated conflicts are with the family members of the probationers, rather than the subjects themselves. I personally loved so much how you expanded on that marginalization, and the feeling that your voice is not being heard is really when you said that temperature starts to rise. That's a great red flag. What is not being heard or validated? A question: what do you do with an individual that's either unwilling or unable to let go of their side?

Bernard: Mediation must be a voluntary process. People do get stuck. The conversation gets stuck. One simple tool is to reflect back. A person will hear themselves and how they sound and very often adjust because they realise how they sound to others. Another tool is to ask questions that take us to a deeper level, something like, "What are you feeling? What is the emotion behind that?" Or, "What is your belief based on?" It helps not only the person speaking, but the entire a group to open up to a deeper, more real conversation, not just an argument about facts and about laws and about regulations.

Speaker: In our group, we noticed that you set the stage, set the scene, because you interviewed different individuals so that you can make sure you had everybody in the room that needed to be there to discuss the issues at hand. I just kind of want to know, how did you come to that through mediation? Did you find that it's what you needed to do, or that it was a good way of going about it? Because it also seems that in dialogue, if we know differences with the parties, we can make sure everybody's in the room that needs to be there.

Bernard: Let me try. I can imagine that it would be the case in an organisation. People may be resisting having this conversation. So, you ask what it would take, or what would help you need to have the conversation with the other side? And often they would suggest that if we have this conversation, we want to make sure that it is safe, that there are rules or, or we want to set the rules together or whatever it might be. So what happens before the meeting, in order to get people into the room, is often a very sensitive negotiation process. And in a way you can see it as a dialogue about the dialogue they will have when they speak directly to each other. It is via the mediator, to find a way in which they can simply enter into the room and speak to each other. So, it's the voluntary nature, which is really important here, and really working with the resistance and honoring it. And valuing it as potential safeguard, because people know what they fear and why they fear it, and you don't. I don't know if it answers your question?

Speaker: It does. I see it as a means of preparation before you even get into the dialogue.

Postscript
The author's reflections, written some months after the conference

When I wrote the initial text, my understanding of the Dialogue inspired by David Bohm was limited. Even though I had read several books by Bohm, read Bill Isaacs' book on dialogue, and had several conversations several people at the Academy, I was constantly confused. I had a sense that there was something that I was missing but couldn't put my finger on what it was. I was trying very hard to understand what this 'dialogue' that everybody was speaking about looked like and I couldn´t see it.

The answer started suggesting itself during the conference and in an unexpected way. It was in meeting people who were practicing dialogue that I realised that I had focused almost entirely on intervention and worked with dialogue as a thing or a tool, whereas the dialogue David Bohm inspired seemed to aim at a new way of thinking and acting.

An image might help to explain this. Specialist doctors and drugs treat the symptoms of illness, but do not address the root of the problem itself. If we know that pollution in the environment is causing health problems, and we only provide the community with good doctors and drugs, we are not solving the problem. In fact, we might be contributing to it by luring people into thinking that medical care is the only solution. In the same way, mediation is a specialist intervention which seldom leads to changes in the system that causes the conflict itself.

In speaking to people who work with the Virginia Correctional Services, I realised that the work that was being done there was changing the way the system works. Above all, it was creating a shift in the way people relate to each other. I came to realise that sustainable change requires a *dialogic approach* and not dialogue as an intervention or a tool. In fact, I started wondering if it does justice to the work being done by speaking of dialogue as a thing, a noun.

My insight? There is value in mediation as a way of dealing with crises, but it is far more important to focus on sustainable change by creating the space for a dialogic way of relating and acting.

Transforming Care for the Elderly through Dialogue

Lars-Åke Almqvist

The development of the Corona pandemic in Sweden has led to an intense debate about elderly care and how it should be designed for the future. Today there is a great consensus among politicians that care for the elderly requires more resources, and employees need better employment conditions.

Government-sponsored elderly care has come into focus now because about two-thirds of all deaths have occurred within that sector. There have been major shortcomings in the availability of protective equipment and in the handling of hygiene routines. In many municipalities, 30-40% of all working hours are conducted by hourly wage earners. This means great staff mobility and poor continuity in the contact between staff and users. The same situation applies in private care facilities.

This paper is a follow-up to my earlier paper, "Economics and Time Management as a Vehicle for Dialogue", written for the 2018 Academy of Professional Dialogue conference. In it I described in depth how our firm, Alamanco, established dialogic practices for all leaders and employees working at several care facilities in Swedish municipalities. Because of their dialogue-centred approach to management they were resilient and open to collaboration, as I have outlined, and therefore well prepared to manage the challenges of past months. In this paper I offer updates and perspective, using examples from three different municipalities who have had no cases of Coronavirus in their care homes or in-home elderly care. Data from health authorities in Sweden shows that, while in those municipalities in which Coronavirus was documented, the three municipalities described here had none. They have a stable organisation with staff, a great commitment from leaders and staff. They rapidly decided to deal with the situation and didn´t wait for directives from authorities or government.

Staff Right

A concept that is fundamental to Alamanco's approach is *Staff Right,* an educational program with the following purposes:

- Develop a common understanding and a common language between management and employees on how to analyse and manage personnel costs
- Develop business management that is based on a holistic view
- Create a consensus on staffing, placement and use of working hours

Work on developing the Staff Right concept began in 2003 in collaboration with Uppsala, which is Sweden's fourth largest city. We wanted to understand why there are so many in elderly care who have a temporary job or work involuntarily part-time. The political leadership also had an interest in developing an organisation with better continuity and quality. All of our Staff Right education uses Dialogue at its core. Because of my own background and career experience, it has been natural to mainly work in municipalities and their organisations for elderly care.

In total Alamanco has worked in 70 out of the 190 municipalities in Sweden that offer elderly care. This means that we have worked with 36.8% of the total. We also had an assignment for a large private care company between 2009-2011, involving about 1800 employees.

How is Swedish Elderly Care Organised?

Sweden has a strongly decentralized social structure. Its constitution gives every citizen a pronounced individual freedom in relation to what decisions an authority can make. This is an important reason why Sweden has chosen a different strategy for the Corona pandemic. Based on our constitution, it is not possible to introduce a general lockdown of society. Citizens have full freedom of movement within the country and across the country's borders. This freedom can only be partially restricted.

The public sector is divided into three levels: state, region and municipalities, with decisions being made at as local a level as possible. The municipalities are obliged through a special law, the Social Services Act, to ensure that citizens who need care for the elderly receive it. About 80% of elderly care is provided by the municipalities themselves; the rest is offered by private providers. The private contractors work on behalf of the municipalities. The municipality is ultimately responsible for ensuring that there is access to elderly care, though they can choose to transfer part of the operation to private companies through public procurement. Some municipalities have introduced models of freedom of choice, which means that citizens can, to a certain extent, choose their providers. All elderly care is financed for the most part through taxes and to a lesser extent by fees paid by users. A number of government agencies carry out inspections and offer advice and instruction on how to care for the elderly.

The elderly care field is a female-dominated labour market, with more than 90% of the employees being women. Many are temporarily employed. Approximately 30-40% of all working hours are performed by hourly contract workers, and only 52% work full-time. This means that there is a great need for recruitment. Up to 50,000 employees need to be hired every year for many years to come.

Sweden's *Municipalities and Regions* is an employers' organisation for the municipal sector. In 2018 they reached an agreement with Kommunal, Sweden's largest union, that full-time employment will become the norm. Employers have calculated how many fewer people they need to hire if each employee wants to work more hours. For Kommunal, it is a gender-equality issue. Women should be able to get a salary that makes them financially independent. This means a major cultural change. It will take a long time to implement.

To this context we add the Coronavirus.

Swedish Elderly Care and the Corona Pandemic

Sweden has received international attention in several different ways because our country has chosen a different strategy than other countries. Because of the decentralized structure of society, as outlined above, the government and authorities have not made any decisions that would entail a lockdown of society. The country's strategy has been based on information and advice from public health officials. While the number of people who may meet in different contexts has been restricted, great responsibility has been placed on individual citizens.

The Swedish Health and Care Inspectorate (IVO) has inspected 1,700 nursing homes across the country. In 91 of these homes, IVO has found serious shortcomings. These mainly relate to the way leadership operates, and to the staff's employment conditions. It is important to have leadership and continuity in staffing. Many temporary employees, who often lack vocational training, make it difficult to maintain good hygiene routines. Those who are paid by the hour cannot afford to shutter at home if they are ill. Swedish employees do not receive sick pay from their employer.

In total, about 5,500 people have died in Sweden due to Covid 19. Of these, 89% were over 70 years old and 49% were over 85 years old. Just under half – 47% – lived in special housing. Another 25% had home care. Added to this, there are major regional differences in how the Corona pandemic has affected different parts of the country. Forty municipalities have been particularly affected and account for almost 70% of the cases in nursing homes.

The developments with the pandemic have led to an intense debate about elderly care and how it should be designed for the future. There is today a great consensus among Swedish politicians that care for the elderly needs more resources, and employees need better employment conditions.

Alamanco´s Work in Elderly Care

An Alamanco assignment begins with us finalizing an agreement with the management. We talk about the management's perception of the organisation's strengths and weaknesses, and their biggest challenges. In order for us to take on an assignment, we require management to be open to all kinds of employee involvement. We talk to local union representatives to get an idea of how the collaboration works between employers and unions.

We work with Dialogue in supporting the development of the organisation, using our Staff Right program to carry out education, as described in my earlier paper. The purpose is to develop a consensus between management and employees on how to staff, locate and use working hours. This requires that we develop a collaborative approach. This is a major cultural change which cannot be done through top-down directives. Consensus can only be developed through a dialogue in which all employees participate.

To change the view on how to use human resources, clear data needs to be produced. Initial work shows that many municipalities are characterised by fragmentation. In elderly care, staff costs make up 80-90% of the budget, even though many employees have only a temporary job. This means that there needs to be close cooperation between the finance unit, the human resources department and the elderly care personnel. This collaboration does not yet exist when an assignment begins. An important goal for us is to make the management aware of the need to develop this way of working together.

Another important aspect of the collaboration is how the employees view their own roles. How do they view their responsibility for their mission, and what benefit it will lead to for users? As mentioned before, we talk to groups about three concepts: the self, the team and the mission. Where do they focus? Is it mostly on themselves, or is it on their work team, or on what they are to achieve together for their users?

This dialogue is particularly necessary in our country: the World Value Survey, regularly conducted to examine people's values, shows that Sweden today is the most individual-centred country in the world!

In order to develop the dialogue across an organisation we work with different models and employee groups. We work as supervisors with entire working groups and their manager. We train managers and employees to be able to lead a dialogue process with the support of our training materials and supervisor guides. Finally, a clear structure is needed for the development work. We agree with management on how the work can take place through a five-phase model, explained in more depth in my 2018 paper. Briefly, these phases are 1) exploring the current situation together; 2) envisioning a shared future; 3) mapping the path to the shared vision; 4) developing an action plan; and 5) following up, some four to five months after the initiation of changes.

The West Bay-Västervik Story

Västervik municipality in the West Bay region of Sweden decided that all employees in elderly care should have the opportunity to maintain a full-time job. As part of this initiative, Alamanco was commissioned in the autumn of 2014 to carry out seven Staff Right training courses for all managers and a number of employees, for a total of about 230 people.

The managers, together with their selected employees, have acted as conversation leaders at each workplace in order to have a dialogue on how to create a consensus regarding staffing, placement and use of working hours. All employees in elderly care and care for the disabled – a total of about 1200 people – have attended Alamanco´s three-day dialogue training.

After each dialogue training, we have conducted a number of follow-up meetings structured as both full and half days. At these meetings, we have worked with individual work teams and their manager to resolve conflicts and develop cooperation. In some cases, these group meetings have affected all work teams within a unit. The right to full-time employment has been gradually introduced in all of Västervik's districts.

The development work in the various districts has naturally gone differently. A crucial factor is how leadership works. After the initial training with Staff Right, it turned out that there were significant differences in how managers took their responsibility to give employees the right conditions to be able to do a good job. We begin by describing an example of how we worked with a nursing home where it turned out that there were major shortcomings in the leadership.

In 2016, we were commissioned by the management of the Social Administration to make a survey of how the employees in one of the nursing homes perceived their work environment. The measurement was carried out with the KASAM (in English, 'sense of coherence') metric developed by Alamanco. It is based on the medical sociologist Aaron Antonovsky's research on our ability to create a sense of coherence in life, based on comprehensibility, manageability and meaningfulness. The KASAM metric is conducted via a web-based interview, during which employees can describe in their own words how they view their work environment. Then they offer answers to a number of follow-up questions that make it possible to create an index for how they perceive the work environment. The results are reported at a group level so that it is not possible to trace what individuals have answered.

On 7-8 June 2016, we held half-day dialogue meetings with all departments, where employees could take part in the results of the survey and have the opportunity to reflect on the results.

Because of the relationship between the manager at this facility and the employees, we judged that it would be necessary for each group to first be informed of their results without the manager being present. This is one of the few exceptions we have made to our normal process of working with the manager and group together.

The work during these seminars covered the following issues:

Current situation: Based on the results of the KASAM survey, where are the group's strong and weak sides?

Future: What characteristics would our group share when it is working best – when everyone comes into their own and we do a good job?

The way there: What will be required for us to achieve this? What would this mean to me as an employee and our group, as well as the leadership and the organisation?

Action plan: What should we do concretely to bring this about? What is our improvement proposal for each area, and our action plan for each?

Results of the KASAM Metric

We prepared KASAM reports for the entire nursing home and for each department separately and delivered them to the management. The results were reported partly in the form of an index that showed how the staff experiences their psychosocial work environment. This index is based on a scale of 0-100, where 50 is the average value we measured in all the measurements that Alamanco has carried out. The average index for this nursing home was only 27, which is among the lowest values we have ever measured. The dialogue with the different groups gave the following sample of results when they got to reflect on the strengths and weaknesses of the workplace:

Current situation: Based on the results of the KASAM survey, where are the group's strong and weak sides?	
Strong sides: • Good cohesion and cooperation in general in the groups of people • A commitment to their work (which, however, varies between the groups). Some are more resigned than others • Years of experience • Good composition of personalities • We are good at our job – humour and joy • Trust in the group • Find solutions • Dare to be straight and say no	**Weak sides:** • Lack of leadership • Frustration and anger • Planning the work • Do more than we should • Takes too much responsibility for other professions • Does not strive for the same goal • Coordinator does not listen, bad schedule • Unemployed posts • Unclear goals • Struggling to get everything done

Future: What characteristics would our group share when it is working best – when everyone comes into their own and we do a good job?	
• Collaboration: The staff helps and supports each other • Good division of labour with clear routines and structure • Whistle when we go to work. Do not feel anxiety • Clear goals – staff the workplace according to care burden • A management that shows interest in the business is fair and consistent	• Job satisfaction • Keep track of the business and follow up on the goals • Well-thought-out and anchored decisions with the participation of relevant staff • Present assistant at the unit who is familiar with our situation • Some 'carrot' once in a while • Structure and clarity in leadership

The way there: What will be required for us to achieve this? What would this mean to me as an employee and our group, as well as the leadership and the organisation?	
Co-worker • Everyone takes responsibility and cooperates • Good communication • Follow decisions made • Find desire and joy, be positive • Look ahead and support each other • Swedish-speaking, trained and committed staff • That we stay!	**Group** • Take advantage of each other's skills • Have a good review with substitutes • Have good routines and structure • Get your own time for group meetings • Become a stronger group, stick together • Work towards the same goal • Respect for each other

Action plan: What should we do concretely to bring this about? What is our improvement proposal for each area, and our action plan for each?		
Co-worker • Develop communication and collaboration • Follow decisions made Take responsibility • Work calmly and methodically • Look ahead, create job satisfaction • Swedish-speaking, trained staff who are suitable for the job	**Group** • Take advantage of each other's skills • Have a good introduction for substitutes • Good structure and clear routines • Follow decisions made • Make time for group meetings	**Organisation** • Another leadership is needed • Dare to be a manager in the right way • Make the right decision and follow up • Develop a dialogue with the staff • Better staff meetings with information, dialogue and follow-up • Get more insight into the business

Conclusions and Recommendations

We reported back to management the results of the survey and difficult conclusions from the dialogue meetings with the working groups. Our research led us to several conclusions:

- There is a great deal of agreement between the results of the KASAM survey and the views expressed during the half-day seminars. It is our definite impression that the employees felt safe to tell us what they honestly think and feel about their work situation.
- There is a very strong criticism of how leadership works in the nursing home. This leads to a lack of trust and confidence from employees, a strong feeling of powerlessness from not being able to influence their work situation and little belief in possibilities for the future. The values reported for work coherence are remarkably low, although there are large differences between the departments.

- Our conversations with employees show that there is no consensus between management and employees on how to staff, locate and use working hours. This means that there is also a lack of a basic consensus on how working full-time as a norm should be implemented. The issues and data that were dealt with during the training days in Staff Right have not been the subject of any thorough dialogue among the employees. There is a strong feeling that there is a lack of co-determination and opportunities to influence the business. The employees are calling for a clear strategy for the development of the business with clear goals. The decisions made today are perceived as short-term, inconsistent and lacking in follow-up.
- This means that leadership different from that in the current situation is required. It needs to be based on a clear strategy for how the business is to be developed in terms of staffing, location and use of working hours. A dialogue needs to be developed between management and employees on how a consensus can be conducted on these issues based on the residents' basic needs. Therefore a restart should be made regarding the issues considered in Staff Right, and how working full-time as a norm can be implemented.
- There is much to suggest that the nursing home should have a coordinator located on-site. This provides the conditions for creating better dialogues on how recruitment, placement and introduction of substitutes can take place in a better way.
- Time needs to be set aside for group meetings in each department to develop collaboration and communication. Good group and staff meetings increase the opportunities to develop the collaboration between management and employees, and to create a greater sense of context.

Based on our report, the manager of the nursing home was reassigned to other tasks. We conducted three Dialogue trainings so that all employees had the opportunity to participate. The new manager participated in each training. After the dialogue sessions, a number of follow-up meetings were held with each group separately with the new manager. At these development meetings action plans were drawn up to develop their cooperation.

Västervik Söder, West Bay South

The next example illustrates what can happen when the right conditions are present from the beginning, because there is leadership that believes in Dialogue and in involving employees.

The area of Västervik South was the first to offer full-time employment as a norm, with the new schedule beginning in September 2016. There are home care services and two nursing homes in the area.

Results: Everyone was involved in the process based on Staff Right and Dialogue education to understand why they needed to work in a different way. They became aware of the financial implications of decisions, and how they could collaborate better on how to use human resources. The charts below illustrate the difference in employment demographics between 2014, before the program began, and 2020.

Nursing Home
Vapengränd

EMPLOYMENT RATE	2014		2014	
	Women	Men	Women	Men
Full time	20	1	53	5
Part time	28	0	3	1
Total	48	1	56	6
Full time	42.90%		93.60%	
Part time	57.10%		6.40%	

Home Care
District 1

EMPLOYMENT RATE	2014		2020	
	Women	Men	Women	Men
Full time	19	0	41	9
Part time	46	2		
Total	66	2	41	9
Full time	28.40%		100%	
Part time	71.60%			

District 2

EMPLOYMENT RATE	2014		2020	
	Women	Men	Women	Men
Full time	6	2	28	16
Part time	11	1	2	
Total	17	3	30	16
Full time	40%		95.80%	
Part time	60%		4.20%	

Annica Mässing, a District Manager since 2001, is deeply familiar with our dialogic approach. She shares her perspective on the results of the work:

Full-time as a norm has led to it becoming safer care. We have regular staff on-site. It will be safer for our users. We have chosen to organise the care with smaller work teams to create good continuity. In the home care service, there are five employees in each work team. Within Vapengränd, people work on a floor basis, and are thus also divided into smaller groups.

The vast majority choose to work full-time. This means that you cover for each other in the event of absence. We have some work teams that are absolutely superb at collaborating. You talk to each other when you want to be free and find solutions within the group for how to cover those sessions. Users are more satisfied with our efforts today. It is a safer business. Our employees are also more satisfied. They also feel more secure when they know what salary they receive each month and do not have to chase hours to get a sensible salary. It is a calmer business.

Full-time as a norm is the biggest thing I have been involved in introducing during my time as a leader. I think it's fantastic that people get organised employment and a salary that you can live on. For my leadership, the dialogue educations have been very important. I spend a lot of time reflecting. I get a lot of feedback from our employees because we work a lot to create trust. We work with adults. We try to create conditions for them to be able to take responsibility in their work. In that work, the dialogue training has been an important support.

Through the resource time we have, it becomes a completely different way of working. We know we have people in place. We do not have to, as before, come up with emergency solutions and next go out and pick up people on the street.

How Has Västervik Municipality Handled the Corona Pandemic?

The municipality of Västervik has had several cases of Coronavirus infections corresponding to a transmission rate of 0.2. It is desirable to be below 0.1. No cases have been registered in Västervik Söder's elderly care, nor have they been documented in nursing homes or in-home care services.

The proportion of hours for permanent employees at Vapengränd was 68.4% in 2014. From January through June 2018 it had increased to 81.2%%. This is despite the fact that sick leave has increased from 9.3% to 12.8%. In 2020 sick leave has continued to increase due to strict guidelines that encourage staff to stay at home with the slightest symptoms of illness.

How has the Corona pandemic been handled with the support of the new way of organising that has been developed over past few years? Below are excerpts from conversations I had with some managers and employees in July of this year:

Emma Säfström, Unit Manager:

We have not had any outbreaks of Corona in our operations.

I feel that in the beginning we became very scared as employees during Corona. We often talked to people who felt an incredible fear. We have group meetings once a month, and then we [review the documentation from our work and] go through everything.

As we go through our documentation we see if patients or staff have reacted to something, and we talk about it. If a group has not documented so much, we ask: Why have you not documented? If you do not document, the next person cannot take any action. It has been a very long journey that is still in process, which we will continue throughout the autumn.

When you come to work the first thing you do is go and wash your hands. You may not have done that before. You are much more aware of where you have been, and you talk about it.

Annika Mässing, District Manager:

At the Vapengränd elderly care facility we have many people of foreign descent. We have a Care and Language and Internship coordinator here in the municipality, located on Vapengränd. Her task is to make it possible for immigrants to simultaneously learn Swedish and receive a vocational education. There is a good atmosphere among the employees, regardless of which country they come from.

It is important to have an organisation with small work teams. It is a winning concept for both special housing and home care. In the small work teams, there is a clear liaison. We have team meetings with rehabilitation and other professional groups. We area managers sit in crisis management sessions every Monday afternoon. We have been doing this since the end of March. The medically responsible nurse decides when to use a mouth covering or visor. At first we had no visors, but we had someone who sat and made them.

When I schedule, I start from the beginning on what is required to run a normal business and then I put in 15% resource time. Resource time means that you as an employee must compensate for absence from your own workplace, or at another workplace. There will be about three shifts per person in four weeks. We continuously monitor the resource time so that it is used efficiently.

In 2017, the home services area was divided geographically into two groups. Here are some comments from these work group personnel:

Robin Lissebring, Assistant Nurse:

We are five people in each work group. There are two contacts in the group and two or three replacements. Since we all work, we have some redundancy that is included in the schedules, evenly distributed over the days of the week.

Special assistance officers formulate an assistance decision for each user. It describes the individual's needs and what to do. Then it is up to the contact person to talk to the user about how to do it.

The very first thing I do is meet and plan together with the user. I go to that person's home so that they know who I am and tell them that I will be their contact person. I am primarily the one the user can contact during the day. During the day, a lot needs to be done. It can be anything from a taxi ride, a TV to be fixed or an operation. I do everything.

All groups have different numbers of users. Everyone needs different amounts of help. We try to make sure that everyone gets the help they want. Not everyone can get help at eight in the morning. We talk about that, and the users understand that. I am the contact person for eight users. The users are divided into areas so that there is not so much driving time in between.

Emma Säfström, Unit Manager:

I think we need to talk about the Free Time concept that was introduced in 2017, in which our coordinator receives an assignment from the development assistance officers, which she gives to Robin. It says what the person needs help with, but nothing about times. If the user needs to go to the toilet, I may take more time than I might normally do.

This is how we must think when we help people. It does not work that an administrator who has met a person once says you get a 15-minute morning visit. I do not think it is dignified because people are different. We removed the time and posted it to the employees. This meant a shift of power from the development assistance officers and from the planner to the user and contact person.

It is the user who knows what they need help with. It is the contact person who is closest to the user and who knows how to help the user in the best way. It does not help if a boss says, "Go and do this or that", because then it is always someone else who sends them on assignment. You do not get the same relationship with the elderly, either.

Rosengården's Nursing Home

In 2013, Rosengården's nursing home got a new manager, Bella Dzabirov. Rosengården is a large nursing home with 102 residents, divided into eight departments. She has collaborated with her colleague Marthe Otterström. When Bella took over as manager, she wanted to start development work. She stated that there was no cooperation among the staff. They did not even cooperate within the same department. Bella wanted the employees to cooperate throughout the house. There should only be one Rosengården.

She started the work of conducting workplace meetings where she mixed staff from different departments. The purpose was for the staff to get to know each other. At the workplace meetings, she put the chairs in a dialogue circle. She began by asking an open-ended question to the employees: "What are you, more than your role as assistant nurses?" This question, of course, aroused great astonishment. What was the purpose of the question? Bella explained that she wanted the employees to reflect on what quality of life the residents would have the opportunity to experience.

A number of planning days were carried out in 2013 in which all employees participated. They discussed how to plan their work in a smarter way, develop the collaboration between the departments and find new ways to set a schedule.

After two years, in 2015, they started to see results. That year, hourly wage earners performed just 6.4% of the total number of hours. In 2018, the share was down to 1.44%. This year during January to August, the share has decreased even more to only 0.27%! This fantastic development again this year has been possible despite the Corona pandemic. Management quickly made its own decisions on how to deal with the pandemic without waiting for direct or external directives. Because staff were used to working together, it was easy to introduce new work routines to prevent the spread of infection.

Rosengården has not had any cases of Covid 19 among either residents or staff. Sick leave among staff has not increased during this year but remains at the same level. Many municipalities have had a sharp increase in sick leave during the Corona period. The municipality of Nynäshamn has had a contagion rate of 0.2 for the spread of Covid 19. Some other nursing homes have had cases of Covid 19 both among residents and staff. Rosengården has had a positive financial result every year since 2015.

Flen Municipality

The municipality of Flen has 15,000 inhabitants. Flen is located in Sörmland County. The county is hard hit by Covid 19. In 2017, Alamanco was commissioned to develop elderly care. First, we conducted a pre-study to create a picture of the situation. We collected data and conducted interviews with managers and employees. The work then began in the spring of 2018 with training managers and employees in Staff Right at all nursing homes. We conducted a large number of dialogue meetings with all employees to develop a common understanding of how to have a better work environment. Towards the end of the year, it turned out that the entire Social Administration would make an overrun of SEK 55 million (£4.6m GBP / €5.4m EUR / $6.3m USD) . The social manager had to end his employment. A new organisation and a new budget model were introduced at the beginning of the year. Fifty people were notified of their dismissal.

In this chaotic development, it should have been virtually impossible to continue the development work. Thanks to the dialogue meetings we had conducted with all employees, they had a common understanding of how to organise their work in a new way. To meet the financial challenges, we managed to reduce the total number of working hours by 21% in 2019, while at the same time increasing the proportion of working hours for permanent employees from an average of 62.71% in 2018 to 74.39% in 2019. The same level applies for January-June, despite Corona.

In Flen there now has been a case of Corona among residents of a nursing home. Our work will continue during the autumn with the nursing homes and to develop a new organisation for the home care service.

Our Own Reflections on the Work with Dialogue as a Process

The Corona pandemic means that our ways of thinking, cooperating and solving problems in our society are at the forefront. This applies not least in the public sector. As I outlined at the beginning of this paper, Sweden has a decentralized social structure that differs from many other countries, with a system of independent authorities and ministers with limited opportunities to control details in a crisis. The responsibility for important societal functions lies with regions and municipalities. A minister cannot take command of the authorities' decisions in individual cases or give autonomous municipalities and regions orders about what to do. The government can primarily govern through controlling budgets, appointing heads of government, and through writing regulatory letters and directives.

The public sector is ultimately governed, then, by general elections and democratic decision-making processes. Our decentralized social system has many benefits. Problems can be solved as close as possible to where the problems arise. The general elections make it possible for citizens to influence the development of society. Disadvantages are that there are often long decision-making processes, with unclear roles for leadership, decision-making and responsibility. People's trust and confidence in politicians and authorities depend to a large extent on the public sector's ability to deliver what is expected. Supporting people in developing dialogue as a part of their practice of governance has turned out to be essential in many municipalities; the improved quality of the workplace environment has helped leaders create settings where the unexpected can be managed far more easily than through traditional means.

The Corona pandemic urges us who believe in the public sector as the basis for good societal development to reflect on how the entire community organisation should be developed to better meet the needs of citizens both in everyday life and in various crisis situations. In the case of this pandemic – and perhaps the next – Dialogue literally can save lives.

Conference Session Extracts
From a conversation with participants considering the paper with Lars-Åke Almqvist

Speaker: Thank you very much. It was a fun coincidence that I was with two colleagues in my small group. We three have in common that we have experience both on the prison side of the Department of Corrections and the Community Corrections side, which gives us a real appreciation for the challenges on both sides. So, in terms of possibilities and obstacles, one thing is that we have an annual employee survey which is a great opportunity to confer, to communicate between staff and management in a lot of detail about our concerns, what things are going well, what things are not going well. That happens every year. We spend more time talking about obstacles.

Speaker: Our biggest obstacle in the Department of Corrections in Virginia is our size. We are a huge organisation and on the prison side that presents a lot of challenges when you want to try to sit down and have a dialogue. Being able to get all of the people around the table that you need is much harder in a prison because the prison operates their business 24 seven. So you, you can't pull people from their duties to sit down and have a dialogue all the time. Whereas the contrast to that is in Community Corrections. If you're in a probation office and you need to involve the Chief in the dialogue, the Chief is down the hall and able to decide to hang a sign on the door to say, we're taking this hour for a dialogue, or whatever meeting it is. It's very different.

Now the challenge in terms of size on the probation side is that it's not just Department of Correction employees, but because it's probation, we have to be concerned about the courts and the judges and the attorneys and localities. They all have an impact on what the probation districts are able to do. We have 43 probation districts with 43 different sets of judges and attorneys and courts and all of that. So size is definitely our biggest challenge. In terms of conditions, one of the things we need is very strong leadership. Leaders, unit heads, who are truly dedicated to the dialogue process in order to make it work. If you have a Unit Head who does not buy-in, that's going to trickle down to impact everyone negatively. Another condition is the importance of prioritizing when you need dialogue, versus when you don't. So many situations can be addressed with a crucial conversation instead of bringing everyone together for a dialogue. Because if you have dialogue all the time it starts to lose its meaning, both for the process and for the employees.

Speaker: We don't have any issues or any kind of conflict that we have concerns about, because our connection with our management team is so strong that if we need to talk to them, we can have those conversations. You know, we don't have issues with dialogues. Some of the units are so small that it's more like a family, so you resolve the issues yourself without even involving the management team. It's so well taken care of and people just kind work together to get the job done.

Speaker: We talked about the influence of religion in the way we behave and understand the power structure. Spain is very paternalistic, as we're seeing with the Covid-19 pandemic crisis. For example in Germany or in Italy, there are demonstrations of people challenging the measures taken against the virus; here in Spain, we accept them as fate. We don't question them or challenge them. This happens in companies where we have unions, but their real power of negotiation is low. The labour laws are not as strong as in Sweden, so they don't protect the worker as in Sweden. I connect that with the Catholic mentality. We have a Catholic mindset, and this idea that God will provide for us. We don't need to care about that. We don't need to earn what we have, and this is what you asked of the state, of the employers, or anyone in authority.

Speaker: We had a quite wide perspective and we talked about the expectations of different generations in work life. What kind of leadership and management are they expecting to have, and what is their relationship to work in general? What is the meaning and importance of work in their life, what kind of work attitude do they have, and how do they behave? Different generations behave in a different way in work life. The most important from my point of view is the kind of an atmosphere you as a supervisor or leader create. Is it possible for employees to come to talk with you about problems?

Speaker: We talked about having a toxic leader who makes that a real challenge. That trust really matters. If you don't have that, and if you have that fragmentation from the top, it's very hard to build meaningful dialogue.

Speaker: I have worked in that situation and it's not good. Everybody's afraid, and there is a breakdown with dialogue. One of the other things that we talked about was staff retention. If you have a challenge with retention, then you're having to re-establish these trusting relationships, these dialogic relationships over and over again. We are now starting to have smaller dialogues on a smaller scale that we're bringing the leader into, but once the leader is there it can still be a challenge.

Speaker: We see an increase of staff members retiring and that has impacted our workplace. We see how critical dialogue has been with managing the pandemic. We have the largest number of positive cases in the department, and we've had the highest number in assisted living, and geriatric offenders in the infirmary. But through dialogue, I'm happy to say that all of our offenders, with the exception of maybe eight, are in a recovery state. We've only gotten to this point through effective dialogue.

Speaker: Some practical things that we've been doing as far as the dialogue is concerned? We've been engaged with all key department heads. We dialogue daily, not only the staff at the facility but also with management executive and regional. We've had medical staff involved, we've communicated with the chief physicians, and even with our regional directors on a daily basis. We've had plans in place. We've communicated with the health department. We've followed the Center for Disease Control guidelines, we've even had visits from the health department. We've had all external stakeholders actively engaged in and involved with us, and sometimes multiple times during the day we've been involved virtually to ensure that we were following the guidelines in every aspect of our operation. We included everyone: food, service, security, medical, every aspect of the operation and where we needed to we included staff.

Speaker: The bottom line is that long-term care in the public sector is a business, period. It's there to make a profit. Staffing is typically done with full-time benefits staff, and with part-time staff to fill in the gaps. They're usually on a rotating schedule with either eight-hour shifts or 12-hour shifts. Back in the seventies and eighties we warehoused our elderly, and we warehoused our serious mentally ill. Now people are taking a greater interest and appreciation for their individual stories and life experience.

Speaker: I just want to add something. I'm not part of the Virginia team, but I've noticed something that Virginia folks have added to these dialogues – the way that you encourage each other through the chats after sharing is beautiful. You have this culture of supporting and encouraging each other!

Postscript
The author's reflections, written some months after the conference

Our conversations during the seminar were about several topics that are important for creating conditions for a lively dialogue in a business. Leaders at different levels have a crucial role. They need to show through attitude, values and, not least, practical action that they believe in dialogue as a process for developing the business. Working with dialogue in a large organisation places demands on organisation and structure. How should leaders and employees have practical opportunities to meet regularly to talk to each other? In what situations and issues is dialogue the best way to communicate? When are there other, better ways to communicate? Are there differences between different generations in the view of leadership, cooperation and what one expects from one's working life?

My contribution to the conference had, as an important background, the Corona pandemic. When the conference was held in October 2020, we had more than six months' experience of the pandemic. It was already clear at the time that dialogue as a process is necessary to be able to deal with all the challenges posed by a worldwide pandemic. Dialogue is needed at all levels in a country, between government, state authorities, regions, municipalities, companies, non-profit organisations and the public. International cooperation between countries and continents is necessary.

While the development of the pandemic shows the need for dialogue, it has in at least two ways affected the conditions for people to talk to each other:

- The opportunities to meet physically have been limited
- Many important decisions have needed to be made in a short time, with little room for dialogue with those concerned

In my work in Swedish elderly care, together with my colleagues in Alamanco, the Corona pandemic has involved many challenges. From March 2020, we had to completely change our working methods. We usually go out to the organisations, working with and meeting leaders and employees at their workplaces. In a normal working year, I drive between 40-50,000 kilometers. From November 2020, we will work exclusively digitally via Zoom. We have succeeded in finding ways that make it possible for leaders and employees to have constructive conversations about how they can develop their business together.

Used properly, digital meetings can save a lot of time and shorten decision-making processes. We have many positive experiences that, during a certain period of time, we can have several short digital meetings to help organisations solve complex problems. With traditional physical meetings, even if they were dialogical, it would probably have taken much longer.

Section Four

Shaping Thinking Through Dialogue

The inaugural paper, "Dialogue – A Proposal" (Bohm, Factor, Garrett, 1991), initiated an enquiry into thinking and thought at the heart of the Dialogue. Without attention to thinking, and the systemic nature of thinking and thought, fragmentation occurs in human consciousness. This condition is now so pervasive that it has become a threat to the well-being or even survival of society – hence the necessity for Dialogue. How do we shape our thinking through Dialogue? Where does it lead us? In this section these questions are addressed in quite different ways by three authors: William Isaacs from the USA, Thomas Köttner from Argentina and Peter Garrett from the UK.

William Isaacs considers professionalism and explores what it would require for Dialogue to become a profession. This is an aspiration of the Academy of Professional Dialogue, and the paper supports and challenges this ambitious intention in a healthy way. Few fields, if any, have achieved the professional status of medicine and law, and there are good reasons for that. The criteria he considers for professionalism fall into two dimensions: knowledge and social. Regarding knowledge, there is a significant challenge for Dialogue as a profession. Since Dialogue involves thinking and thought, it is adaptive as well as technical in nature. An original or first-hand awareness is part of what makes a Dialogue practitioner competent and confident. This essence, and others, have yet to be codified and reliably proven. His paper lays the ground well for a longer future consideration.

Thomas Köttner was a step ahead – he worked online as an executive coach for years before the medium became a necessity for many during the Covid-19 pandemic. Can 'virtual' online work be as 'real' as thinking together in the same physical building and room? Thomas proposes the two are different but just as real as each other, and that online Dialogue has some significant advantages. The focus is on each person's face, which can be seen directly, and the surrounding environment is less distracting. Participants have the safety of controlling their own connection, and the trappings of power, authority and wealth recede significantly. Given the time and cost reduction, Zoom and other audiovisual systems are clearly here to stay. Indeed, Thomas sees an evolution occurring in our ways of thinking, acting and interacting as we have adapted to the online medium.

Peter Garrett walks through a series of different vignettes in his life to identify and name a common developmental pattern. Whether starting a new employment role, consulting to executives, reviewing his whole career, learning to ski or participating in a Dialogue, he has discovered four phases of development. These phases are experienced both internally and externally, and correspond to an enlarging 'container', or spaciousness. He notes how the transitions from one phase to the next are significant shifts that require energy and attention, and result in very different potential opportunities. How one thinks and feels is different in each phase and in each transition. This is simple, but not simplistic, revealing how to help oneself and others on the developmental journey through life that Peter claims is common to all people and social systems from birth to death.

– P.G.

What is Professionalism in Dialogue?

William Isaacs

The Context for Establishing Dialogue as Profession

Dialogue has developed over a long intellectual and practical trajectory, reaching back to the ancient Greeks in Western society. Over this time, it has appeared in varying forms in many indigenous cultures around the world, where it is experienced not only as a means of communication but also as an intimate part of community and spiritual life.

Over the past three decades, the practice of dialogue has emerged as a distinct field based on the integration of experience, research, and theory-building from numerous initiatives and practitioner efforts around the world. The various threads of activity in this field include explorations of dialogue in groups and as a component of collective social intervention (Isaacs, 1999, Garrett, 2018); as a means of fostering deliberative democracy (Fishkin, 1991), as a supplement to negotiation (Susskind, 2003); as an approach to diplomacy (Saunders, 1999); and as a means of stimulating organizational development (Bushe & Marshak, 2016). There are multiple paradigms underlying these and other approaches, and a wide variety of methods that flow from them. While there is a surface similarity to all of these, there are important differences in intention, world view, and method among them.

What is striking, however, apart from the enthusiasm and engagement of the practitioners, is the lack of a shared set of standards for what constitutes excellence or ethical performance; there appears to be no unifying set of ideas about the knowledge that underlies these efforts. This context is driving the Academy of Professional Dialogue's efforts to professionalize dialogue by establishing a more coherent approach to the field and its practices, with the intention of producing reliable outcomes and ethical standards.

Turning dialogue into a profession—an aspiration for many occupations and vocations—requires a careful and deliberate inquiry into the criteria that constitute a profession. This includes ways for assessing the quality of outcomes and the means for developing current and future practitioners. This is especially important, given the increasingly contentious terrain of professional knowledge itself. Professions increasingly face a crisis of confidence and legitimacy, particularly where professionals have misused their formal authority, made famously poor predictions, failed to produce promised results and, as a result, produced disastrous unintended consequences (Schön, 1983; Tenner, 1997; Zakaria, 2019). As Donald Schön wrote in 1983,

> *In public outcry, in social criticism, and in the complaints of the professionals themselves, the long-standing professional claim to a monopoly of knowledge and social control is challenged—first, because professionals do not live up to the values and norms they espouse, and second, because they are ineffective.*

Schön traces the failure of professionalism as traditionally conceived to a core problem, that of the nature of standard ideas about professional knowledge itself. This problem is rooted in a model of technical rationality that consists of "instrumental problem solving made rigorous by the application of scientific theory and technique." According to this model, professionalism rises or falls on the merits of its rigor and application of scientific methods. The so-called "minor" professions (like social work or librarianship, to use Nathan Glazer's terminology), have inconsistent, ambiguous ends and unstable institutional structures as compared to the "learned" professions such as medicine or law (Glazer, 1974).

The paradigm of technical rationality operates from the perspective that professional practice is a process of problem-solving. There is, for instance, a "standard of care" in medicine for broken bones. Physicians are generally trained to recognize and address this kind of problem, understand what methods to apply, and reliably predict and measure the outcomes of their established protocols. Problems like these do indeed benefit from the application of scientifically grounded principles where the solutions, while complex, may be discovered through research and procedural effort. Once discovered, they can be applied reliably. However, not all problems come so neatly bundled. Such problems, like those faced by Dialogue Practitioners, bring with them ambiguity, uncertainty, instability, and conflicting values. Complex social settings are typically inhabited by many different actors, each of whom have different world views that lead them to define the situation differently. This is true in settings organized by an apparent hierarchy of control, as in many organizations. It is even more true in settings where there is no single authority, where the people do not like or trust each other, and where they do not agree. In all these cases, as Ronald Heifetz (1994, 2017) has pointed out, the problems require an "adaptive" approach. No single technical, expert solution will work. Answers in these cases can only arise from the community or collective context overall, and they require learning and new capability from everyone. While technical rationality can provide a basis for action in some contexts, its limits have become increasingly evident. In every field, professionals are having to confront the requirement of improvisation and the handling of uncertainty.

The need for methods and approaches that can reliably begin to understand and address complex adaptive problems has never been more relevant for Dialogue Practitioners. Dialogue as a profession is well suited to address the very challenges that have been framed as problems within the framework of technical rationality. Dialogue, as I will define it here, holds the potential to offer a disciplined, professional approach that can begin to shed light on and transform the adaptive problems that technical rationality fails to address—and indeed can now be seen to have been exacerbated by that approach (Alexander, 2012).

For dialogue to achieve this result and move toward becoming fully professional, it will need to do four things. First, it must develop and articulate its knowledge base as a grounded, disciplined body of thought from which general principles can be derived. Second, it must provide a clear and specific set of practices by which these ideas reliably can be adopted—and, in so doing, distinguish dialogue from other forms of engagement. Third, it will need to show how it is distinct from and addresses the problems of technical rationality that underlie the commonly held perception of professional knowledge. And fourth, it will need to develop the social components of a professional community, including a distinct system of education, accreditation, ethical supervision and peer governance. This paper focuses on the first three of these requirements.

Defining the Profession of Dialogue

Many fields make the claim of being a "profession." Few, if any, have achieved the same status as medicine and law, even as the claim of professionalism has been asserted in fields ranging from real estate to social work to management to warfighting. The problem of definition is complicated by the fact that the meaning of professionalism varies as a function of the context in which it is performed (forensic vs. clinical psychology, for example), and in the way different stakeholders perceive it. So many fields claim to be "professionals" that the term has drifted towards meaninglessness.

Efforts to define professionalism have a long history and can be traced back to the Middle Ages, where clerical education was considered to endow people with specialist knowledge and a distinct social status, enabling them to assume roles as church leaders (Crook, D. 2008). The emergence of the "learned professions" of medicine and law, considered to be "major professions" by some sociologists, became the standard of what the term *profession* meant (Glazer, 1974):

> ["Major" professions] are based on knowledge which is not generally available to the layman and is gained by formal education, have a distinctive organization of the profession with some power over access to the profession . . . as well as a special code of conduct referring to the professional person's access to aspects of individual's lives which are regarded as private.

There have been numerous efforts by sociologists to define the criteria for what constitutes a profession. Edgar Schein (1973), following this tradition, articulates a set which identifies a professional as someone who:

- Is engaged in a full-time occupation that comprises his principal source of income
- Has a strong motivation or calling and lifetime commitment to it
- Possesses a specialized body of knowledge, acquired through a prolonged period of education and training
- Acts from general principles, theories, or propositions
- Operates from a service orientation, focused on the objective needs of the client, with an absence of self interest
- Is focused on the objective needs of the client, from a detached perspective, in a relationship of candor and mutual trust, and the absence of moral judgment
- Assumes a stance of autonomy of judgment of his own performance, reviewed by peers and enforced by a clear code of conduct
- Participates in a professional association that defines criteria of admission, educational standards, and domains of action
- Focuses on a limited and defined body of knowledge, and does not make claims to be acting outside of his training

There have been extensive debates about which of these criteria, and in what order, determine the *degree* of "professionalism." But most approaches coalesce around a selection from these factors. Some professions, like medicine, fit all the criteria, while others, like management, very few.

Examining dialogue in light of these criteria, most do not yet apply. There are few practitioners who are fully employed in this field. There is not yet a clear set of accepted general principles from which Dialogue Practitioners act, or a clearly defined and specialized body of knowledge acquired through a prolonged period of education and training. There is not yet a tradition of working from a detached perspective to apply these principles, or a peer community that validates the standards and quality of the performance of practitioner. There is, however, now emerging a professional association for dialogue that is developing these and other elements.

The criteria that define a profession can be separated into two dimensions. The first is a *knowledge dimension* that focuses on the principles, methods and standardization of a particular accepted and developed body of knowledge, where members are trained in that knowledge and have achieved an acknowledged level of mastery. The second is a *social dimension* that focuses on the requirement that members participate in an accepted process of education; admission to the profession is carefully controlled, and members are expected to function with a high degree of ethical and moral clarity.

While the social dimensions of a profession are important, the balance of this paper will be toward the clear articulation of the knowledge dimensions, as they are particularly critical in the formative stages of a profession.

Towards a Dialogic Paradigm of Professional Knowledge

One of the central factors in determining the importance and distinctness of a profession corresponds to its grounding in a clear body of knowledge, and its ability to apply a general set of principles to practical problems. To Wilbert Moore (1970), a profession can be defined by its ability to produce a distinct set of results because of its specialized, bounded, scientific, and standardized nature:

> *If every professional problem were in all respects unique, solutions would be at best accidental, and therefore have nothing to do with expert knowledge. What we are suggesting, on the contrary, is that there are sufficient uniformities in problems and in devices for solving them to qualify the solvers as professionals . . . professionals apply very general principles, standardized knowledge, to concrete problems.*

As outlined above, the quest for general principles grounded in science and applied to practical problems provides the central basis for the accumulation of professional knowledge, and the mastery of this knowledge gives practitioners their standing. Schein (1983) explains it this way:

> *The ultimate criterion of professionalization according to most sociologists is the achievement of "autonomy," which implies 1) knowing better what is good for the client than anyone else because of extended technical education or training, 2) subjecting one's decisions to the review of colleagues, and 3) setting all one's standards pertaining to the jurisdiction of the profession and entry into it through peer group associations.*

Autonomy arises principally because of deep clarity in the underlying body of knowledge, and in its systematic transfer to practitioners. This makes establishing clarity for the emerging field of Professional Dialogue particularly important.

Yet it is in this very domain of autonomy that professional knowledge, as commonly defined, runs into difficulties. The technical rationality paradigm, which is rooted in Positivism, maintains that empirical knowledge is the only real form of knowledge, and has as its goal the technical and scientific control of the natural environment (Habermas, 1987). Professional knowledge based on this view will seek to ground itself in one of the traditional disciplines of science. In this light of this, it is critical that those who wish to refine the concept of professionalism operate with clear and unambiguous ends and have stable institutions of practice. In doing so they will be able to access both the rigor of the scientific method and the relevance of adaptive solutions.

Technical rationality in its own context takes for granted that rigor consists of the disciplined application of general scientific principles. But as I am suggesting, it is becoming clear that in day-to-day practice the improvisational reality that professionals encounter in any field requires far more interpretation, novel reflection, and adjustment than is ever represented in the traditional approaches to knowledge. This is especially the case for Dialogue Practitioners. At their core, the problems they face are socially constructed, dynamically complex, and subject to ambiguous and shifting interpretations. These problems are further complicated by competing values and widely differing goals and mindsets held by a wide variety of stakeholders. The very notion that there is a single expert technical view ignores the complex social reality that comprises the problem space facing dialogue professionals.

As our adaptive challenges intensify and become more abundant, professionals need to be able not only to solve problems, but also *to set and define them.* This requires on-the-spot improvisation and reflection in novel ways that no training or protocol can anticipate. More than this, the very nature of the social contexts out of which problems arise is itself incoherent; practitioners must have the ability to explore this underlying incoherence in a manner that is rigorous, perceptive and effective. If we define *professionalism* only as grounded in technical rationality, we will remain incapable of addressing the most important problems we face. We need a new approach, and a widened perspective, which builds on the rigor of science and at the same time expands the frame in which it is embedded.

Just as good science is grounded in close observation, deep inquiry, and thorough testing of assumptions, these same elements can be brought to bear in collective inquiry and reflection, which is the heart of Professional Dialogue theory and practice. We can address adaptive problems while expanding the frame of knowledge and inquiry by which insight and solutions are generated.

A Paradigm for Professional Dialogic Knowledge and Practice

To articulate a clear set of ideas upon which Professional Dialogue can be based, we need to focus on three questions: 1) What are the components of professional knowledge in dialogue, and how do they fit or relate to other fields? 2) What is the work of dialogue—that is, what domains does it focus on, and when is it needed and not needed? and 3) What tactics and practices identify how the work of dialogue is done?

David Kantor (2012) suggests one way to build a rigorous model that can take this complexity into account. He identifies three distinct knowledge components: A theory of the "thing" (the entity on which the model focuses); a theory of change, which articulates how change is brought about in the model; and a theory of practice, which suggests what actions should occur, and in what order.

The "thing" of medicine is the human body, and it is focused on the work of diagnosis and healing. In Western medicine, this is largely dominated by a molecular, mechanical view of the body. In this view the physical systems of the body interact in complex ways that can, to some degree, be articulated causally. Medicine often involves finding the right "molecule" to treat illness, providing a well-established focus, for instance, for the pharmaceutical industry. This too illustrates the theory of change in medicine—the application of the right methods to allow the underlying systems of the body to heal. In this analogy, the theory of practice would be the application, in the right sequence and in the right ways, of the skills, techniques and processes held in the body of medical knowledge.

What, then, is the model of knowledge for dialogue? The *theory of the "thing"* for dialogue consists both of the work of dialogue and the components of knowledge that comprise it. As outlined, the work of dialogue is the activity of engaging complex social settings that hold adaptive problems—ones that do not entirely submit to technical solutions but rather require both technical *and* adaptive solutions. The *theory of change* here has to do with catalyzing the unfolding of potential by means of inquiry into the underlying identity narratives and social dynamics that have led to patterns of fragmentation. The application of the work—the *theory of practice*—is to create and manage holding environments where inquiry can allow human beings in complex social settings to move from fragmentation to wholeness.

Over the past three decades my colleagues and I have developed a body of knowledge and experience that integrates these three related theories into a single approach.

First, our *theory of the "thing"* is informed by the world view articulated initially by David Bohm, that reality is comprised of an undivided wholeness that manifests as an explicate set of factors. These factors are in a constant state of enfolding back into an implicate, differentiated and patterned reality. This "implicate order" then unfolds back into explicate form (Bohm, 1980). In this view, every situation has a distinct potential which is constantly unfolding into initially subtle, and then more concrete, form. Dialogue is one vehicle, or aperture, through which this unfolding movement can be known. A Dialogue Practitioner can always ask, "What is the potential yet to unfold in this moment?" This is very much as a physician might ask, "What is the underlying biological reality underlying the symptoms we are seeing?"

Bohm's view was that the underlying unfolding-enfolding structure was holographic, meaning that each situation contained a microcosm of the larger context in which it was operating. This is also a practical principle for practitioners who can see each aspect of the social context in which they are working as providing insight into, and informing and being informed by, a wider context. Bohm ultimately saw this principle as extending to the whole of consciousness, which also further delineates a clear stance that a Dialogue Practitioner can take by asking, "What is the nature of the consciousness in me and the people in this circumstance, such that the situation appears as it does?" This can lead to question, "What would it take to let this situation shift?" Self-awareness and cultivated self-perception become central dimensions of the focus of this world view, which sees the nature of consciousness itself as arising from an inherent undivided wholeness. This wholeness includes and informs what emerges within human beings, as well as what unfolds around them.

Second, we build on the theory of thought Bohm initially articulated, and that has been further developed since that time (Barfield, 1988; Bohm, 1992; Isaacs, 1991 and 1999).

According to Bohm, thought is an individual and collective "system" that presents experience as it if were literal, when in fact it is a mediated representation. Human thought creates divisions which are artificial fictions useful in managing our affairs; however, these fictions take on a larger sense of reality that cannot be distinguished from direct experience. As Bohm put it, "thought creates the world and then says 'I didn't do it.'" We experience a thought-made world—in fact, nothing we experience has not been impacted by human thought. But these processes are invisible to us. Therefore, fragmentation in experience proliferates between nations, political tribes, units in organizations. They bypass or mask the underlying wholeness, preventing us from being aware of the processes that keep us from it. It is only as this whole system of incoherence can be examined that it becomes possible to create different results. This dimension of the "thing" that needs exploration and transformation is the nature of the system of thought as it is manifesting in any particular complex situation. Dialogue Practitioners must both understand and develop perception and skills to inquire into the incoherence of thought and its impact on the social contexts in which it is operating.

Third, we focus on the micropatterns of behavior that appear in social settings, and the underlying constructs that inform these behaviors. Chris Argyris and Donald Schön (1989) articulated the idea that "rules-in-use" that inform practice—the often-unconscious but patterned schema that determine the way local behavior unfolds. These patterns can be mapped and identified, in both macro organizational contexts and micro individual and team settings, to illustrate the operating structure that produces the observed behavior one may find. The discipline of mapping the social structural rules that control and inform human action brings significant rigor to a dialogic inquiry and makes it possible to liberate frozen patterns of action. By understanding and mapping the individual and organizational "defensive routines" that may be operating, one creates the basis on which to develop new approaches to transformation and change.

These three together present the beginnings of an integrated foundation of knowledge on which a profession of dialogue can be built. In combination they provide a way to understand the underlying nature of the collective thought that operates within any social system. As these patterns are understood they become amenable to close observation, measurement and change.

The *theory of change* we have developed in dialogue is based on the notion that action arises out of underlying social fields, which we call holding environments or "containers." It is out of these that social phenomena arise. I have described elsewhere a theory of the unfolding of these fields (Isaacs, 1999). The central idea is that fields evolve as a function of the energy and quality of attention of the participants in a dialogue, and that the evolution of these fields progresses through a clear and discernable sequence. Dialogues begin in "politeness," where collective memory patterns of engagement dominate. They then move into a pattern of disturbance and even breakdown as individuals begin to surface "what they really think," and as the holding environment becomes psychologically safe enough for these elements to be articulated. The group then has a choice: they can either retreat to politeness or to inquire into and "suspend" the disturbance. This unfolds into inquiry, a third phase of dialogue, where individuals begin to surface and reflect on their underlying theories-in-use, their underlying individual narratives, and their motives. The dialogue can then move into a collective "flow" state, where the group begins to transform its own narrative about itself. As the group matures its perceptive ability, it can surface insight that might have previously been censored or hidden from view. Such insight is the result of qualitative change in the underlying thought system such that people are no longer caught in automatic or hypnotic repetitive patterns. Critically, this process can be objectively observed, guided, and experienced by groups of people. Change occurs as people allow the underlying field in which exchange and thinking appear to evolve and become more refined, conscious, and coherent (Scharmer, O. and Kaufer, K. 2015).

Finally, *a theory of practice* for Professional Dialogue must outline methods, tools and practices for dialogue that are both effective and testable. A first critical dimension of a theory of practice is the articulation of an overall goal. For dialogue the goal is to inquire into and make accessible the underlying wholeness that is being masked by patterns of fragmentation in thought, feeling and action, and that is causing the manifestation of unintended and unwanted outcomes. Practice theory must go well beyond merely identifying a set of techniques, to specifying how practitioners should function in both space and time relative to the situations in which they engage. For instance, a theory of practice must pinpoint the "stance" the practitioner takes relative to the system they are in. Unlike approaches based in technical rationality, where the position taken typically is one of a distant expert, a Dialogue Practitioner assumes an engaged process stance, one where self-reflection within themselves and with the situation itself are all active parts of the approach (Schein, 1993; 2013). Also, one of the most common failures of practice theories is the absence of any treatment of time, the lack of any indication of what technique to use when, or how the phases of activity unfold over time, and how different techniques are appropriate at different junctures.

The theory of practice for dialogue therefore includes the following dimensions:

1. *A disciplined approach to internal "self-reflective" or "first-person" knowledge.* Technical rationality sees problems and their solutions as resident in the actors and systemic forces of the situation. A dialogic approach sees behavior as a function both of the internal meaning-making of the actors and external causal factors. This makes the disciplines that build self-reflection and awareness, both individually and collectively, central to Professional Dialogue practice. This approach takes seriously the idea of understanding the "microcosm in the macrocosm"; that is, the understanding of how factors within one part of the system are impacted by the wider whole. For instance, a Professional

Dialogue Practitioner would continuously cultivate awareness of their own qualitative inner state and note that the depth of their internal inquiry profoundly determines and impacts the unfolding dynamics of the dialogue. As a result they would sustain a disciplined approach to continuously refining their own inner clarity. They would also note the way qualitative factors in one subset of the system mirror factors in the larger whole.

2. *A distinct approach to problem-setting* that seeks a systemic characterization of an underlying problem and that neither takes for granted nor privileges any one articulation. The dialogic approach takes as given the reality that different actors define the challenges and the situation differently, making problem-setting and reframing, not problem-solving, a central focus of the approach. It also holds that the need is to create conditions for a collective inquiry into the unfolding order in the system as a whole, noticing that fragmentation masks that potential. Problem-setting is not an expert process, but a shared collective effort.

3. *Awareness of and ability to set and hold collective "social fields"* in which the practice emerges. The art of setting and holding fields in which small groups, teams, and systems operate is a central part of the practice of dialogue. Creating these holding environments entails an ability to perceive the subtle dimensions of thought and feeling that are at the source of human experience. Behind the overt thoughts and feelings are more delicate impulses and patterns of movement that can be discerned and held by a facilitator and ultimately by a group. Developing an understanding of this subtle space requires training and practice, similar to the training that might be required to lead meditation or other forms of reflection. A professional in dialogue would have achieved some level of mastery in this domain, both in calling attention to it, surfacing implicit factors within it, and guiding collective reflection that emerges from it.

4. *A clear set of practices and methods that evoke dialogue,* as distinct from other forms of social engagement. This includes knowing a set of tactics like inviting a group to form and center its energy before a session and to reflect afterwards; knowing how to invite a group to speak to the center, and not to each other; and providing opportunity and guidance on how to explore and inquire into disturbance. This approach to dialogue is very different to models that focus on interpersonal dynamics and the improvement of social relationships, for instance. Dialogue is fundamentally not about interpersonal engagement per se, but the expansion and clarification of the individual and collective consciousness of the people engaged in the dialogue. Dialogue facilitation requires a measure of detachment and skillful reflection, but also an understanding of the underlying theory and world view behind this approach. It also requires an understanding that every dialogic exchange follows a creative rhythm that permits or prevents certain kinds of exchanges at different points. The timing, aesthetics, and sequence of moves made

by participants in a dialogue is highly material to its quality and impact. Good practice involves knowing what to do and how to function through this unfolding cycle. An essential dimension of dialogue practice, finally, includes the ability to hold and manage the disturbances that unfold as human beings converse. Because adaptive problems arise out of fragmented social systems, where there is often conflict and intensity, no single agreed definition of a problem, and no unifying point of authority, practitioners must know how to lead an inquiry into, not suppress, deep difference and disturbance as they present themselves in these settings.

5. *A systematic design approach for how dialogic interventions unfold and scale.* The model my colleagues and I have developed for how dialogue unfolds over time, we term the "Generative Spiral." It consists of three phases: the creation of a holding environment where it becomes possible to surface, map and diagnose the conditions and systemic patterns of meaning-making and acting in the organization, in ways that are recognizable to the participants in the system and accepted by them; a phase where habitually held organizational collective memory patterns and structures of thought are actively transformed, leading to the emergence of a new narrative about the identity of the organization; and, finally, a third phase in which new habits and routines begin to be propagated and new capacity developed, to enable the scaling and sustained deployment of a more coherent approach to the adaptive challenges they face. These same principles can be applied at multiple scales, beginning with one-to-one relationships, extending to small groups and teams, to units of organizations, to whole organizations and beyond, to national governments in regional or global contexts.

Taken together these dimensions comprise a focused approach to practice that takes time, study, and experience to develop. It also presumes an enhanced self-awareness that goes beyond what is typically required of technically rational professions. Adaptive problems require a disciplined approach to collective inquiry, one that focuses both on the problem structures and substantive content, but also the underlying system of thought and identity narratives that have given rise to the situation. This kind of inquiry is done *with* participants, not *to* them; its effectiveness and the results that emerge are a measure of the resonance between the practitioner's internal coherence and their external actions. Effectiveness here requires objectively developed authenticity.

Conclusion

Dialogue, when understood as a process of drawing out and reflecting on the underlying system of thought that has produced social fragmentation and incoherence, can become professionalized if elements such as those outlined in this paper are expanded and extended to more formal study, further articulation, and rigorous testing. Moving dialogue in the direction of a formal profession will require much greater elucidation of the elements of the knowledge dimensions of dialogue, as articulated here, but also the social requirements for professionalization. These include the continued formulation of a training and education process, accreditation, and the formation of a peer-based review and governance process.

Dialogue practice, if developed, holds the promise of offering a rigorous means to address the adaptive problems facing organizations and the wider society. Turning dialogue into a profession could expand our concept of professional knowledge and make it possible to make progress beyond that which can be achieved by professional action grounded in technical rationality. In practice we can supplement the traditional problem-solving focus with a new way to understand and address the contextual factors that emerge out of the fragmentation of thought and incoherent social fields that professionals are called upon to address.

References

Alexander, C. (2012). *The Battle for the Life and Beauty of the Earth: A Struggle Between Two World Systems*. Oxford: Oxford University Press.

Argyris, C. & Schön, D. (1989). "Participatory action research and action science compared." *American Behavioral Scientist*, 32(5), 612-623.

Argyris, C., Putnam, R., Smith, D. (1985). *Action Science*. San Francisco: Jossey-Bass.

Barfield, O. (1988). *Saving the Appearances: A Study in Idolatry*. Middletown, CT: Wesleyan University Press.

Bohm, D. (1980). *Wholeness and the Implicate Order*. London: Routledge.

Bohm, D. (1992). *Thought as a System*. New York: Routledge.

Bushe, G.R. & Marshak, R.J. (2016). "The dialogic organization development approach to transformation and change." In Rothwell, W. Stravros, J., & Sullivan R. (eds.), *Practicing Organization Development*, 4th Ed. (407-418). San Francisco: Wiley.

Crook, D. (2008). "Some historical perspectives on professionalism." In Cunningham, B. (ed.), *Exploring Professionalism*. Bedford Way Papers. London: Institute of Education, University of London.

Fishkin, J. (1991). *Democracy and Deliberation: New Directions for Democratic Reform*. New Haven; London: Yale University Press.

Garrett, P. (2018) "Engaging fragmentation, subcultures and organisational powers," in *The World Needs Dialogue One: Gathering the Field*. Chipping Campden: Dialogue Publications.

Glazer, N. (1974). "The schools of the minor professions." *Minerva*, 12(3), 346-364.

Greenwood, E. (1957). "Attributes of a profession." *Social Work*, 2(3), 45-55.

Habermas, J. (1987). *Knowledge and Human Interests*. Cambridge, UK: Polity Press.

Heifetz R., (1994). *Leadership Without Easy Answers*. Cambridge, MA: Harvard University Press.

Heifetz, R. & Linsky, M. (2017). *Leadership on the Line: Staying Alive Through the Dangers of Change*. Cambridge, MA: Harvard University Press.

Isaacs, W. (1991). "The Perils of Shared Ideals." University of Oxford D.Phil dissertation.

Isaacs, W. (1999). *Dialogue and the Art of Thinking Together*. New York: Currency.

Kantor, D. (2012). *Reading the Room*. San Francisco: John Wiley & Sons.

Larson, M.S. (2017). "The rise of professionalism: A sociological analysis." In The Wiley Online Library: https://doi.org/10.1002/9781119395485.ch20.

Moore, W. (1970). *The Professions*. New York: Russell Sage.

Parsons, T. (1939). "The professions and social structure." *Social Forces*, 17(4), 457-467.

Parsons, T., & Shils, E. (1959). *Toward a General Theory of Action*. Cambridge: Harvard University Press.

Ridington, R. (1996). "Voice, representation, and dialogue: The poetics of Native American spiritual traditions." *American Indian Quarterly*, 20(3/4), 467-488.

Ritzer, G. (1975). "Professionalization, bureaucratization and rationalization: The views of Max Weber." *Social Forces*, 53(4), 627–634.

Saunders, H. (1999). *A Public Peace Process: Sustained Dialogue to Transform Racial and Ethnic Conflicts*. New York: St Martin's Press.

Scharmer, O. & Kaufer, K. (2015). "Awareness-based action research: catching social reality creation in flight." In Bradbury, H. *The SAGE Handbook of Action Research* (pp. 199-210). London: SAGE Publications Ltd.

Schein, E. (1972). *Professional Education: Some New Directions*. Carnegie Commission on Higher Education. New York: McGraw-Hill.

Schein, E. H. (1993, Autumn). "On dialogue, culture, and organizational learning." *Organizational Dynamics*, 22(2), 40+.

Schein, E. Humble Inquiry (2013). *The Gentle Art of Asking Instead of Telling*. San Francisco: Berrett-Kohler.

Schön, D. (1983). *The Reflective Practitioner: How Professionals Think in Action*. New York: Basic Books.

Tener, E. (1997). *Why Things Bite Back: Technology and the Revenge of Unintended Consequences*. New York: Random House.

Susskind, L., Fuller, B., Fairman, D., Ferenz M. (2003). "Multistakeholder dialogue at the global scale." *International Negotiation*, 8(2).

Weber, M. (1968). *Economy and Society*. Totowa, N.J.: Bedminster.

Zakaria, F. (2019). "The end of economics?" *Foreign Policy*, Winter 2019.

Conference Session Extracts
From a conversation with participants considering the paper with William Isaacs

Speaker: I was part of the coaching movement for a long time, and became a member of the International Coaching Federation. Two years ago I decided to drop out of that because it had become such a procedural thing. It imprisoned coaching into a set of ways of doing that are very limited and very technical. If we develop a profession, we should try to avoid that. And another thing, I wondered what would be different between a dialogue professional and, for instance, a person trained by Otto Scharmer as a systems interventionist? How do we differentiate ourselves?

William: I think you're right on. We're being quite ambitious here. What we're saying is that there is a thing called dialogue in the room, but there's something much more expansive, which is not just organizations as systems or networks of organizations as systems, but the whole thing. It's very possible to impact the collective narratives of large regions. I think it's purely a matter of building capacity now.

Speaker: I'm thinking that we have to really be transparent and conscious about something. Are we in the exploration and development of the profession—or are we in sales and attraction for the profession? One piece that I think ties in with that is this notion of vulnerability versus credibility. I don't see them as mutually exclusive, but if I try to relate this to Kantor's languages of communication, it seems to me that we started off this conversation in the beginning of this session in the meaning space, right? Then it seems like there's this tendency to flip over into the power (doing) space. I think that is part of the confusion. I don't know if *confusion* is the right word. I'm trying to surface what I think is underneath the surface. I think we have to be really conscious of that because there have been mixed sessions where we say we're going to have a dialogue, and then we talk about how we attract more members. So which one are we doing? And part of this to me is a little bit more about the vulnerability versus credibility. Could we get professionals to really talk about the times where they've missed handling the disturbance? We're humans. We have triggers. Can we have that conversation without being concerned that if you expose a misstep you're no longer credible?

William: Well, just to say something about that. I don't think we're necessarily talking about trying to expand the thing today, or getting better at it, but more getting clear what is it and what isn't it. In my mind, one thing that we would be taking seriously is the expectation of mastery for the profession that would be knowing that there is a continuous process of transforming fragmented parts of myself.

That must be shifted for me to continue to be effective. If you're not ready for that, you are not ready to be in this gig.

Speaker: I'd like for us to recognize that what we're doing here right now is part of the process. And let's acknowledge that these conversations benefit our goal of trying to make this more of a professional and respected profession. And then the other thing is we're talking about is how we encourage people to value what we do, and how we encourage ourselves to be invested in what we do. I'm reminded that's really paramount to *why* we do what we do. How do we find the right people who want to come on board to work as dialogue practitioners?

We want people who are invested in understanding the spirit of dialogue, I'll say for lack of a better way to say it. Once someone becomes immersed in it, they may realize there is value to this process, not just to me personally but to others that they care about. So, I think it's really important in this process, as we start thinking about how to make it more of a profession. I think we really have to reach out and look for ways that we find value it ourselves. And if we exemplify that value to others that we work with, they in turn can find value in it. I'm thinking about how other work was done and became a profession. We didn't just magically call people doctors. We figured out a process that eventually we recognized when we have had a health need, we would call on someone who was a doctor. So I think that same process can work for us in this context, but we need to help others understand and value the work that we do.

Speaker: It sounds to me like we don't yet have the rigorous body of knowledge and we don't yet have the social part, that committed group of people who are farming the way. So, in about three years' time, how would we move towards that, with the two spaces of moving forward together?

William: I think that's right. I think that's really right on.

Speaker: I'm struggling with this because what I see in the work that's being done in Virginia, for example, is that this is really coming from the inside out. It's growing in groups. It's like creating healthy people. It almost like they don't have to go to the doctor. I think what we're facing is people, your clients, expecting something to be done for them. How can I fix or address the issue? That's the expectation we face a lot of the time.

William: I think we need to take all this complexity and get it simple. I don't mean that we oversimplify it. I think we are in the business of solving adaptive problems by definition. That means none of us have the answers. We don't solve all kinds of problems—we solve the adaptive problems. They are a very special kind of problem. It could be at any scale from you or your family to a nation. We have to figure out what it means to do it.

Speaker: What do we need to move forward? One of the things that we need in simple language is case studies. We certainly have a wonderful case study in Virginia, and Bill, you've written about your work in Asia. If we had enough case studies we could look across them, and I think there's things we could learn across those case studies. Then we'll have a more measurable outcome. Virginia certainly has measurable outcomes in terms of the changes in their recidivism rate and changes of attitude that show up in their annual survey and so forth.

Speaker: But, in addition to that learnable set of skills, is there not also an underlying understanding that has to be there around it?

William: A hundred percent! This is the missing bit that I was trying to bring out in the paper. There is an underlying understanding. The ground is actually very solid. It is not the case that we were just making this up. There really is a solid theoretical and a deep body of understanding that is articulable and learnable, that then translates into a set of techniques and practices. But there's something behind it. The techniques alone are not enough. That's the point.

Postscript

The author's reflections, written some months after the conference

My paper attempted to outline the conditions required for the successful establishment of a professional approach to "dialogue." As I have reflected on this effort over the past year, I have had several new insights and would make several changes to what I have said previously.

First, the "theory of the thing" as articulated in the paper leaves out a critical—and yet central—dimension that remains unstated in the emergence of effective dialogue practice. At the center of this theory is the idea that the way the collective system of thought works fragments the world, producing incoherence and destructiveness. Within this system there is but little capacity to notice and correct these flaws. This system of thought is pervasive and seemingly immune to change. However, new levels of subtle intelligence can be activated through dialogue that can bring awareness of these limits in thought and catalyze transformational shifts in the internal collective thought infrastructure, making possible previously unimaginable and seemingly impossible change.

What is missing, however, is the recognition that the subtle forms of intelligence that can guide and help correct the system of incoherent thought emerges from *something* itself. That something is the Self, individual and collective, present at the core of everyone. This Self is coherent and shares a set of characteristics and qualities that are immediately knowable and recognizable. These qualities include compassion, calmness, confidence, courage, creativity, and clarity. The "theory of the thing," to be complete, needs to articulate the living presence of the Self, and to acknowledge that fragmentation extends to the human experience of self. The human understanding of identity is fragmented by the incoherent system of thought, sometimes experienced as our having different "parts" of ourselves that are at odds with each other, or that have differing agendas and reactions. This multiplicity of internal "parts" emerges from the fragmentation of thought, a connection that has not previously been well articulated.

More significantly, the healing and transformation of this condition emerges through the activation and presence of the Self, and through the subsequent subtle intelligence that can shift fragmented thought and feeling.

This insight impacts both the way change is understood and the practice of dialogue itself. Change now implies assisting people to consciously activate an experience of Self, which can enable them to compassionately embrace the multiplicity of selves and their narratives. Dialogue is a practice that activates the experience of Self, individual and collective, which leads to the intensified emergence of subtle intelligence that can transform the incoherence of thought and the fragmentation of identity that has cut off human beings from the experience of wholeness.

Developing Online Professional Dialogue

Thomas Köttner

I invite you to an exploration into the ways the Digital Ecosystem—the interrelated web of thinking and technology—may promote a step forward for deep Dialogue, and for Professional Dialogue expansion.

The Origins of this Writing

The year 2020 will probably be remembered as an unusually intense, life-changing year in our history. The Covid-19 pandemic has generated an intricate web of systemic impacts, some of which will clarify and stabilize, and others which—having arrived in an unexpectedly sudden way—will take time to understand. For the first time in modern times, most of our social, relational, conversational and work-coordinated interactions outside of our living places are being held online and in so-called remote ways.

This time has been life altering and life changing for many people.

I am one of those for whom very little has changed during the pandemic, since I have spent most of my last ten years living and working online, holding deep conversations with executives around the world, meeting, presenting, negotiating, closing deals and generating strong relationships and friendships with persons I have never met personally.

Many events, relational behaviors and challenges that were once considered exceptional have become commonplace, seemingly overnight. They are changing our work, education and social interaction forever. Dialogue, our ancestral way of sharing, storytelling, learning, thinking and creating new meanings and thinking together, will unavoidably be influenced by the way in which digital technology has disrupted our lives.

I am very grateful to share some perspectives of my journey in living online in dialogue-based professional work over the last two-and-a-half decades. Throughout the early 1990s my professional fields were always on the humanistic side of business. Because I was eager to learn what was going on in the "developed" world my work often involved long, costly and tiring trips to very different parts of the world.

Living in Argentina, in what is called the South Cone of South America (Uruguay, Chile and Argentina) has always been the acorn of opportunity on the branches of the oak-strong challenges. Ours is a complex country often characterized as "once first-world, turned into third," far away from many academic, scientific and economic centers. Those of us with sufficient interest were always looking for creative ways to narrow the gap in order to get "closer to the action" of the newest states of many arts and disciplines. By 1996, Internet-based technology had turned solid enough to become a life-changing opportunity. Since then the online world has been a central means of conversational interaction. It has also allowed sharing a lot of work over audiovisual channels around the world.

My professional journeys were all driven by an underlying interest in human behavior. With the arrival of the Internet, I found the interaction of human behavior and the digital environment very attractive, and it led me to get involved in consulting and management for high-end e-commerce platforms. In 2010, after my various interests had consolidated into the field of learning and development as an executive coach, I was invited to join the start-up of CoachReady, the world's first digital and fully online executive coaching company, of which I am a managing partner and Coaching Strategies Director to this day.

During the first ten years of development of CoachReady we faced much skepticism about how our online-based, face-to-face human interaction was creating a fruitful, close and warm relationship—often in better ways than the usual in-person meetings, which were the rule in those days. We have learned the practice and philosophy to support the effectiveness of online development approaches, and today we serve some of the largest and most demanding global companies on five continents, working and connecting in what has only recently become the new normal.

I hope I can ignite some curiosity and insights that might make us look at the apparently cold digital world in a new light, and discover not only new platforms but also new ways for Professional Dialogue to become both necessary and unavoidable in the near future.

What is the Impact of the Digital Revolution on Dialogue?

I'll venture to say that the cost / benefit equation of the way we offer dialogue as a practice in business, education and institutional life will be a central concern. But what kind of cost, given that monetary costs are often *reduced* by converting in-person gatherings to online?

The central cost in the digital world is measured in time expectations. Many online sales businesses go bankrupt, for example, not because they do not have the quality or the quantity of the desired product, but rather because they cannot match the shortened patience threshold cultivated by a world where things are available seemingly instantly, "anytime, anywhere." If we are above the age of 20, it is difficult to understand the demand for speed that is central to a young person's life. Where postal mail takes days, digital communications take nanoseconds, with corresponding expectations of reply. Dialogue, which requires time to develop, would at first glance seem to be incompatible with the inclination toward speed. We'll explore that premise in this paper.

Black-Swan Technology

Sometimes a slowly growing trend is hit by a black swan—an unforeseen event with big consequences—which accelerates the evolving trend and establishes it as a new reality, seemingly overnight. The Covid-19 pandemic is a kind of black swan, one of those completely unforeseen situations that disrupt the preexisting world, and it has forced the acceptance of a new world as a mandatory life condition: you and I cannot speculate anymore about the possibility of staying in the well-known world that has passed.

Many of us (at least in the developed world) have been put in the situation for several months now of communicating mostly and centrally over digital devices. Travel is still not possible in many countries, and financial considerations are keeping a strong hold on costs and expenditures. This will very probably mean that travel and accommodation budgets will not be available in the same way they were. We are already facing the twin scenarios of the sad disappearance of many usual customs and, at the same time, of exciting new possibilities for those creative minds that take advantage of this moment of further digital transformation.

Dialogue in the Digital Era: The Challenges

We face the paradox that the more Dialogue becomes necessary for making sense and meaning of all the changes, the more the concepts of Dialogue need to be reviewed and perhaps changed to fit the new times. As the Academy of Professional Dialogue dedicated to the support and development of Dialogue professionals, we are certainly responsible for the education of the next generation of practitioners. The ways we adapt to the unavoidable impact of digital communication will have a strong influence on the way that Dialogue develops in the time ahead.

We are in the midst of not only a revolution in speed, but also an overwhelming abundance of information and communication itself. This overabundance of permanent information means that the scarcest good in the world today is not time, nor money, but attention—the "cost / benefit" ratio I mentioned earlier. Digital speed and connectivity creates the challenge of being highly aware and discerning of what is really worth paying attention to. The aforementioned relationship with speed as a value is affecting even language. Millennials (widely considered to be those who this year will be 22 to 39 years old) and generation Z (the oldest ones of which become 23 years old this year) do already communicate in new and time adaptive languages. They save letters and they save words to send short messages to convey what they find necessary in the moment. And while I wonder how much time is saved by writing "Thk U" instead of "thank you," (and even more so how that time saving is applied!), it is a fact that the main communications between young people are brief messages sent and answered at lightning speed.

Communication continues to rapidly evolve, particularly as many people are entering a state of cognitive fatigue, sometimes referred to as "Zoomed Out," due to the inordinate amount of time spent in videoconferencing. For such people it is a relief to trade the computer screen for written, brief chats. Feelings and states of mind, life moments and experiences, welcomes and dismissals can be transmitted with a series of emojis, and—this may seem surprising—is actually not very different from hieroglyphic expression.

Meaning and sensemaking through such forms of communication are based on first impressions, and further depth is seldom invited. Remember that saving time is the essence of the digital world and, as we become accustomed to immediacy, we may not realize how impatient we may become when something delays things beyond our expectations. This is probably the main challenge we face when wanting to create calm, reflexive and dialogical spaces. The digital world enhances and promotes several effective communication possibilities, but it may very possibly limit our current understanding of some dialogue perspectives, Bohm's included.

In the face of all this, how do we cultivate the necessary spaces of time, of silence, required to make sense at a deeper level? How do we resolve these paradoxes?

How Do We Translate Dialogue for the Digital World?

How will we develop the new generations of digital natives for meaningful and deeper dialogue, given a new world of digital hieroglyphics and language? To begin, we will need to learn to adapt our current understanding to the world of digital space and time. For example, many people I have come across over my years in online conversation have, and still do, refer to any kind of computer-based interaction as a "virtual" event to distinguish it from "genuine" interaction, even though the people communicating via computers are very much alive and real. As words solidify the images we create and see, the label *virtual* appears as something visible, but not real—often, even, as something of questionable quality, or imaginary.

I invite you to become aware that the conversations we have are anything but unreal. We are two or more persons seeing ourselves face-to-face at a synchronic moment and interacting in real time. Some virtual spaces are imaginary or may be only partially interactive by design; online games based on imaginary lands or universes are virtual. Prerecorded video, even though it broadcast online (such as a YouTube video or a recorded webinar) may be partially or wholly virtual. But online, real-time video, with enabled face-to-face conversations, are very real. They are just online.

Similarly, we may consider that remoteness does not automatically imply the need for different behaviors than in physical contact. There is no difference of content in our conversations, and they require that we behave the same and pay attention to the same details we pay attention to in physical realms.

I refer to *online* as everything that is enabled by the Internet as the medium for communication. By contrast, a phone conversation may be remote, given the participants not sharing the same physical space, but it is not generally considered to be online (Voice over Internet Protocol—VoIP—calls possibly excepted!)

What's Good about Online Interaction

In spite of the challenges outlined, and the radical changes in understanding often required to participate in online dialogue, there are many benefits to embracing this inevitable migration. Persons will often seem more open online than during physical contact. For many it seems that the screen acts as a protective interface which provides a kind of psychological safety that is not present in the same circumstances in physical face-to-face communication. In his always-witty manner, Oscar Wilde said, "Man is least himself when he talks in his own person. Give him a mask, and he will tell you the truth." The psychological safety mask, helpful until we can become more trustful and then let it down, is present in the online relationship because I can interrupt the contact immediately if I feel uncomfortable, just by the touch of a button or by closing my laptop.

I note that when I am communicating online I get way more focused on the other person, because she occupies my visible screen with a scene that is centered on herself. We are not exposed to the potential distraction of observing a far wider visual spectrum, with the added stimulation when we are in physical settings. I have also noticed that I can delve into our subjects in a more fluent way, because online many of us are more purpose-driven. This may go against our assumption that Dialogue should begin without any set purpose, but in my experience this intensity of focus and purpose actually instills a more dialogical attitude in a shorter time. We are more relaxed because we feel in governance of our space, thus allowing for a more inviting attitude and postures.

Multi-participant dialogues become more democratic. Power, authority or wealth positioning, which are always present in the physical settings, disappear. The power office with its exclusive furniture and private elevator, the rich home and the fancy cars, whatever expressions of wealth or power cannot be displayed in their fullness in the little same-sized rectangles we all appear in. The CEO will have the same screen real estate as any employee when their meeting happens online. In the digital world we can make a contribution just by who we are and what knowledge, ideas, or helpful insight we may share.

As I mentioned earlier, the digital-social ethos may put some pressure on our tendency toward immediacy. Emails, WhatsApps and Instant Messages of many kinds are expected to be answered as soon as possible, ASAP (hopefully with some other acronyms, so that we save writing and reading time!) But on its positive side, this quick communication allows a lot of flexibility for rescheduling and time reallocation.

Mobility also allows us to be able to choose our settings for an online conversation. In the digital context, meaning-creation and sense-making are also partially related to the way we present ourselves on screen, beyond the trappings of status. We can design our digital environments in ways that pay the same attention we would offer when receiving someone at home or at the office. Years ago, when jackets and ties were still the dress code in many companies, I decided that, even when I could work from home in a more relaxed manner, I should still use a jacket or something which corresponded to a certain formality and could express a respect for the situation in which we were both engaged. It was respect without solemnity; attaining to a certain dress code sends a message.

Digital online dialogue also usefully raises the question of how to handle the perception of ourselves. In our traditional ways of dialogue we may feel inclined to forget about ourselves, particularly if we are just engaged with our partners in dialogue and forgetting about ourselves. Almost all video conferencing platforms have a feature which shows ourselves together with other participants. This creates, or at least allows, an awareness of ourselves. This does not happen when we are sitting in a room with others. We do not see, nor have any chance to see ourselves. This new self-perception is almost a reflex reaction which we need to get accustomed to in order to manage (or disable online). Such self-consciousness is common with those new to video technology, in some ways like people facing their first long distance calls on the phone would raise their voice when talking (as if shouting would make the voice to be heard over the distance separating caller and receiver—we haven't yet grasped the potential of a new environment. So many of our behaviors are ancestral, and we need to adapt to the ever-new technologies and their particular aspects.

Since the screen is the frame for our upper torso and usually just our head and neck, facial expressions become the body language of emotions and visual feedback of what is being exchanged. It takes some practice to let go of the perception of ourselves in order to focus on others and create the necessary empathic energy. I believe this is an important part of developing a new kind of proprioception.

Designing the Online Environment and Preparing Ourselves

What we have set aside in physical presence and familiar cues in the traditional shared physical places for dialogue, we can capitalize on if we pay attention to certain aspects in our video conferencing spaces. When I moved to the house I live and work in, I built a room which would become my daily place in the world. It was a place where I could put all the books that had previously been dispersed in different places of my previous home into one library, where I could work, read, listen to music. In that way, I am sharing my world with my client or friend when we meet.

Similarly, when I meet with a person in their setting, I also have some clues about their space, some of which might catch my attention and inspire me to get a bit more personal, perhaps asking about some interesting picture or object. This creates a dose of closeness, which is most often welcome and brings warmth to the inevitable unfamiliarity of a first meeting.

When we prepare to promote adequate perceptions, it does not mean that we are pretending or faking something. We all know that authenticity and genuine expression of ourselves is of the essence of deep Dialogue. We can pay the same attention and put the same love toward creating an online environment as we do when we are the hosts of a Dialogue circle in the "offline" world. The digital, online world is primarily audiovisual, so meaning is built with an increased accent on certain clues that will help the adequate creation of meaning. We can design our digital space and setting by paying attention to similar design clues that we use when designing our work or living space, thus helping to build a container that promotes feelings of warmth, proximity, familiarity and attention.

Specifically such meaning-creating modes are possible in some of the following areas:

- I propose paying attention to visual design clues: colors, perspective, your presence in the foreground in relation to your background. Good digital thinking starts with caring for a beneficial outcome for all involved, particularly for others. Ask yourself: what is the other seeing ?
- Most of us create neat and tidy spaces when we prepare for a physical dialogue circle, yet we may have all witnessed that the same does not always happen online. We may certainly not have the most adequate space for video conferencing, given that we may be at home, guarding ourselves from interference from other members staying in the same home or office. But whatever space we decide to present ourselves in, we may still care for making it a clean, tidy and non-distracting or disturbing view in our backgrounds.
- Several online videoconferencing platforms offer digital screens to be used as backgrounds. Their benefit is that we can choose something neutral that does not distract our senses and may cover up for some background we may not particularly like. But be aware that it has a cost, in obscuring the always-welcome genuineness of showing yourself in your own world, thus adding to the authenticity and trust involved in the relation.
- Audio design, related to voice clarity, includes an adequate microphone that helps ensure distortion-free sound quality. Paying attention to resonances in the room, which may produce echoes, is always welcome.
- Spatial design clues: Some spaces create intriguing, amusing, inspiring, serious, joyous impressions, each appropriate to different conversations. What is yours ? Design of your dialogue ecosystem is not something that needs to be contrived or overdone, but rather it is something that reflects yourself, in the same way you may pay attention to dressing up in a certain way.
- If we want to create warmth, we will need to appear on camera. Not doing so would in many cases appear as disrespectful, given the need for the visual feedback offered by

our facial expressions and gestures. As mentioned, this implies that we will also be seeing ourselves on screen together with our dialogue partners. Instead of trying to deny our proprioception, we may turn it positive by paying attention to our posture, gestures, and expressions that may help carry our message and emotions across to others.

It may not necessary to mention the relevance of clarity in our verbal expression, the authenticity in our meanings and feelings, and the coherence we may need to bring into a space where we have to turn a three-dimensional presence into a plain screen of distributed flat images. However, most probably we will one day, not too far from now, be meeting in 3D holographic ways!

How Digital Dialogue Connects with the Quantum Energy Field

Richard Feynman, who won a Nobel prize for his work in the field of quantum mechanics, is reported to have commented, "I think I can safely say that nobody understands quantum mechanics." So in no way will I pretend in what I write to understand the depths to which David Bohm and all the other theoretic physicists who were related to him may have reached.

I was always curious about the fact that so many of these scientists have become interested or involved in the field of dialogue. Our "offline" world is based on the habit of *seeing in order to believe*. The quantum realms are, for most of us who grasp some basic concepts of theoretical physics, basically a matter of *believing in order to see*. For so many of us quantum physics amateur readers, the concept of the unified energetic field and our conception of ourselves as parts of a whole universal energy, makes just enough sense as to grasp the idea.

I have always been aware, before an online meeting, that my distance to my fellow person is the distance from my head to my computer screen. If we were in physical presence, we would likely feel we were invading the private space of the other. Yet if for whatever reason the thought of being 9,000 miles away appears to create any feeling of personal distance, our awareness that we are connected is what gets us close again. In this sense, my chair is connected through the sustaining structure of my house, to the ground . . . which is the same ground that supports your house and your chair, even when we may seem separated by an ocean that covers part of our shared space.

I invite you to consider this thought and check how it improves your feeling of physical connection and relatedness in dialogue, whether in person or online. Once again, we are all an integral part of the whole. Our mind, our brain and our heart aligned makes us connected in our intention and energy field, thus allowing us to create a warmth in us. I have no doubt we are very able to transmit this between us.

Awareness and Ethics in Relation to Online Dialogue Practice

Much of our best thinking starts with our perspective for the future, our purpose and our design of the steps involved to create what we have envisioned. I understand this is a central aspect that differentiates the free-flowing and fully open outcome of Bohmian dialogue in relation to client-requested Professional Dialogue facilitation.

This means that, as Professional Dialogue Practitioners, we need to become much more aware of our deep purpose in facilitating dialogue. We shall avoid letting our biases interfere with where the dialogue needs to go or where it may arrive. We need to be alert to how a client-defined objective might inadvertently steer a dialogue, and how designing a process to reach that outcome might become self-referential.

If we let this happen, it could produce in manipulating approaches, which are so present on social networks and in the whole world of digital applications, where information is increasingly tailored to resonate with our prejudices and preconceived ideas. It looks like users are the beneficiaries, when it is frequently quite the opposite.

Introspection and awareness from the practitioner is central, and I would say mandatory for the conscious professional practitioner using a medium that lends itself to helping to shape consciousness.

What Does this Mean for the Profession of Dialogue Facilitation?

What might the future of Dialogue in organizations and institutions look like, particularly in contrast with the customary ways we have organized and delivered dialogic interventions?

As I have emphasized, we will need to be aware of our perceptions of time, and create dialogue spaces and ways of dialogic interaction that allow us to think together in shorter timeframes. In a Digital world, where expected outcomes and purpose are of the essence in every line of consciousness and thought, Dialogue will probably need to become more purpose-driven, while still seeking to connect, explore and discover together. It will move toward a directional outcome.

I predict that dialogue spaces will be requested to help ad hoc teams for very specific projects. Such new teams will not have known each other before, and will possibly disperse once the project is completed. To satisfy such needs we will need to keep researching and practicing in order to understand the impacts and attitudinal changes, if any, of geographically diverse and multiculturally influenced online dialogues. This will create a beneficial, even necessary, collaboration for cross-cultural dialogue facilitation teams; these will also require new collaborative models for professional intervention.

Will purely local teams, which by definition may share the same cultural blind spots among them, be effective for dealing with cross- and multicultural team dialogues online? If we believe so, how will we promote meaning-creation agreements among participants? For example, how will we deal with language-influenced metaphors, images and understandings if done from a single cultural perspective?

In that sense, what are the implications if we choose one or the other alternative cultural understanding? Will the local team of facilitators imply that professionals of a certain culture should just work with local companies that impact solely their local society, institutions or businesses?

An End to this Paper and the Start of a Journey

As with everything unexpected, the lockdown and the emerging online scenarios point to a future with a lot of changes in our ways and habits. Many spaces, places and ways we were familiar with will decay and disappear. But many new ones will come as interesting opportunities. Dialogue will be more necessary than ever, and the future invites us to find the most adequate and effective ways to engage with it.

Research and understanding of new approaches and practices will be a necessary and interesting field if we allow it to be. Our facilitation work possibilities will expand without limit if we learn to bring the spirit of Dialogue of the ages to the digital world. If we are bold and curious, we will encounter an exciting time for everyone involved in this professional field.

The Internet is creating a kind of mutation, and our ways of thinking, acting and interacting will have us either adapting to or collapsing under the unavoidable big wave. I invite you to join me on the bus to the beach so that we can surf the wave together. Let us enjoy the thrill of creating the future of our human understanding through dialogue with the abundance of resources we have at hand.

Additional Reflection:

On Our Relational Nature and Communicating Analogically
Note: For those who may be interested in some of the background thinking that led me to write this paper, I am including some notes on what I call Analogic and Digital thinking. The paper stands on its own, but I am following the practice of suspending my thinking "in the middle of the room" for others to see.

From the moment our earliest ancestors realized that being together was better for staying alive than going alone and being eaten by stronger beasts, we, as a species, have stayed in relationship, communicating and coordinating actions for an expected outcome. Our first coordinated conversations, then, repeated and situation-specific, were through movements and sounds. They could be said to be *instinctual*, based in the instincts necessary for survival and relationship.

Sounds evolved, and our tongue movements created new versions of speech; with this, our brains evolved for progressively more sophisticated ways of human messaging. In this, the technology of fire was a critical organizing medium, keeping us warm, fed and ultimately alive; it was a central aspect for helping us remain together and close to the tribe. We might say that this is how our *Analogic* thought journey began to emerge from intuitive thinking: the process of combining images, sounds and words in relationship with each other was at the foundation of brain development, thought and rational memory.

As I am using it here, Analogic thinking is evolutionary, and it is less about technology than it is about thinking itself. It creates expansion by improving what exists, creating or adding new features or experiences. Analogical thinking also starts with ourselves. It brings things forward from our past approaches to similar situations in the present. When we have to solve something, our brains search for analogous (from the Greek *analogos*, meaning "proportionate") memories, experiences, knowledge, information, data—anything that might be available to us. Intuition may of course be a part of it as well, but intuition also brings together the accumulation of our past experiences.

Analogic thinking is based, then, on the weave of our integrated data, information, knowledge, wisdom. Our genetic and rational memories come to us to allow for analog categorizations that organize our thought and actions.

The Analogic world is our past coming to the present in the way of thinking and thought.

What is Digital Thinking?
As I am using it here, Digital thinking is not only about technology, and neither is it synonymous with "binary thinking." From a conceptual perspective, a technology may be anything that allows us to achieve more with less, whether we call it *Analogic* or *Digital*. A myriad of devices across the millennia could be considered technologies, and actually some of them even created mutational evolutions in our brain structures. The wheel, for example, jump-started immeasurable creative developments in transportation, exploration, migration, commerce and many other fields. Similarly, Gutenberg's printing system extended knowledge, the sudden abundance of which generated significant development within our brains.

Technological and digital devices have made for many of the improvements in comfort and practicality we experience today, as well as for increased efficiency and faster manufacturing processes, for economically sound processes and developments and for unlimited and easy transportation. Technological hardware and digital programming has allowed for all the almost real-time communication, education and transcultural exchange that many currently enjoy. And the Internet, with a similar or even more anthropological mutational power than the wheel and the printing press, has provided us with a modern library of Babel.

But I want to emphasize that the central quality of Digital thinking is *not* about devices, appliances or code-based programs and content. It is a different way of thinking about everything, because it *starts with the future* and depends on reverse thinking and reverse engineering to bring the future to the present. In this future orientation, Digital thinking can be used to look ahead for the benefit of the others or the world at large. Because it does not depend on the existent, Digital thinking is disruptive. It creates something completely new, something that may only be appreciated once it exists. This new creation may be something the majority of the population hasn't yet asked for, because it has not generally been imagined yet.

Digital thinking has created many technology companies which, in turn, have helped create new disruptions. Four of the ten most valuable companies in the world did not exist 25 years ago, after decades of this list being populated by corporations more than a century old. Many of the top new companies were conceived on the basis of Digital thinking. They provide us with good examples of how far and how highly conceptual their conception has been.

Alphabet, the holding company for Google and all its later derivations, was founded in 1998 with the vision that one day there would be so much information produced and sent into cyberspace that it would be necessary to organize it to make it findable or useful. Analogic thinking would have put a librarian's perspective to work in order to *catalogue* content on each of the different platforms by subjects. Digital thinking caused Google to *search* for the desired information in the online multiverse.

Ali Baba was formed in 1999 because Jack Ma wanted to create more trust in commerce in China, where such social emotion was very scarce at the time. Digital reverse thinking helped him understand that Internet would, over time, either accelerate trust building or fail completely. So, following that premise, he started an online commercial exchange marketplace which became the largest retailer and e-commerce business in the world.

Elon Musk founded Tesla—now the most financially valuable car company in the world—in 2003 as a clean-energy producing company to create a new understanding for an unprecedented global energy matrix. When he started to think about how to realize his vision, he decided to work through one of the most contaminating industries to create an electric car company. He did not to create another car company, he wanted to create a clean, electricity-driven transportation system which included electric supply stations and transformation of urban transportation design.

To understand the difference between Digital and Analogic thinking in car manufacturing, Daimler Benz provides a good example: it is also designing an electric car, but it is doing so on the basis of the existent and known. Tesla, through Digital thinking, conceived and created a completely new, unprecedented perspective by designing an energy system that *includes* the vehicle. This is a disruption for the car industry and for every industry which will be changed by those with a further purpose than just accumulating capital and delivering value to their shareholders. Where Analogic thinking is sourced in the past, Dialogic thinking is rooted in the future.

In a certain way, Digital thinking follows a similar path to artistic creative thinking. First, you envision what you want to create and then think in reverse, learning what needs to be done to produce the envisioned outcome. What do we want to do? For whom will we do it, with what kinds of innovation, and with what life-changing purpose in mind?

Once the end-users and beneficiaries are defined, thinking processes go in the direction of the need for making that happen, and then to shaving off steps and then some others in such a way that the processes are made as simple as possible. This is the main reason why Digital thinking is behind the acceleration of almost everything. Time becomes of the essence for anything that intends to produce satisfactory results. This creates a huge impact and unavoidable difference with our longtime ways of living, working, socializing and communicating.

Conference Session Extracts

From a conversation with participants considering the paper with Thomas Köttner

Speaker: I was just noticing that for me, with so many of us on this screen, as Thomas said, the scarcity is not money – it's attention. And it's very hard to hold somebody in attention online with so many faces, and for no more than just a few seconds then it's somebody else and then somebody else. So I really appreciated being in a breakout room with four people. It was such so relaxing. But I realized I'm a child of a past century really. Further depth is seldom invited.

Speaker: But one of the things that I do find attention-grabbing in online dialogue is silence, and just slowing the pace down. Certainly when we're doing autistic dialogues, we ask everybody just to take the pace down and leave a gap between speakers so that there's time for processing. It's really around the suspension piece, and enabling the listening.

Thomas: There's something to learn from this, and for how the conference is designed. I had a dialogue last week in this small room where silence was the right thing. It brought people almost to tears just because of the depth that had been reached. The silence allowed for us to absorb what had been shared. I think it's an important thing to take into account on our online dialogues, because being digital is about speed and obtaining immediate results. We have a natural expectation of something to conclude and happen immediately. We have to make a conscious allowance for silence.

Speaker: I've worked both in-person in the room and now quite a lot on the web like this. As a group of individuals become more familiar with the environment it becomes easier for them to use it. Early on I've experienced a lot of intention to try and fill the space, but after a while it seems entirely possible to experience those moments of silence and connection and intimacy, even amongst quite a large group. But it's taken a while for people to become comfortable with the online environment which is different to the environment when you're in one room, as we have all known since we started.

Speaker: What's interesting is that it strips away some of the distractions that are present in physical settings. That has the advantage, I suppose, of at least making possible an awareness of a whole lot of other factors that would normally be missed. There are a whole lot of subtle components that are less present when we are moving our bodies around the planet, opening up other ranges of awareness.

Speaker: Now I am running into a certain dilemma because I have to watch the time, I have to watch the conversation as it goes on, and I also see in the chat that there's another question to Thomas, and I don't know how to handle that altogether without doing any harm to one or the other. So what I will do is I will just read the question for Thomas: Having worked online for 10 plus years, are you surprised to see this become a new wave of communication? What, during this transition of communication, has changed for you having done it for so long?

Thomas: This is here to stay! Why would businesses absorb office costs? Why would they absorb a lot of other things that are involved? Why would they still absorb travel and accommodation costs if things can be done remotely today?

Speaker: I liked what you said in your paper about this becoming more problem-solving oriented. That makes much more sense, especially when you put it in the context of how my 21-year-old is upstairs texting and playing games and all of that. I mean, it's just a whole new way of doing things. I believe where we're going with dialogue is identifying and solving problems. It's a little harder to be more generative, but I think this environment is definitely much more suited towards problem-solving and Working Dialogues, as we do in Virginia.

Speaker: I may have to bypass the question of whether dialogue should have a purpose, with an objective, because the way that I have run dialogue groups in the past few years, I squarely put them in the field of adult development, and the development of one consciousness. We take topics that are really very hot topics in society. We share what we think, what we want to see happening. The idea is to really find ourselves in front of our automatic responses, our presuppositions, and to get to know ourselves when these presuppositions are being questioned. So for me, Bohm Dialogue in its original way is a fantastic method for the development of consciousness.

Sometimes we get into a flow and all kinds of new perspectives open for everybody. These are magical moments, but sometimes it's a struggle, a struggle between who I am in relation to what we are talking about—and who are the others? The struggle itself is a way of learning. I know there are young people in groups that are used to just seeing a question and an answer. But after a while they engage in this slow process of getting to know themselves and getting to know what all the suppositions are in the group that we haven't seen. So it's truly an educational tool for me in my professional life.

Speaker: I think that's a good point because there's a lot of upside to this dialogue in the future, and the communication and sharing our thoughts. But communication is not just about conversing or sharing ideas. There's an energy, a spirit and a soul that I don't think that dialogue online will ever be able to encapsulate, so that's something we're going to lose with it. I'm looking at this screen right now. I can't tap into any of you and feel your energy. When I'm in a room with people, even with the most silent person I can still feel something from them that, as a Dialogue Practitioner, I can draw from them. I can help them to express themselves, but I can't do this in a virtual room. With the artificial, you cannot ever replace the human spirit, the human energy. So that's what I have to figure out because I do this for the benefit of people. I have to figure out how I can do that most effectively on a platform that doesn't allow that.

Speaker: These little moments of connection are a little bit lost, but on the other hand what I think is a big plus, especially for this work of dialogue, is that we are a little bit more with ourselves. We are in our own space for taking care of our own selves. I think this opens more space for self-reflection. I find myself reflecting more. Like you mentioned before, who am I in this? What does that change in my perspective? And then I can bring these perspectives back into the group.

Speaker: I was in one of the breakout rooms yesterday that really threw me back when there were people who have said, "Yeah, I'd rather be like this than be amongst people in a larger group."

Postscript

The author's reflections, written some months after the conference

The 2020 AofPD conference included a significant diversity of professional and personal provenances, all of which had in common the understanding that online Dialogue has entered our lives forever. The pandemic accelerated a process which accepts little, if any, opposition.

Since the conference, as time has passed, I have been able to observe what has improved, stayed as it was, and what has been changed for better in regards to online Dialogue.

My belief is that what has improved is the more relaxed attitude, giving up the beliefs that real Dialogue can only happen in person. What has stayed as it was, for the moment, is the technology. Of course some devices, software adaptations and gadgets have appeared, but none really impacts the essence of the Dialogue experience.

My longtime interest in dialogical interaction was the aspect of human connection, and I believe that it is in this field where I could observe the most significant progress in the online Dialogue experience.

I have learned that, despite the perception of technology as a conditioner, it is still the human qualities, transcending the technology, which enable deeper connection.

Humility, accepting uncertainty of outcome ,welcoming diversity and dissent to understand common and non-common grounds . . . all these attitudes, which enrich offline Dialogue, require an additional dose of awareness to create energy and connection online.

We do not enter the room alone; we enter it with our space and circumstance. It is important to bring our environment to the online meeting space, sharing where we are, allowing others to have a glimpse of our world at that moment, thus getting closer and fostering empathy. Leaving microphones open can also help in perceiving each other's lives as they happen.

Awareness of time differences, moments of the day for each participant should be considered.

An additional dose of awareness and intention to the creation of ambience, and graduating intensity of voice and rhythm, creates the energy adequate for connection. Deep connection can happen online, and it has the same magic and power as offline.

We can alternate generative space with purpose-driven space for best results. Letting it happen may take some additional time, but it should probably be brought into the timing for the intervention.

We are always learning. *No matter* how experienced we are in Dialogue practice, the online world will bring new possibilities as well as challenges. Let us register every learning after every Dialogue.

The Container Development Model
Peter Garrett

I recall starting a new job when I was in my late 30s. I had been running my own business importing women's fashion clothing into the UK and wholesaling it to upmarket independent women's dress shops from a fancy display unit in the rag trade area, behind Oxford Street in London. Then the supply end in South Africa failed to deliver. As I was closing things down and letting the showroom, I thought how much I would enjoy working with property. An old friend was now running the property development side of his family's business, and an opportunity opened up for me to join him. I did not have much experience, so I prepared carefully for my interview with his uncle, the founder of the much-larger conglomerate of construction businesses. I related to him how I had purchased and developed a residential property (which happened to be my own home) some years previously to get myself out of debt. The story was impressive enough for him, and I was hired at a good salary.

The property development company had a total staff of nine, including the partners and the clerical support staff, and was housed in a prestigious and delightfully ornate four-story brick building in South Audley Street, Mayfair. This is just one block away from Park Lane; if you have played the English version of Monopoly you will know this is an expensive area. I had a well-appointed office, and an experienced personal assistant called Thelma. This was back in the days when executives used Dictaphones and their PAs typed their letters for signature or amendment. The whole environment was different and new to me. I didn't really know how things worked in property development, and I knew that I didn't know. I feigned a confident and relaxed air whilst watching everything going on around me very carefully for all the clues I could get. It took me nearly an hour to work out how to use the Dictaphone! This was a highly professional business that made good profits developing commercial and residential property across the UK. They had a dozen or more large and active developments under way at any time, and expected to sell a number of properties every month. The best architects, solicitors and estate agents were keen to have our business.

The role I was expected to play was explained to me on my first day. My brief was to clean up a mixed portfolio of dormant parcels of land that had at some point in the previous 30 years been reserved for later development, thought worthless or simply forgotten. I would have to search in the hard-copy paper archives for evidence we actually had the title to the various pieces of land, then use my initiative to turn them into profitable developments. In addition I was given two active sites. I was learning fast – largely learning that there were yet further areas of the business about which I knew next to nothing!

On my second day at work I found myself attending a meeting in a barrister's chambers, since I was now a Project Development Manager and this was a key meeting for my active site in the south-coast port of Dover. We held an option to buy development land there pending the gaining of planning permission. Our planning application had been refused, and so we were taking the application to appeal with the Department of the Environment who could, in certain circumstances, overrule the County Council's planning decision. I had to instruct the barrister on how to proceed with our case. Clearly I was naïve in the matter and almost out of my depth. The stakes were high and mistakes could be very costly. I was accompanied by one of our solicitors, whom I met as we entered the chambers, and then it dawned on me what to do. I delegated the briefing of the barrister to him. That way my own inexperience was less obvious as I started to understand the situation and what was involved. They knew I had been recently appointed into my role, and attributed more experience to me than I felt I had.

Over the following months I came to understand the situation more clearly and took on the briefings of the barrister myself. My inexperienced but creative thought and challenges helped to define the arguments that led to us gaining planning permission for an out-of-town retail shopping park in Dover. It was a significant success and I was starting to show up as a confident and competent player. I negotiated the purchase of several further tranches of land from a neighbouring farmer, to our mutual benefit. Then I worked with the architects on the extensive development, tendered the building contracts, project-managed the construction work, let the completed units to top supermarkets, DIY retailers and so on. I completed the process by selling the properties to a pension fund with sitting tenants, yielding a steady income for the new owners. By this time I was the real thing – an experienced Property Development Manager. My main portfolio of forgotten tracts of land had become valuable sites that realised good income: much sought-after car parking in a congested town; a ransom strip (similar to an easement) that provided access to a large residential development near London; a golf course; a cemetery; a cluster of combined live-and-work units for new start-up businesses in Yorkshire, among others. I had found a way of doing things that was effective, and I enjoyed the work.

Inner Development

Stepping back, it is possible to see a growth within me alongside my outer career development during the three-year period I have just described. There is a sequence of phases. As I began I was naïve. I didn't know what I didn't know, and fortunately I was very receptive to learning. This is when I was *realising myself*. The name I use for this first phase has a deliberate double meaning – it was I who was realising how things fitted together, and I was starting to make my own potential contribution real. It involved talking with people, asking questions, reading files, speculating, theorising and knowing there was more to be seen and learnt. The second phase I now call *showing up*. I was progressing. At times I stepped into the spotlight as I led project management considerations, made new proposals in our partners meetings, recommended investments we might make and represented the company to others. When I got it right I was well acknowledged, and when I didn't I tried to recognise how I could have done it differently (sometimes reluctantly), and endeavoured to learn from the feedback I received. I was lucky to have so many projects to activate and to learn from. I had to respond to circumstances, like moving gypsies off one site to regain possession.

Then I started to find my own direction and purpose. In a run-down part of London where we owned a couple of boarded-up derelict shops, I felt the area had lost its heart. It lacked pride. I imagined a covered street market alongside a shopping arcade that would give it a lively centre and attract people who wanted to be there. I began to acquire the additional neighbouring units, and options on others, to pull this off. This was the phase of *occupying the ground*. My inner confidence, purpose and commitment were now defining my own way of doing business, and I was good at it. In a further phase, people could see I knew what I was doing and started to come to me for ideas, advice and guidance. I had become influential within the company and beyond, and I helped to define the spirit, purpose and integrity with which we worked and were known to work. I was now *affecting the field*.

I have experienced and seen these four phases unfold naturally in this sequence many times: *realising yourself, showing up, occupying the ground* and *affecting the field*. In each new situation or initiative the phases are similar, even though there is a different content of learning – whether as a child learning to ride a bicycle, as a parent having a first child, as a university student landing a first job, as a warden taking charge of a prison for the first time, as a busy CEO taking over another organisation, as an employee stepping into retirement, or as a widow having just lost her husband.

In the Context of Dialogue

I have found my understanding of these phases particularly helpful in my Dialogue work. Generally the inner development leads the outer growth of effectiveness. For example, typically as individuals *show up* more opportunities come their way. My favourite role is coaching an executive and his or her team on how they work together and with others to deliver a result though the best use of open Dialogue. In these dynamic processes, change is under way everywhere: in each of the individuals in the Dialogues; in the relationships between them; in the dynamics of the whole group; in their relationships and responsibilities with others; and in the overall situation and circumstance. The four phases provide a framework for understanding this complexity in order to be helpful in any transition. An individual may be an old dog in their current role, but still realising themselves in digital skills, or they may be occupying the ground with their family and the arrival of children, but still showing up in their new leadership role. The team may be showing up, whilst their larger organisation may still be realising itself. To be effective in Dialogue one has to understand the relationship between what is happening internally and what is happening externally. That is the key to releasing the dynamic value of Dialogue.

Supporting the Development of Others

Let's step forward ten years in my life. I am now working as an independent consultant to the European division of an international energy company. I have been successfully coaching Tim, the chief executive, and his leadership team, drawn from across southern Europe, including Turkey, Spain, Portugal, Greece and Italy. Their business meetings start late, with espresso and strong cigarettes. They are informal and conversational, effective, and finish late in good humour. Then the announcement is made that they are about to be absorbed into (actually taken over by) a larger business unit to the north, including the sterner and more disciplined northern European powerhouses of Germany, Austria, Poland, France, UK and the Netherlands. A new cycle had begun.

I met the new incoming chief executive who would be replacing Tim to lead the enlarged business. I agreed to support him in this new role. Ewan is a pleasant man, a Scott with a broad accent, and a qualified accountant. I noted that he is honest, enthusiastic and astute, and that he is entering unknown territory in his job. This is larger, more complex and more socially demanding that anything he has done before. With this new initiative he was clearly in the phase of *realising himself*. I had a good idea what he would be going through during the coming year or two and how to help him.

The leadership handover was beautifully orchestrated. Normally decision-making stops when news breaks of a change of leadership, as those who will report to the new leaders wait to see what changes he or she wants to introduce, and how to position themselves to be seen to be of value. I had seen gaps of three or four months where all major decisions were on pause. So I counselled the two of them to minimise the handover period. We called a two-day meeting of the enlarged Executive Leadership Team meeting two weeks later in Istanbul.

Tim, the outgoing leader, led the first day. He reviewed the state of the business with everyone. Ewan was seated quietly in the background listening carefully and starting to realise the situation. In the evening we took a boat down the Bosphorus. It was a balmy summer evening as we sat on the large open deck watching the Istanbul suburbs drift past on our outward journey. We ate and drank, then dropped anchor to celebrate and acknowledge the role Tim had played. He was popular, good at his job and sometimes absent-minded, which all added to the good humour of the occasion. He appreciated the gifts he was given. Then we raised anchor for the return leg, and as we did so Tim symbolically handed over the leadership to Ewan with a firm shake of hands. We sailed back, and before breakfast Tim had departed.

Ewan led the second day of the meeting. We had talked about how he would show up in that meeting whilst he was still realising himself, and designed a good way to manage the situation. He began by saying that he was not Tim, and clearly he would do some things in a different way, because he was a different person with a different history and a different set of skills, but first he needed to understand their thinking about the business. We had two rounds where everyone spoke in turn. In the first they introduced themselves and said how they would like to see their part of the business develop over the next year. In the second round they were asked what, if anything, they would like to change during the next month. It was a clever way to start. He had put the initiative in their hands, which was sensible since they knew more than him, and sustained the momentum by asking to hear about immediate decisions to be made by them. He had managed his own naïve phase of realising himself without giving away his authority.

As things worked out, the business flourished. It had the advantage of a full European trading presence and rationalised its investments in a different way in consequence. Then the larger multinational organisation made the strategic purchases of two strongly branded competitors in Germany, thereby adding these businesses into Ewan's remit and significantly expanding his turnover. He was now showing up as confident to lead the integration of the new German businesses into his existing portfolio. There were cultural issues to face, however, before he could do so and fully occupy the ground. I called on a German colleague to co-facilitate some of the sessions as we resolved this.

The challenge was that Ewan valued thinking openly with everyone before making a decision. The new German executives, on the other hand, had just suffered a takeover by Ewan's parent firm and presumed they should agree to whatever he wanted. So he was encouraging open thinking and they were careful to agree with everything he said or might mean. It was politely frustrating for everyone. Once they realised what he was actually calling for, they acted quite differently, often disagreeing and opposing him in strong and blunt terms. At some point Ewan would make his decision and want to move to action, whilst his German colleagues were still making alternative proposals. It became like a three-legged race again, and everyone became quite frustrated with the lack of flow and progress. I had to intervene and make clear distinctions between each part of the meeting. So in the first part they agreed the issues for consideration, in the second part it was open thinking with no decisions made, and in the third part Ewan defined the decision and they explored the implementation of it. Everyone had to play a somewhat different role for this to work. On Ewan's part he had to be clear when he was ready to call a decision, explain his logic and be explicit that no further alternative proposals were welcome after that point. Gradually people understood this process and enjoyed the easy progress they made in consequence. Ewan had begun to occupy the ground in his own unique and effective way. I stayed with Ewan through perhaps half a dozen further business roles and he became an influential leader in his larger organisation.

Transitioning to the Next Phase

I had a good feel of how to be helpful in my executive coaching because of this simple sequence of *realising yourself, showing up, occupying the ground* and *affecting the field*. It revealed the developmental needs of the individual in a particular initiative. I have coached many different individuals, and on entering each new situation they ran through a similar sequence. I could see it in others, and I experienced it repeatedly in myself. There was the time when I took up skiing, for instance. Between the idea of skiing and first getting onto the piste, or ski run, there was a significant phase of realising myself. It is a period of private enquiry. Am I fit enough to do this, or is there some set of exercises I should find at the gym? What do I wear? Is my walking anorak OK or do I have to invest in an alpine outfit in flashy colours? I didn't know what 'normal' looked like. I asked people if they were skiers and found people who knew a bit about it. Younger people used snow boards and older people skis. My age placed me firmly in the skiing group. I discovered some resorts are better for learners than others, and the prices vary, but it is not inexpensive.

Eventually the day arrived when I was dressed in my full new dazzling yellow and black kit (covering new 'wicking' underwear and thermal vest), helmet and reflective goggles. Of course I had tried it all on at home in my bedroom to reassure myself, and I was satisfied I looked good. But now I was at the ski resort in full view of everyone and I felt highly visible! What I had not taken into account was the boots that lock into the skis. They are designed for the skier to be leaning forward at an angle, and as a result it is very difficult to walk wearing them whilst carrying the skis. So I hobbled from the ski hire shop to the snow, with the skis and poles slung awkwardly over my shoulder. I locked the boots into the skis, and there I was, ready to go. What happened next? Well like any typical beginner, I slid a few yards and fell over. So this is learning through mistakes! Pleased I also booked some lessons . . .

Getting from *showing up* to *occupying the ground* in skiing is more difficult than I had imagined. This is because you have to learn to move your body in a way that initially is counter-intuitive. If you try to remember which way to move, by the time you tell your body it is too late and you have fallen over. You have to feel the motion in your body. Let me explain the problem. When I learnt to ride a bicycle as a youngster, I leaned to the left if I wanted to turn left, and I leaned to the right if I wanted to turn right. That is the way to maintain balance. I later did the same on a motorcycle at much faster speeds. On skis it is the other way around. If you intend to turn to the left, you lean to the right! The outer right edge cuts into the snow increasing the friction, and that turns you to the left. If you lean the other way you have no cutting edge, slide wildly and fall. Understanding this is only a small part of doing it. But there is more. If you are about to drop down a steep slope, intuitively you lean back, as you do going down an incline in your hiking boots. But on skis you will fall if you do that. Instead you have to lean forwards, propelling you even faster down the slope – and the steeper the incline the further forward you have to lean to keep your balance. This is scary stuff! But without mastering these two rather elementary requirements you cannot occupy the ground, because you find yourself instead lying on it. It takes more than skill; it takes an adventurous courage to be any good, and there are more than a few would-be skiers who lose their nerve. I found that the way to get there is to stop thinking and instead to feel what is needed. And it really helps to watch those who know what they are doing. They can help you to sense the way to ski better. In that way they are affecting the field, and being in that field you can really benefit from watching them at a distance.

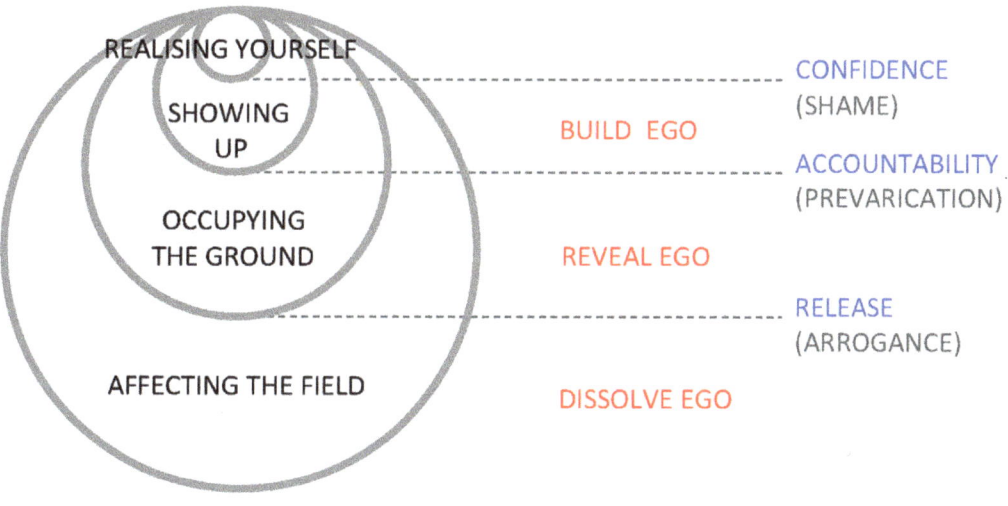

Acknowledgement: W Isaacs & P Garrett © Dialogue Associates, 2011

The Work To Be Done

It is probably becoming apparent that one does not simply drift from one phase into the next. There is a definite barrier to break and an internal shift to occur as you move into the next phase. *Realising yourself* is a private matter. Your enquiry proceeds at whatever pace you choose, or whatever time you have available to you, exploring whatever sources you can find. You can read, ask, experiment and speculate, without anyone else knowing what you are up to. When you show up, however, it is apparent to others. You are visibly taking a position and people may or may not like it, and they may or may not agree with you. If you have done your work realising yourself, you will have good reasons for doing what you do, and it will help you if you explain them to others. Essentially it has been a phase of building the ego.

So the challenge of *showing up* is one of confidence. It is about revealing the ego. If I have failed at something I wanted to do in the past, and in particular if I have been shamed or ridiculed by others, then showing up can feel like a dangerous step for me. It is worth considering this in an organisational context. I don't know how many times I have seen a junior rise to the challenge of expressing their different view in an important meeting, only to be slammed by the most senior figure in the room. It results in feelings of humiliation in the meeting, tears in the washroom and the future withholding of relevant information because of the proven dangers of expressing one's view. This is not at all uncommon. As a result, an essential organisational skill in leadership, facilitation and coaching is helping individuals successfully through the barrier of *showing up*. It is important that individuals gain the confidence to do so and, generally speaking, that ease is more important than whether the views they first express are 'right' or 'wrong'. As they get confident showing up they will express their views more clearly, and the thinking behind the views will be more logical. Without hearing from the people affected, however, leaders and decision-makers will be largely flying blind.

Sometimes people are expected to show up before they have done the preparatory work in the previous phase. When this is the case they come over as hollow, because they know the words but not the meaning. They spend hours rehearsing their lines, or use PowerPoint slides to remember what to say because there has been no corresponding inner developmental work. So we have the outline of a coaching model whereby we can recognise where an individual, team or organisation is in a particular initiative, and help them to fill out that phase and move into the next.

The shift from *showing up* into *occupying the ground* is a different challenge. As a manager or supervisor you will have noticed bright juniors who will soon be ready for promotion. They show up in meetings in a convincing way, and have initiative and self-confidence. Perhaps you recommend they apply for a promotion, but they may or may not do so. Showing up is something you do at the right occasion. You may even perform on the stage several times a week, but that is not all day every day. Everyday consistency requires real commitment. A girl might have a boyfriend for a summer, but having a child is for a lifetime. This is about sustaining the ego. A promotion may result in better pay and conditions, but it has responsibilities and accountabilities attached to it. The new role may put that individual in sole charge of some activity or part of the business, answering to more senior people, and that requires a different stance. In my 20s I worked temporarily as a barman in London, and loved it. Later, in my 30s, I held the liquor licence for the 20-bedroom hotel I was managing. They were similar but completely different roles. As the barman I locked up my bar at night and went home without a care. As the hotel manager I was paid more, but I was continuously accountable. I had calls in the middle of the night and had to get up and deal with them – the police advising a break-in, or a guest complaining that the bath water in their room was only lukewarm!

There can be a tendency to prevaricate and procrastinate. People avoid or put off stepping into the next phase of occupying the ground. The person involved may be quite capable of doing a more senior job, but they may not be ready internally to take on the responsibility. If they do eventually bite the bullet and occupy the ground, they do find that there are consequences. When you are the only one responsible, you have to find a way of managing things. There may not be anyone there to advise or guide you, but still you have to act. You start to gain some first-hand knowledge beyond simply doing what you are told or following the rules. Your way of doing things will be different from others because of your personality, experiences and cultural inheritance. Something else occurs, which is unexpected. When you occupy the ground some people come closer because they are attracted to your way of working and your commitment. They want to work with you. Others move further away from you. Your commitment is an inherent challenge to *their* prevarication and procrastination, and they are uncomfortable being too close to you. So occupying the ground develops a kind of intensity that attracts and repels. It is hard to predict who will come closer and who will move further away, but a sorting out definitely starts to occur.

An Expensive Lesson

Occupying the ground for an extended period builds a body of knowledge and experience about how to manage a particular activity successfully, and what not to do because it will be counterproductive. How do I know? Because I have done it! That is the typical stance of someone who has occupied the ground extensively. But there is a further phase – namely, *affecting the field*. Again there is a barrier and challenge in making this transition. It is necessary to release some aspects of your experiential knowledge whilst remaining fully committed to others. Let me give you an expensive example where this did not happen. I was invited to intervene in a joint venture pilot that was intended to result in a US $5bn manufacturing business. Two leading companies in the field, from Canada and South Africa, had joined forces to develop an innovative technology. Both had proven prior experience and knew that they knew how to do this work well. The problem was they had different methods and different organisational cultures. They were unable to listen to each other and to learn from each other because they already knew! It was not just a failure of communication – it was a failure in the developmental work needed within each organisation to move beyond their arrogance of having occupied the ground. They could have affected the field internationally with their innovation, but instead the joint initiative simply failed.

The fact that you and I really do know how to do something, and have proof that it works, does not mean that our way is the only way to do it. Finding God through Catholicism does not mean that others cannot find God as a Jew, Hindu or Zoroastrian. If my way definitively excludes other ways, then I cannot affect the field. Whilst remaining committed to the essence of the work, I have to release my ego – my attachment to *my* way being *the* way, if my influence is to be extended further into the field. Reputation is a powerful thing. There is not one way but a thousand ways. Each person and each situation is unique, and an intention to foster the unique work of others is what underwrites the ability to affect the field.

The Developmental Phases in Conscious Awareness

Let's drop into a different endeavour. Back in 1984 I was working with David Bohm on understanding the workings of human consciousness. We believed there was a pervasive defect that took the form of fragmentation and it broke up the sense of common meaning between people. It was the root cause, in our view, of most of the problems facing society today. We used *median*-sized groupings of 20 to 40 people (that are too large for family dynamics and smaller than societal ones, as originally advocated by Patrick de Maré) to identify and talk about our own changing state of conscious awareness as it occurred. One thing we noted is the difference between thinking, which is new, and thoughts, which are replayed past-thinking. Thinking is slower, whilst thoughts can be prompted very quickly by association, provocation, threat or desire. Thinking is a higher level of living, subtle awareness, that can influence which thoughts to entertain and which thoughts to let be. Thoughts, on the other hand, are replayed from the past and cannot manage immediate thinking. Although both are needed, we found that thinking is quite rare. George Bernard Shaw once proposed that most people think only two or three times in a year, and that he had made an international reputation for himself by thinking once or twice a week! We found we were thinking much more often than that, because that is what we were intentionally setting out to do, but it was still quite rare for many participants to get beyond their memory.

I have not forgotten one delightful evening when a group of 25 of us were in Dialogue together in a friend's apartment in Kensington, in London. A colleague, Mike, began to see what was happening for the first time, and he spoke about it in a delightful way. He said, "A thought coming towards you is very different from a thought moving away from you!" He explained what he meant as we all talked about it together. He had felt his initial impulse to think. It was the start of an energetic movement that as yet had no form. It was emergent and urgent, although it was unclear just what it was. Gradually it began to form itself into an idea with purpose, and to be meaningful to him and perhaps to what we being considered in the room. He found words appearing to clothe the idea in language, and as he listened he started to choose some sentences to place his idea into the Dialogue. I find it hard to think of a better name for this first phase than *realising yourself*. He had described what he called 'a thought coming towards you'. It was actually a subtle thinking process that was emerging into articulation through words, which are thoughts.

Then he spoke a few sentences, adding his contribution to the ongoing conversation. From that point he was showing up. The private process that had been occurring within him had become a public one now occurring in everyone. It was entering the awareness and thinking of others in the room, and they did different things with it. Some liked his idea, some liked the intention but not the words, some thought what he had said was irrelevant to the main theme of the conversation, and so on. This is what he called 'a thought going away from you'. It was now with other people. He could feel his own impulses to explain more, to defend his idea, to laugh and to be silent. He had the opportunity to continue to think, and to continue to describe the movements in his consciousness, including what occurs when someone else's thought moves into him. By doing so it would lead to him into occupying the ground – in this case the ground of conscious awareness. That is exactly what many of us did, and thereby we affected the field in terms of the emergence of a new kind of Dialogue. What was very evident in that Dialogue meeting was that the live description of his thinking deepened the atmosphere in the room significantly and drew others into a more subtle sensitivity. Past thoughts were less inclined to flood in to fill the space, and instead people were listening to themselves and each other in a more receptive way.

Container Development

We later called this atmosphere the 'container'. Why the container? Well, if you consider it carefully, consciousness is simply its content, including the unfolding and enfolding flow of that content. The container is the content and flow that is commonly held by those involved. This container can be expanded and deepened to enable a greater common content and a freer flow of understanding. What is not commonly held is fragmented, and held by some participants but not by others. So the four developmental phases I have been describing are a container development model. The starting point may be largely internal and unseen, like the seed in the soil. It is not apparent to others how things are unfolding and what is emerging until the shoots emerge and some form appears. Then it develops with fuller growth, deeper roots, flowers and eventually the fruit that yields the next seeds to affect the field.

I use this container development model widely in all my work. The container development phases are depicted in many of my models – they are the expanding grey developmental circles, for example, in this graphic of our Dialogue practices, which are at the core of my Dialogue work. They are a reminder that each of the practices develops through the four phases as you grow your own personal container and capability. The same is true of a team that learns to listen better as the container develops, for example – not only to what is said but to what is meant and to the process of thinking and feeling behind that. This is the way into a deeper Dialogue.

A Developmental Framework for Consulting

The framework informs my consulting intervention work too. Here I combine it with a number of other key models derived from my practice. On being invited into a new situation to help, I am very conscious that at the outset I am naïve. I don't know what I don't know, and I am carefully attentive to all the clues I can find as I start to realise myself in that context. I am willing to learn from anyone and everyone. I enjoy my naïvety because it is a time when I can ask about peculiar anomalies and contradictions without being either clever or stupid. It is a valuable time that only happens once in an intervention and is soon lost. This is a time of enquiry, not a time of advocacy. If I understand why things have unfolded the way they have, then I can intervene in a way that enables them to unfold more generatively in the future. Showing up in intervention work is necessary to gain the authority to learn with people in the organisation or community. We will all learn more if I show up in the right spirit. Occupying the ground allows me and others to attract a core grouping to do the work needed in terms of the support and challenge of the existing patterns of relationships and containers. It starts to be apparent why we have what we have, and how to intervene for it to change generatively. This needs authority and right use of the organisational power structures. Affecting the field goes broader and deeper.

And a Career

Perhaps a final example is how the sequence of phases helps me to reflect on my own Professional Dialogue career as a whole over 35 years. The *realising myself* phase was during the eight years I worked with David Bohm in private Dialogue Weekends. I started to show up in corrections with my Prison Dialogue work, starting with a nine-year stint working in an English prison (HMP Whitemoor), and in organisations starting with my work partnering with Bill Isaacs (the Leadership for Collective Intelligence programme). My 20 years of partnership with my friend and colleague Jane Ball has led to the substantial ground we have occupied in our joint consulting company, Dialogue Associates, and the design of the Integrated Dialogue Model. Then we and others deliberately started the Academy of Professional Dialogue in 2017 with the intention of affecting the field.

And that is what we are starting to do . . .

Conference Session Extracts

From a conversation with participants considering the paper with Peter Garrett

Peter: What does Realising Yourself mean in a few words? (*Various responses:* Finding a new need and putting yourself in a learning position; self-actualization; preparing yourself for your future endeavour; understanding; as you begin you are naïve – you don't know, and know you don't know.)

Speaker: When you think of someone who's newly promoted into a leadership position, they are going to have to find themselves and work out how they fit into this new role moving forward.

Speaker: Maybe a supervisor who has been in that job for a considerable time, but they've lost their ability to show up. They may need to be reminded of the importance of being visible, showing up.

Speaker: In our small group I made the point there are a lot of really professional, well-educated women that take a lot longer to show up, perhaps, than their male counterparts.

Peter: Why do you think it is, in some organisations, that women have more difficulty showing up?

Speaker: I can only speak for myself. It took me a long time to learn to show up and then actually experience how beautiful it can be to occupy your ground and see what effect it can have on others. I don't know. Maybe it's how we've been educated, maybe family relations or whatever, an experience that nothing's ever really good enough. Maybe it's also cultural in Germany, but I notice it in a lot of women that I've come in contact with, where I see the brilliance and they sell themselves short.

Speaker: I'm working with a senior leader right now who's had to step in to be the head of something, because one of the partners in the firm left. She knows how to do this, and she was really comfortable before, but there's this question of confidence. So I think you're right. It really is a point of sustaining the ego to occupy this new ground.

Speaker: I think that we in Finland have this cultural problem that you are expected to go from realising yourself directly to occupying the ground without the showing-up phase. And that's a real problem. People are not allowed to test their skills and their ideas, because everybody's expecting that if you are showing up, you should know your stuff, be really confident about it. I think that's harmful for new entrepreneurs and emerging experts.

Speaker: Occupying the ground is really embodying your role confidently, effectively relying on your own impact. If you are going to occupy the ground, you have to take accountability. You have to say, okay, this is my job. I'll get this to work.

Speaker: In occupying the ground. I think it's a good opportunity to look at how you can improve something. You're actually trying things out, seeing what worked well, what didn't work well, making the adjustments. In the first stages you're gaining the knowledge, then in occupying the ground you're wising up. But you actually learned that by occupying the ground in my mind.

Speaker: I think sometimes you see that people have potential, but they don't have the confidence to step out. So as leaders, it's your responsibility and due diligence to align them with the opportunities to extract that potential. It is twofold – you're helping them, but what they're doing will, in turn, help the organisation. It also allows them to have buy-in to what you're doing.

Speaker: Affecting the field effectively means we go back to a place of being humble, because it's almost like where you were before realising yourself, but in a different way. You have humility, but you have the confidence at the same time – it's a conscious humility of giving space to others.

Speaker: I give myself six months as a new Director to show up and to get to know the agency. After I have realised myself, I show up and then I am prepared to do what I was brought to do, which is to begin to occupy the ground. And part of that is building a team, shifting the culture and doing all those things necessary to get the outcome ultimately. In Virginia the data and research will show you how our culture shifted over the years. That's an example of how you come in – you begin by realising yourself, then showing up and occupying the ground causes those things to happen on the back end. So that's the way it plays out in my mind and what we have been doing.

Speaker: Peter, when I read your paper, I really thought about the idea of selflessness as you move into that area of affecting the field. It's a choice you make to do that. And I think about it in terms of an organisation. You recognise the value and purpose of the organisation, the impact of the organisation is greater by bringing others in and sharing that information and knowledge with them. To a certain degree that can be at the expense of the individual potentially, but it makes the organisation better and it helps the organisation accomplish whatever its mission or purpose is.

Speaker: So the Virginia Department of Correctional Justice could be affecting the field of correctional justice in the entirety or in parts. How, how are you doing that?

Speaker: Yes, we are achieving that effect on the field in the US. Last year over a dozen corrections agencies from other states came to Virginia to take a look at what we're doing. So we are leading the cutting edge. I am sought after to speak often at meetings of directors and so forth. Other members of our team and overstaff are being called upon to share what they're doing and their expertise too. Four years ago, I went to the National Institute of Corrections and spoke at a class of people aspiring to be leaders of corrections. I spoke about dialogue and a lot of the things that we are doing to change the culture of the organisation. This past Friday, four years later, I received an email from a gentleman in Arizona who was a member of that class who is now preparing to be a CEO, and he wants me to spend time with him helping him to go over all those notes that he took from me in that class four years ago. He has been watching us from afar and sees things are working. He liked what I said then, and he wants to put some of those things into place in a different state.

Postscript

The author's reflections, written some months after the conference

The four phases of the Container Development Model were generally well recognised by participants, and there was some interesting exploration about the challenges of showing up in an organisational context. Also culturally, it seems in Finland there is an expectation that when you have realised yourself in some field you now occupy the ground – but without the intermediate phase of showing up. I believe this is true in some other cultures too. It is not uncommon for people to claim or pretend to know more than they do to hide the fact they are actually still showing up. This is unfortunate because the successes and failures in showing up are an essential part of learning, without which one cannot occupy the ground. Pretending one already does so usually makes people particularly sensitive to any lack of acknowledgement.

It set me thinking about how one learns and develops during the 'realising yourself' phase. The container is smaller and private. The discoveries may be largely vicarious or informed more by the experience of others rather than one's own. This is particularly the case in traditional forms of education, where reading and being familiar with the existing literature is a requirement for graduation, and graduation seems to imply occupying the ground. Describing what others have done, however, is very different from being able to do it yourself.

This is about different qualities of knowledge that are available in each phase. In the realising yourself phase it is often third-hand and derived from people you have not met, describing things. This may be fine for technical matters, but not regarding personal development. Watching and hearing directly from someone else about their own experience provides access to second-hand knowledge. This is more helpful, because you can sense the context, weight and authenticity behind what you are hearing. Both forms provide guidance that can be adapted and incorporated, but neither are first-hand. That only comes from showing up and trying it 'live' for yourself. Your experience and reflections are then very different.

Showing up involves a much larger container that includes others, and they will respond and react to what you do. Therefore, you have much more to handle when you show up, along with a far greater learning opportunity. Acknowledgement seems such an important factor in this transition and I am left wondering: just why?

The World Needs Dialogue!
2020 Conference Participants

Screenshots of a sampling of the 500 participants in the conference.

www.ingramcontent.com/pod-product-compliance
Lightning Source LLC
Chambersburg PA
CBHW042358280426
43661CB00096B/1155